FIRST LADIES
of RUNNING

FIRST LADIES
of RUNNING

22 Inspiring Profiles of the Rebels, Rule Breakers, and Visionaries Who Changed the Sport Forever

AMBY BURFOOT

RODALE.

RODALE *wellness*

Live happy. Be healthy. Get inspired.

Sign up today to get exclusive access to our authors, exclusive bonuses, and the most authoritative, useful, and cutting-edge information on health, wellness, fitness, and living your life to the fullest.

Visit us online at RodaleWellness.com

Join us at RodaleWellness.com/Join

Rodale books may be purchased for business or promotional use or for special sales. For information, please write to:
Special Markets Department, Rodale Inc., 733 Third Avenue, New York, NY 10017.

Printed in the United States of America

Rodale Inc. makes every effort to use acid-free ♾, recycled paper ♻.

Book design by Carol Angstadt

Photo editing by Liz Reap Carlson

Photograph credits can be found on page 261.

Library of Congress Cataloging-in-Publication Data is on file with the publisher.

ISBN-13: 978–1–60961–564–2

Distributed to the trade by Macmillan

2 4 6 8 10 9 7 5 3 1 paperback

Follow us @RodaleBooks on

We inspire and enable people to improve their lives and the world around them.
rodalebooks.com

To the pioneering women runners
without whose courage and generosity
this book would not have been possible

CONTENTS

FOREWORD

GROWING UP IN BOULDER, Colorado, and just outside Boston, Massachusetts, I was surrounded by great runners and renowned races like the Boston Marathon. Strangely enough, however, I didn't actually know a lot about running.

That's because my parents never talked much about their running careers, or pushed me to enter races. It's almost like they didn't want me to get into running too early in life. They wanted me to discover it naturally and on my own. Nevertheless, they always supported my interest in basketball, swimming, soccer, and all sorts of physical activities.

Looking back, I'm so glad they didn't encourage me to focus on running too soon. I think this allowed me to build up the passion and momentum I have felt since I turned pro in 2004. It's taken a lot of hard work and tenacity to win the 10,000-meter bronze medal in the 2008 Olympics, to compete in the Olympic Marathon in 2012, and to continue pushing my boundaries. In September 2015, I set a new American record for 10,000 meters on the road.

If my parents had pushed me into running at an early age, I don't know if I would still be exploring my potential and chasing fast performances. I'd probably be injured or burned out. Instead, I'm still excited about my running, still challenged to improve, and still hungry to achieve my goals.

To some extent, I was raised in a running store. In the early 1980s, my mother and father both worked at the Frank Shorter store in Boulder. It seemed like the center of the running universe. So many famous runners passed through that store. Of course, I didn't know who they were at the time. I just thought they were friends of my parents, or Frank's friends, and that everyone wore running shoes.

I didn't know my parents were fast and famous. I just thought they liked to run a lot.

One of my mother's best friends was Lorraine Moller. I didn't realize she was an Olympian and the 1984 Boston Marathon winner. I just thought of her as my favorite babysitter.

I also had no idea that my mother, then Cheryl Bridges before she married my father, Steve Flanagan, and changed her name, was a one-time world record holder. In 1971, she was the first woman to break 2:50 in the marathon.

My father wasn't too shabby either. He ran a 2:18 marathon and competed in the World Cross-Country Championships three times. Yet neither of my parents ever talked about their running. It might seem a bit unusual that I knew so little about my parents and their racing records, but I guess that's just the way they wanted it.

In high school, I had a poster of Grete Waitz on my wall. I thought she was amazing with all those wins in the New York City Marathon. She was so consistent—a goal I later adopted for myself. She became a role model to me, and I knew that my mother admired her, too.

Later, when I met Joan Benoit Samuelson, we talked about training programs. I think she was very intuitive—very good at listening to her own body and its needs—and I've tried to follow that approach. I also know that she trained like a beast.

It wasn't until college, when I started to immerse myself in the sport, that I began to uncover the amazing truth about my parents. I can remember times when I went rummaging through the back of closets and found medals, old pairs of running shoes, and musty Team USA uniforms. I thought the uniforms were cool. They were so retro that they seemed hip to me.

Anyway, I learned more about my parents running histories once I started asking them about the stuff in the closets. My mother would tell me stories about how uncomfortable it was to run in heavy cotton clothes and sweat suits, and without a sports bra. When I got my first shipment of running apparel from my sponsor, Nike, she was absolutely flabbergasted by the fit and function of all the technical clothes.

She also told me that it wasn't unusual for her to be pelted by cans or bottles from passing motorists. I don't know how she and her fellow female pioneers handled it all. Those were hard times to be a woman in the male-dominated world of competitive running. I'm not sure I would have had the guts to pursue running without any real support, and I can't fathom how they managed to persevere. They were very strong and courageous.

We've made such amazing progress since those early days. I can't say that I've ever felt any disadvantage compared to my male contemporaries. My running is so much easier than my mother's was. I am able to do what I want to do and to pursue my dreams. I have so many opportunities that might never have existed without my mother and the other women runners like her. They paved the road for all of us to follow. I feel so deeply appreciative for all they have contributed to the sport.

And they didn't do it just for Olympians like me. They did it for all women runners. Because one of the things they learned is that running improves your self-confidence and can give you a sense of possibility that carries over to all parts of your life. Running certainly changed the trajectory of my mother's life—it gave her so much more confidence. And it has done the same for countless other women.

That's what I tell the women runners I meet at road races. It doesn't matter how fast you are. It doesn't matter how long it takes you to reach the finish line. It's all about personal excellence—striving to be the best you can be. That's what we're all aiming for. That's what the First Ladies have taught us.

Shalane Flanagan

Shalane Flanagan won a bronze medal in the 2008 Beijing Olympic 10,000 meter race and holds the American record for 10,000 meters on the track and on the roads. She has a marathon best of 2:22:02. Her book, *Run Fast, Eat Slow*, will be published by Rodale Inc. in September 2016.

Thanks to the First Ladies of running, millions of women around the world now enjoy many road-race opportunities.

INTRODUCTION

GO TO ANY 5-K, 10-K, half-marathon, or marathon and take a look around. You'll see a complete cross section of humanity: men and women, teenagers and septuagenarians, lean-as-greyhound speedsters, and others who are round as an apple. Roughly half the runners will be females. Some will be leggy teens with ribbons in their ponytails. Some will be strong and muscled—women in their twenties and thirties who look like they just stepped out of a CrossFit class or a triathlon training session. You'll see pregnant women enjoying a relaxed aerobic stroll and new mothers pushing their running strollers. They'll be chatting with leaner, gray-haired women who run with a crisp, efficient stride.

It's hard to imagine that running didn't always look this way. But it didn't. For running's first 2,700 years, dating back to the ancient Olympic Games, women were completely excluded from most events. They couldn't run in any official distance races at all. Consider a few events from the 1950s and 1960s.

- In the mid-1950s, an Ohio farm girl named Grace Butcher dreamed about running the mile, like her heroes Glenn Cunningham and Wes Santee. Her dream died on the vine. Women were prohibited from running any track distance longer than 200 meters.
- In the early 1960s, Smith College runner Julia Chase wanted to run the Manchester (Connecticut) Thanksgiving Day 5-miler as her mentors John Kelley and George Terry had done. Her entry was refused. The rules forbade her participation, she was told.
- Five years later, in 1966, Roberta "Bobbi" Gibb wrote away for an entry application to the Boston Marathon. She had grown up outside Boston and had watched the marathon several times with her father, feeling a strong kinship to the graceful rhythm of the runners. However, Boston Marathon officials rejected her request. Women were incapable of running 26.2 miles, she was told, and were barred from entering marathons.

Fortunately, Butcher, Chase, and Gibb refused to give in. They persisted, eventually achieved their running ambitions, and opened the doors for all who would follow in their footsteps. The progress came slowly, and sometimes painfully. The old men who controlled the sport of running—members of the International Olympic Committee (IOC) and the Amateur Athletic Union (AAU)—insisted on sticking to bygone regulations and unproven health concerns.

At times, the rule makers actually pushed the clock backward rather than forward. The first Women's Olympic 800-meter race was held in Amsterdam in 1928. It should have advanced women's running. Instead, it shuttered progress for another three decades.

In that pivotal race in 1928, one finisher collapsed briefly to the track. Several others looked tired and bedraggled after the all-out, two-lap effort. No one pointed out that this was also true of the men who had run a hard 800. Newspaper sports writers, all males of course, expressed horror over the sight of the sweaty women. One paper actually used a primitive form of Photoshop to scare readers with the sight of the women's contorted faces.

The IOC promptly banned the women's 800. It wasn't until 1958 that the IOC announced the event's reappearance in the 1960 Rome Olympics. At last, Grace Butcher and other women had a chance to prove their endurance abilities. The 1960 U.S. Olympic Track Trials in Abilene, Texas, in July 1960, stand as an absolutely crucial event in the history of women's running.

It is here that women were allowed to participate in the 800-meter race for the first time since 1928. (During this era in the United States, running races were measured using the U.S. customary system. For ease of reference, I refer only to the metric distances in this book.) For the first time, women who had no talent in the sprints were given a chance to test themselves in a middle-distance event. Although little attention was actually paid to the women's 800, the event served as a springboard for all future women's distance races—the 800 was where the first baby steps were taken, and soon these steps would change into powerful strides.

However, Olympic officials continued to drag their heels when it came to giving women runners full parity with men. The women's 1500 meters was not added until 1972. The marathon came in 1984, after a particularly inspired campaign by many running groups. Even so, women were not given the opportunity to run the 10,000 until 1988, the 5000 until 1996, and the 3000-meter steeplechase until 2008.

After the 1960 Olympic Track Trials, the pioneer women runners turned naturally to cross-country and road races, held in public parks and on public roads. Indeed, in the spring of 1967 a new event called the World Cross Country Championships was organized, and it included a women's division. (This event, now semiannual, has also been called the International Cross Country Championships, among others. I have used only the current label, World Cross Country Championships, to describe these significant races, held in March since the 1950s.) Still, progress came slowly. Each runner had to wage a solitary battle in her own region. Luckily, these women were made of strong stuff. They might have gotten rejected time and again, but that didn't stop them. They kept returning to the races.

It wasn't just that they received little encouragement. It was far worse than that. They were widely ridiculed and routinely warned about permanent physical damage. Running might prevent healthy pregnancies, they were told. They were warned that it would surely turn them masculine, overly muscled, and unattractive.

How wrong could a group of so-called experts be? Let me just say this: I began my running career in the mid-1960s, and I met many of the women pioneers. The Boston Marathon and other East Coast races introduced me to Bobbi Gibb, Kathrine Switzer, Sara Mae Berman, Nina Kuscsik, Charlotte Lettis, and others like them. Anyone could see that they were bright, engaging, and beautiful in every way. As you will soon discover, their stories are both incredible and inspiring.

I met the West Coast runners less often, but I find their stories among the most amazing in this book. Take a look:

- Doris Brown took a red-eye flight from Seattle to New York City for the 1976 New York City Marathon, the first to go through all five boroughs. I've never heard of another elite runner doing this. The next morning, she finished second to Miki Gorman, and apologized for being a little tired.

- Southern Californian Judy Ikenberry began her track career in the 1960 Olympic Track Trials 800. She was 17 at the time, raw and wild. Fourteen years later, having gravitated all the way up to the marathon distance (an unusually big jump), she won the first National Women's Marathon Championship.

- Cheryl Bridges grew up in Indianapolis, where the board of education decided she could run on the high school campus—as long

as she stayed far away from the boys so as not to distract them
with her flowing blonde hair. She moved to California, kept on
running, and, in 1971, set a marathon world record. Her daughter,
Shalane Flanagan, won an Olympic bronze medal in the 10,000
meters in Beijing in 2008. Shalane has run far faster at all distances than her mother ever achieved, though she has never held a
marathon world record like her mom.

After my competitive racing days, I had the good luck to land an editorial
job at *Runner's World* magazine where I continued to follow the women pioneers of running. I watched Grete Waitz, Patti Catalano, and Joan Benoit
raise the women's running torch ever higher and wrote frequently about
their brilliant performances. Francie Larrieu and Mary Decker seemed to
show up at every National Track Championships and Olympic Trials.

I was sitting in the press section of the Los Angeles Olympic Stadium on
August 5, 1984, when Benoit ran onto the track well ahead of her marathon
rivals. This was the long-awaited day—coming 88 years after the first Olympic Marathon for men—and emotions ran high. Looking up and down the
media row, I saw many fighting to hold back the tears. I didn't bother fighting; it was futile.

However, Joan didn't launch the boom in women's running. The real
tidal wave of women's running didn't get started until the mid-1990s. What
happened then?

So now we must talk about Oprah Winfrey. Oprah ran her marathon 10
years after Joan's. In other words, her race happened well outside the time-
line I have used to organize this book. But I was there to watch Oprah run
her 1994 Marine Corps Marathon in Washington, DC. In fact, I ran the last
23 miles with her. And I can assure you that it was the most courageous
marathon run I have ever seen. So I have no hesitation about including
Oprah with these pioneer women runners.

To begin with, Oprah came from a troubled background. Second, she
was not raised with sports. And third, she is a woman from an ethnic group
that, in the United States, has not been associated with distance running.
Few American black women, beyond Marilyn Bevans, ran long-distance
races. What's more, Oprah had a weight problem that was visible every day

Joan Benoit races the last lap on the track in the 1984 women's Olympic Marathon—the first for women, coming 88 years after the first Olympic Marathon for men.

on national TV and every week on magazine covers at supermarket check-out counters. She was about to turn 40, and she wanted to do something epic—something that would challenge every fiber of her being.

She decided to train for a marathon. And once she made the commitment, she stuck with it to the very end, just like all the other women runners in this book. Oprah succeeded, and in early 1995, we put her on the cover of *Runner's World* magazine with the headline, "Oprah Did It, So Can You." Maybe it's just a coincidence, but that's about the time when thousands, and then millions, of women began running.

People often ask me to summarize the shared qualities of the pioneer women runners. That's not a fair question—not to me, and especially not to them. They broke through the gender barrier in good part because they were fiercely independent; each is a unique individual. They don't fall into pat categories.

Still, if forced, I would probably come up with these following five shared qualities. They don't apply to all the pioneer women, but they do apply to many.

1. First and foremost, they ran because they loved to run. They told me dozens of insightful childhood stories that made clear their early attraction to running. It was an activity that gave them great pleasure—a soul-satisfying, physical pleasure—and they couldn't understand why anyone would want to deny them such joy.

2. They had supportive parents. This wasn't universally true, of course. Several came from troubled family backgrounds. But most of their parents imbued these individuals with strong values, particularly a fierce work ethic.

3. All were changed by their running. Not just in terms of strength and endurance, but emotionally as well. Again and again, I heard variations on this theme: "Before I started running, I was very shy and insecure. Running gave me a sense of self, and a voice to express that self."

4. They were smart and successful in other areas of their lives. An astonishing number of these runners, from the 1960s, in particular, earned MDs, PhDs, and other advanced degrees. They became doctors, veterinarians, college teachers, and impressive business and community leaders. They were either born leaders, or they had learned through running that they could lead and influence.

5. They didn't run as a form of protest. They weren't trying to overthrow some regime, or even the odious early bosses of the AAU. (Although this mindset changed somewhat in the 1970s.) They just wanted the right to test themselves freely in competitions with other runners. Some never protested the discrimination; they lined up quietly on sidewalks and behind bushes. Others took on

the burden because it represented the only way forward for them, their sisters, and their daughters.

The First Ladies of running changed the running world, unleashing a pent-up demand that eventually opened the floodgates. They never intended to force themselves onto the male-dominated sports pages or into the male-centric business world. Those things just happened. As a result, women runners have had an impact beyond track meets and road races. If women can run 10-Ks and marathons, as these First Ladies so ably proved, then, to quote a popular phrase: "Who says women can't run the world?"

I feel incredibly fortunate to have grown up running with the First Ladies. I was able to witness their accomplishments at close range, and to call many of them good friends. They have made running a more exciting, rewarding, and inspiring sport for everyone.

Throughout this book, I've written about the First Ladies primarily using their first names. I believe this makes for clearer reading. (Yes, they got married, divorced, and remarried just like the rest of us.) I've used the surnames they carried during their prime running years. I mean no disrespect by taking this shortcut, and I hope none is taken. I mean only to champion these incredible women, and I hope that this book gives you a chance to learn more about them.

Grace Butcher sprints off the final curve to win the 1959 National Championships 800-meter race—the first such championship for U.S. women since 1928.

"Running and writing both seem like a calling to me—something I've done ever since I can remember. One is for the mind, the other for the body. It seems as if I have to do both to be who I am. They run like parallel streams through my life."

GRACE BUTCHER

Born: January 18, 1934

MAJOR ACHIEVEMENTS

- First modern American 800-meter runner
- Winner, National Indoor Championships 800-meter, 1958 and 1960
- Winner, National Championships 800-meter, 1959
- Participant, 800 meters, 1960 U.S. Olympic Track Trials

GRACE BUTCHER ALWAYS KNEW she'd be a great runner. "I just had a certainty about it, as if it were meant to be," she says reflecting on her childhood in the early 1940s. "As far back as I can remember, I ran. First, I played horse. My toothpick legs were the horse's legs, and the rest of me was the horse's body. I galloped through my childhood."

Grace's life took an abrupt turn when her family moved from upstate New York to a small town in Ohio, and she was forced to leave behind her best friend, Eva. In a world more than 50 years before Facebook or Twitter to keep them connected, the two became fervent pen pals to stay in touch. They remained close friends and kept their dreams alive with each letter— Eva signed all of her notes "FSA" ("future sports announcer"), and Grace signed hers "FOS," which stood for "future Olympic star."

1

In her new home in Chardon, Ohio, Grace plastered the walls of her bedroom with photos of great distance runners such as U.S. milers Gil Dodds and Glenn Cunningham, and the famous Finnish star Paavo Nurmi. She was ready to compete just as they had and saw no reason why she couldn't become one of them. Yet, she noticed there was something missing in her montage of heroes: a woman. Grace recalls that she didn't know any other girls her age who ran, and didn't even know if any professional female runners existed.

"I imagined that surely there was some mystical kingdom where girls wore warm-up suits, and ran laps, and sweated, and had muscles," she remembers.

So, on her own, she attempted to organize a girls track team at Chardon High School. But her efforts were blocked by an old catch-22 circular argument: "We can't have a girls team because other schools don't have a girls team. You won't have anyone else to compete against."

Grace's mother took action. To find a team for her daughter, she made countless phone calls until, in the spring of 1949, she finally made a connection. Grace's mother located a program in Cleveland, nearly an hour's drive from the rural farmlands of Chardon.

"This was an era when parents didn't automatically drop everything to take their kids 40 miles to music and sports practices," Grace recalls. "But my mother did."

Grace's father was less involved in her training. He was a Harvard-trained mechanical engineer whose first Depression-era job was digging ditches for a road crew. Sometimes, he tossed a football with Grace in the backyard or helped her with homework, but he always seemed to become impatient with her and to have little time for her extracurricular interests.

At 15, Grace and her mother finally arrived for her first official track practice. Grace could scarcely believe her eyes. The handful of young women stretching, warming up, practicing their sprint starts, and working on their hurdling form was exactly as she had envisioned. This was the Polish Falcons track team, coached by Stella Walsh, 100-meter gold medalist at the 1932 Olympic Games, and the 100-meter silver medalist in the 1936 Olympics. While continuing to compete herself, Stella supervised the team, which competed in local and regional meets organized by the Lake Erie Amateur Athletic Union (AAU).

At her first practice, Grace learned the most important of all track skills: How to use a garden trowel to dig a proper starting hole. This sounded simple enough, but she quickly discovered there was a specific technique. "You had to scoop out cinders at a right angle to the track," she remembers. "That would give you a vertical surface at the back of the hole, so you could push off hard."

Grace tried all the events that Stella offered: sprints, hurdles, high jump, long jump, even the javelin. At the end of practice, Stella asked Grace which event she would most like to enter. "The mile," Grace answered, with no hesitation.

Stella was taken aback. She hadn't expected this response, or anything like it. She figured Grace would want to do one of the sprint events the girls had been practicing. "Oh, no," Stella explained. "You can't run the mile. There's no mile for women. The longest distance is 200 meters. But with your nice long legs, you could be a hurdler."

Although disappointed at first, Grace decided to pursue training for the 200-meter race and hurdles. Her excitement to finally have a team to run with, and an Olympic champion as her mentor, inspired her to push harder with each workout. She wrote in her journal on May 16, 1949: "What a workout—hurdles and broad jump. It was worth every bit of sweat to get the praise I did from Stella."

Stella further demonstrated her confidence in Grace when she loaned her protégée a pair of her own track shoes to wear in practice. Less than a month later, Grace ran in her first track meet. Dressed in the Falcons team uniform—a shiny white satin singlet and matching shorts—she finished third in the 200 (which Stella won) and fourth in the hurdles. The best came last: She ran on the Falcons' 4 x 100 relay team, along with Stella, and they finished second. However, the track meet didn't fulfill all of Grace's fantasies. In her active imagination, she envisioned herself racing in a packed stadium with wildly cheering fans. But, in reality, the small meet only attracted about six loyal mothers. Still, at 15, Grace was already competing on a track against a world-class athlete. "To run in the same race with Stella!" Grace wrote in her journal. "To see her take off her warm-up suit struck me as rather like seeing a statue unveiled."

Two months later, Grace won the Cleveland Junior Olympics hurdles title. It wasn't the mile; it wasn't the event she dreamed about winning. But she remained hopeful. She told herself this was just the beginning of her journey toward a great track career and the Olympic Games. Instead, it was almost the end.

Life changes quickly when you are 15. The next year, Stella Walsh left the Falcons to pursue other interests. Without Stella, the Polish Falcons' track team dissolved, and there was no longer an activity for Grace to throw her energy and passion into. She drifted away from running and track practice.

Two years later, Grace fell in love with a local boy from Chardon and rushed off to marry him in Louisiana, where he was stationed with the army. When the couple returned to Chardon several years later, they were the parents of two, dark-eyed, curly-haired boys. The once-close world of track and field now seemed like a distant dream. Grace nonetheless stayed physically active by playing basketball, riding horses, swimming, and even racing motorcycles.

"It seems that I was born with my adrenaline button stuck in the 'on' position," she says. "I always had to be doing something intensely physical. I didn't drink or smoke or party hard. What else was I going to do with myself?"

Until the mid-1950s, Grace rarely thought about her early track racing days with Stella. Her schedule was plenty full without running—she now had a husband and two small children to manage. But one day, she saw a local TV program that featured Harrison "Bones" Dillard, a Cleveland native inspired by Jesse Owens, also from Cleveland. Dillard, who had won four gold medals in the 1948 and 1952 Olympic Games, mentioned several track programs in Cleveland, including one for women, the Holland Athletic Club (HAC). Grace decided to focus her attention on one sport—her first—track. She joined the club shortly after seeing the TV program and wondered if she might find an outlet for her still-unsatisfied love for distance running. During her first year with the HAC, Grace was coached by the club founder, Bernice Holland. Afterward, she worked with first one Hungarian immigrant, Alex Ferenczy, followed by another, Julius Penzes.

Penzes's workouts were grueling, seemingly endless, and quite different from the training methods of today. But the Hungarians' system of the 1950s and 1960s produced world-record results by way of highly structured interval training of varying distances. A workout might begin, for example, with 10 strides of 160 meters each, followed by a series of 200-meter repeats at a much faster effort, finishing with a different distance and a new pace. The runner never knew what to expect next, since the coaches revealed only one part of the workout at a time. "When I talk to the runners of today, I often feel that I'm disappointing them, because they always ask how many miles I ran each week in the late 1950s," Grace says. "We didn't do many."

In the 1970s and beyond, most coaches advised runners to build their strength and fitness by logging as much distance as possible. Everyone counted their weekly mileage; that was how runners compared themselves with each other. "We simply didn't count miles. We did only track work, and it was all speed, speed, speed. I never ran anything longer than two miles continuously at a time, but I did speed workouts that just about killed me."

Grace had to push herself especially hard in these workouts, because she was a natural distance runner who was forced to compete at shorter distances against runners with more speed than she had. But at the time, she had no other options. The longest event for women in the Olympic Games was 200 meters. Although the games previously included an 800-meter race for women at the 1928 Olympics in Amsterdam, officials quickly dropped the event from the schedule after several participants collapsed at the finish line (an act that is commonplace among both male and female runners who give the race their all). Though virtually alone in her efforts in the mid-1950s, Grace wanted to bring back the 800 meters for American women. While the event didn't exist in the Olympics, European women still ran it quite regularly. It didn't seem to kill anyone, and it gave women track runners a bigger stage on which to test their abilities.

"I wrote letters to everyone I could think of," Grace recalls. "I wrote to other athletes, to the AAU, and to public figures who I thought could help us. I don't recall that anyone objected. Everyone seemed to agree that women deserved more opportunities at longer distances." But still nothing happened.

———

By the summer of 1957, Grace had made enough noise that she was allowed to run in an exhibition 800 at a local outdoor meet. No other women entered.

Since it was an exhibition, and no one knew what might happen, track officials allowed her male coach to pace her through the first lap. Grace then went solo the second lap. She finished in 2:57.8. It was, as far as anyone could determine, the first time in 29 years that an American woman had raced two laps (800 meters) around a track.

Grace wasn't particularly proud of her time. She knew that she and others could do better, if given more chances. But she had finished, and she didn't collapse or horrify any of the spectators. "At least we showed that a woman could complete the two laps," she remembers.

At about the same time, the International Olympic Committee announced that it was going to add the women's 800 to the 1960 Rome Olympic Games. The U.S. track organization, the Amateur Athletic Union, quickly took note, hoping to uncover some American talent for Rome. The 1958 AAU Indoor Championships were slated for Akron, Ohio, and a women's 800 was included. Again, it was billed as an "exhibition" rather than an official event on the racing program.

But at least the women's 800 would become part of a national championship event, which meant it would open more doors and attract more attention to women's middle-distance running. However, the effort didn't happen as readily as Grace and her friends had hoped. And the national publication for track and field didn't show much interest. "Women's track is definitely not men's track," said a *Track and Field News* magazine editor at the time in 1959. "We cannot sacrifice magazine space to cover 'fringe' activities. Personally, I can't get very excited about girlish athletics."

────────

Nonetheless, 10,000 enthusiastic indoor track fans did get excited, along with Frances Kaszubski, the AAU national chair for women's running. A handful of women toed the start line, including Grace and 47-year-old Stella Walsh, her first coach. With the starting gun in the air, Kaszubski interrupted the proceedings to make a brief plea to the competitors. "Ladies, please don't collapse and embarrass us," she said. "Run under control and with a smile on your face."

Grace can't swear that she followed directions that day. She only remembers finding herself in the lead midway through the distance, somewhat to her surprise, and that she pushed hard the rest of the way to maintain her margin. She broke the tape in 2:48.6, a new personal best. Later that evening, Kaszubski slipped her an official AAU winner's medal, even though the race had been labeled an exhibition.

After her 1958 indoor win, Grace set her sights on the 1960 Rome Olympics, just two years away. She would be 26. Across the country, dozens of other young runners got the word about their new Olympic possibility. In another 24 years, women would finally be allowed to run an Olympic Marathon. But the first big step forward came in 1960, and the distance was 800 meters.

Grace intensified her training, running twice a day, six times a week, sometimes worrying that she couldn't afford to take a rest day. In particular, she obsessed over her need for increased speed. In that regard, many of her competitors had an advantage over her. They could run 400 meters in 58 or 59 seconds, while Grace's best was 63. She might have beaten them at a longer distance—1500 meters or the mile—but races at those distances still didn't exist for women. When not training with Penzes in Cleveland once a week, Grace sought out area high-school tracks. The local coaches supported her, and even loaned her "workout boys" to pace her during intense interval training. "The coaches soon figured out I was serious and hardworking," she says. "They would tell the boys they could get in really good shape by running with me."

The hard training began to pay off. Grace won the 1959 National Championships 800 in 2:21.2, a big personal best. That gained her a spot on the U.S. team that would compete against the Soviet Union, then the highest honor in American track, short of an Olympic berth. This was the Cold War era, and the United States versus the Soviet Union track meets were televised every year, with huge national audiences tuning in. Every American runner on the U.S. team was given a singlet, shorts, warm-up suit, and navy blue travel blazer. It was almost more than a small town girl from Chardon, Ohio, could believe.

Grace attended a training camp in Cleveland, where her hotel and meals were paid for, and she received $2 a day in spending money—she was finally treated as an elite athlete of the time. Then, the team flew to Philadelphia's famous Franklin Field for the big meet. It began with an opening ceremonies spectacle just like the Olympics.

"It was thrilling to march into the packed stadium in a parade behind the flags," Grace recalls. "We realized the Russian women were better than us because they had so much more experience, but we were also proud to be the best Americans. We felt we would catch up with the Russians once we had as many years running the 800 as they did."

While the experience was enthralling, Grace's race was not. In the previous weeks, Penzes had increased her training program to three workouts a day. Excited about the progress she had made, he reasoned that an extra dose of training would drive her to an even higher level. The plan backfired. One day Grace's foot exploded in pain, as if she had wrenched it in a hole. With her foot heavily taped, she ran in the meet anyway, but fell short of her best efforts. The injury continued to plague her off and on for a year. When the foot was healthy, she trained intensely, aiming toward the National Championships and National Indoor Championships, followed by the 1960 Olympic Trials. She knew she was returning to good form when she won the 1960 Indoor Championships in 2:26.8, followed by a 2:24 July tune-up race in Chicago.

It seemed as if her training and racing were coming together at just the right moment. But walking off the track in Chicago, she felt a sharp pain in her foot once again. Despite the injury, and filled with dread, Grace flew to Texas for the two biggest races of her life—the Nationals and the Olympic Trials. At Nationals, two other runners broke 2:20. This was new territory for American women in the 800, and Grace couldn't match their pace. That left only the Olympic Trials, where each runner had to finish first, second, or third in the first-round heats in order to advance to the final. The first three finishers in the final would go to the Olympics, provided each attained the international qualifying time.

The throbbing pain in Grace's foot continued, and she found it impossible to run with her normal stride. A sympathetic coach tried to help by giving her a shot of novocaine, and then wrapping the foot as tightly as he could to minimize its movements on the loose-cinder track. But these hasty remedies were to no avail: Grace finished fourth in her heat, failing to make the finals. As it turned out, only one American, race-winner Billie Pat Daniels, ran fast enough to earn the trip to Rome. She broke the tape in 2:15.6, a new American record. The second and third finishers didn't achieve the Olympic qualifying time.

This proved what Grace had known and argued from the beginning. The best U.S. women, denied the chance to run the 800 for so many years, would need time and opportunity to catch the rest of the world. The point wasn't to win medals the first time around; the point was to start the journey, and then let history unfold as it would. The wisdom of Grace's vision proved true just eight years later when the United States' Madeline Manning, also coached by Julius Penzes, won the 800-meter gold medal in the 1968 Mexico City Olympic Games.

After the 1960 Olympic Trials, Grace returned to Chardon, back to her husband and two young boys, and waited for her foot to heal. After several months, she returned to the track, starting the laborious process of getting back in shape. With her Olympic dream lost, she struggled for motivation. "I remember that I was out on the track with no one else around on a hot late-summer day," she says. "And I felt so very lonely."

But she didn't give up. It is the way of the athlete to return to the struggle, to start over again, no matter how difficult or solitary. You run again, because you must. It is something you feel deep in your core, something difficult to describe to others. Is it physical? Is it spiritual? Does it matter?

"I developed a sort of life motto, 'Keep on keeping on,'" Grace says. "I believe we're all here to discover our life's purpose, and then once you've discovered it, for Heaven's sake, get on with it. The saddest words I know are, 'If only . . .'."

In the early 1970s, occasional road races began popping up around Ohio. Grace was in her late thirties, but entered many 5-Ks, and even the races that occasionally stretched to 15-K. No other women in Ohio competed in these races, but Grace wanted to test her limits.

"Mentally, I loved the idea of running longer distances," she says, "but physically, my body didn't like it—I always tightened up badly and had to take three or four days off to get rid of the pain in my calf muscles. I think I just ran too much on my toes the way I did on the track."

Fortunately, that same running form served her well in masters track and field competitions, which was gaining popularity. Over the next 20 years, Grace continued running and writing, eventually teaching at several universities and publishing many poetry books.

"Running and writing both seem like a calling to me—something I've done ever since I can remember," she says. "One is for the mind, the other for the body. It seems as if I have to do both to be who I am. They run like parallel streams through my life."

Denied an official race number, Julia Chase displays perfect form—and a nice Smith College gym uniform—in the 1961 Manchester Road Race in Connecticut. She ran the 4.75-mile distance at a 7:10 minutes-per-mile pace.

"Running puts you in touch with your primal self and your deepest resolve. You learn how to deal with pain and other obstacles. You realize that it's not important to do conventional things. You can do whatever feels worthwhile to you."

JULIA CHASE

Born: August 24, 1942

> MAJOR ACHIEVEMENTS

- Participant, 800 meters, 1960 U.S. Olympic Track Trials
- First woman road racer, Manchester 5 Mile (Connecticut), 1961
- Finisher, 50 years later, Manchester Road Race, 5 Mile, 2011

BEFORE 1961, THERE IS no record of a woman ever finishing an American road race. When Julia Chase became the first—completing a 6.5-miler on Veterans Day in Chicopee, Massachusetts—the newspaper stories dripped with sexism and ridicule. "Julia Chase, an attractive, 19-year-old Smith College student is causing almost as much dither these days as Amelia Bloomer did when she introduced unconventional ladies garments in 1849," read an article in the *Boston Globe* newspaper. The Associated Press described her as "the curvaceous, 19-year-old sophomore."

Headline writers, in particular, enjoyed making fun of Julia and her running. The *New York Daily News* used its famous back page to proclaim: "She wants to chase boys." Julia had neither wanted nor expected attention from the press. She ran the small race in Chicopee to build confidence for a much bigger event later that month—the Manchester Road Race in her home state of Connecticut.

The Manchester Road Race took place on Thanksgiving Day, and the 4.75-miler was perhaps the country's second most famous road race, second only to the Boston Marathon. Manchester annually attracted 150 runners, only 50 fewer runners than Boston, and its field also included Olympians and elites. But Julia's desire to run the Manchester race was a personal matter—just one year earlier, in 1960, Manchester had denied Julia entry. Race officials told her to try again the next year, with an earlier registration. She hadn't been permitted to register for the Chicopee race, either (it was against Amateur Athletic Union [AAU] regulations for women to run more than 1.25 miles). But when she showed up anyway, the race organizers treated her respectfully and let her run along with the 34 official entrants (all men, of course).

After a couple of miles, she passed one of them—the first male ever to be passed by a woman in a road race. What was his reaction? "Good work," he said, "keep it up." Julia finished 28th overall at Chicopee. Surprised and impressed by her performance, the officials even dug up a trophy to award her. However, the good will ended when word spread about her effort. Reporters called her at Smith in Northampton, Massachusetts, several times a day. Julia, raised to be polite and helpful, gave them as much interview time as they wanted, although some questions could be painfully cringe-worthy. "For a college sophomore, all the questions just became excruciating," she recalls. "They kept trying to come up with different motives for why I ran." They all asked the same kinds of questions, most of them implying that she must be "different," and not in a good way.

Why would a woman want to do this thing that no other women do? Was she looking for a husband? Was she trying to make a statement about female superiority? Was she an "Amazon woman" with some strange genetic makeup? The answer to all the probing questions was a resounding no.

"For me, I was doing something completely normal, something I loved," Julia says. "I had grown up running through the woods. Humans have been running from the beginning of our history. I thought it would have made more sense to ask: 'Why doesn't everyone run?' "

———————

Julia began her running as a youth in Groton, Connecticut, on the edge of the Thames River and Long Island Sound. Both her parents were ill much of the time, so she lived on her grandmother's 8-acre homestead and was less supervised by adults than most youth. If she missed the bus to school, she had to get herself there, so she jogged the 1.5-mile distance.

"It was easy," she recalls. "It was simply the way we got around in those days. Besides, I loved everything about it. I loved the aesthetic of being outdoors, running a forest trail, jumping over a stream, and wondering what I'd encounter around the next corner."

She remembers how her grandmother, at age 75, encouraged all her various enthusiasms—from outdoor exploration to running. "Granny was warm and supportive, as curious as I was, and always interested in learning new things," Julia recalls. "If I discovered a bird's egg in a nest, she'd take me home to look it up, and we'd figure out together what kind of bird it was. She told me that I should aim for a full life, and to do good for others."

As a teenager, Julia spent much of her time outdoors with her four brothers. The five of them would play baseball during the day, play hide-and-seek in the evening, and go swimming at night. Growing up as the middle child in a family of all boys, Julia learned quickly to pick up a variety of sports with skill that rivaled most boys her age. In school, she recalls that gym teachers often picked her to show a group of much-older girls how to put a good spin on a softball. "When it came to sports, I like to think I held my own with all the boys in the neighborhood," she says.

During the spring of 1957 when Julia was 14, she and her father headed to mass every morning for Lenten services. It was on these drives that she learned about another near-religious practice—morning runs. Every morning, like clockwork, Julia and her father would notice a solitary runner logging miles on his daily workout. But it wasn't just any regular road runner hitting the pavement for his morning miles. It was local marathon star John J. Kelley, the best distance runner in the United States at the time.

The sight of Kelley's slim-but-energetic figure bounding along the road entranced Julia—he blended seamlessly into the scenery. He appeared unfazed by the whir of passing cars, the monotony of unending distance, or the unpredictable spring weather. A month later, on April 20, 1957, Julia was quietly reading in her bedroom when she suddenly heard her father bellow up the stairs: "Johnny Kelley just won the Boston Marathon!"

The news astounded her, particularly after her father explained the magnitude of the Boston Marathon. It was hard to comprehend that the short, youthful-looking runner she had seen on local streets had won a race of worldwide importance. She could scarcely imagine someone covering 26.2 miles on foot. The distance seemed overwhelming.

At the same time, Kelley's victory also caused Julia to begin thinking about her own limitations—or lack thereof. Maybe the seemingly impossible was not, in fact, that far out of reach. She began to ask herself: "I wonder if I could do something like that someday?"

From that day forward, Julia clipped every headline and story that noted Kelley's accomplishments. And even though a knee injury would hold her back from running for three years, she would still walk to the nearby golf course where John Kelley and fellow runner George Terry ran their hardest fartlek workouts. She would scout out the best vantage point, sit herself down, and watch them fly past. "I can't really explain it," she says, "but I would almost shake with excitement [when they ran past]."

By 1960, her knee had strengthened enough that her doctors gave her permission to resume exercising again. So, she started by running alongside the railroad tracks where she had often seen Kelley, in hopes that she might spot him training. She was happily rewarded one day when he came churning toward her on the tracks and stopped to chat.

"Do you think women can run long distances?" she asked eagerly.

"Why not?" he replied.

Kelley invited Julia to meet with him and Terry to talk more about distance running and training. Julia relaxed at the kitchen table at Kelley's Mystic home, and hung on each word the two experienced runners spoke. They explained why there weren't women running road races. Common wisdom held that endurance exercise was beyond a woman's physical abilities. Worse, strenuous training for endurance events might actually destroy a woman's physical health—imperiling her reproductive organs and threatening her ability to have children.

That was the conventional thinking in 1960, and the conventional practice at the time was for women to focus only on, well, "womanly activities." But unlike the masses, Kelley and Terry dismissed these theories. They told Julia that there was no proof or substance to any of them. How could there be?

Because women weren't encouraged or even allowed to run long distances, there had never been a tried-and-true test of the bad-for-you hypotheses. Unlike cross-country and road races, track meets did allow a limited schedule for women. Women could run as far as 200 meters. And in 1960, for the first time since 1928, there would be an 800-meter race for women in the Olympic Games.

Dreaming of a bid for the rare Olympic opportunity, Julia asked the two men if one of them would coach her for the 800 meters. Kelley demurred, focused as he was on his own efforts to make it to Rome in the marathon, his second chance at an Olympic medal. But Terry stepped forward and began devising a plan to get Julia in shape for the 800 meters. The duo attended their first track meet together, the New England AAU Championships on July 4, 1960, in Providence, Rhode Island. This meet took place just two weeks before the Olympic Trials would begin in Texas.

Julia toed the start line for the New England 800 meters, but she started way too fast (the curse of many first-timers). Luckily, Terry chased her around the track and caught her attention, signaling her to calm down. She slowed, but still found herself ahead by a large margin and sailing to a clear victory, until the last straightaway.

As Julia turned for the final stretch, she saw a couple strolling down the first lane, holding hands, and kissing every few seconds. "They looked to be very much in love," she recalls. "But I didn't know what I was supposed to do. I had never run a race before, so I fell back on my best manners, and said something like, 'Excuse me. Could you please move to the side and let me through?' This was before I learned that you're supposed to just yell, 'Track!'" In spite of all this, Julia won the race in a New England record time, 2:42.

Two weeks later, still knowing almost nothing about track racing, she was en route to Abilene, Texas, for the women's Olympic Track Trials. Friends and townspeople quickly raised funds to cover her travel expenses. The Olympic Trials would be her second track meet ever.

Julia and Terry's road to the Olympic Trials had the makings of a movie—a mix of near disaster, comedy, Hollywood-esque glitter, and inspiration—that began with their plane catching fire. Luckily, the plane managed to land safely. Unluckily, this meant it would take nearly a full day to reach Abilene.

Once there, Julia found herself among seasoned female track athletes for the first time. She was particularly taken with Wilma Rudolph and her Tennessee State Tigerbelle teammates. They carried themselves so elegantly—tall and proud, almost regal. Their bright uniforms turned Julia's head even more. "The outfits were new and very striking, making them all look like professional athletes," she remembers.

Julia's attire was "rather shabby," she says. She donned a pair of her younger brother's brown shorts, a white T-shirt, and a decaying pair of George Terry's track spikes (that were also three sizes too large). To keep the spikes on her feet, Julia and Terry taped them snug with rolls of wide adhesive tape.

But even duct tape couldn't fix the annoyance of Julia's ill-fitting bra. Mere moments before the start of her event, Julia had to devise some serious damage control. Her bra felt like it was suffocating her. She raced under the grandstand, turned away from the crowd, and quickly removed it. Hurrying back to the track, she lined up with the other women in her heat and listened closely for the starter's commands.

The gun fired, and they were off, sprinting wildly down the cinder track. Each runner focused her gaze straight ahead, channeling an all-out effort into a single goal—placing in the top three to secure a spot in the final, which would be the race to select potential Olympians.

Julia fell short, finishing fifth in the qualifying race. Still, she improved her time by 10 seconds to 2:32, and, at just 18, learned firsthand what more experienced women could achieve on the track. Later that summer, Julia continued traveling with Terry and friends to several track meets in Providence, eventually lowering the New England record in both the 400 meters and 800 meters. The meets never had a locker room or other facilities for women, so the men created a makeshift changing area for her. They circled the car, forming a wall with their backs pressed against the windows. Once all windows were blocked, Julia awkwardly—but privately—changed into her racing outfit.

On Thanksgiving morning, 1960, Julia drove to the Manchester Road Race for the first time, accompanied by John Kelley (a multiple Manchester winner), George Terry, and fellow racing friends from Groton, Connecticut. She was prepped and trained to run five miles with ease, and she was ready to go. She never imagined that she'd be barred from registering for the event—she had, after all, competed in the Olympic Track Trials several months earlier.

But Manchester officials saw things differently. They claimed that AAU rules prohibited them from allowing a woman to enter the road race—women belonged on the track only (and only up to 800 meters). In the face of this strict interpretation, Julia didn't press her case. She wasn't one to create a scene or be marked a troublemaker. Besides, the officials placated her and Terry by implying that they would reconsider her entry into the race the next year, if she entered early. "I didn't put up much of a fuss that first year at Manchester," she recalls. "I thought, 'Let's just let the race get going.'"

Julia watched, frustrated, from the sidelines, as a record 114 men crossed the finish line. On the drive home, Julia's friends fumed over the way she had been denied entry. "They were saying, 'That wasn't fair. The organizers should have let you run. They were still registering beer bellies and eight-year-old boys. You could have beaten them easily.'"

But for someone eager to sprint toward finish lines, Julia was a master of patience. She knew her time would come. She came from a long line of family members who didn't tolerate discrimination. Her great grandfather was president of the American Woman Suffrage Association in the late 1880s; her relatives were abolitionists who helped slaves flee to freedom on the Underground Railroad; and her grandmother, Mary Foulke Morrisson, gave a seconding speech for Herbert Hoover at the 1920 Republican Convention and worked to found the League of Women Voters.

Julia shared their steely determination in the quest to overturn injustices. She set her sights on the next year's Manchester Road Race—1961 would be her year. By early November, Julia's secret was out. She made strides toward Manchester by first running the Chicopee, Massachusetts, 6.5-miler. A short newspaper story flashed across the newswires, and soon she was receiving calls from reporters around the country. She answered all with her natural courtesy and thoughtfulness. A *New York Journal-American* newspaper reporter wrote: "It was frightening to interview Miss Chase on the phone today. Sporting writers are conditioned to other athletes throwing out two or three cuss words per sentence. Miss Chase spoke in a cultured voice. She was logical, frank, humorous, and intelligent. (It usually takes four athletes to get that combination.)"

By the morning of the 1961 Manchester race, Julia's story was headline news across the nation. Dozens of papers sent reporters to cover the race, including the *New York Times*. *Sports Illustrated* magazine even assigned a

Manchester race director Pete Wigren tells Chase and Dianne LeChausse
that they can't run. They do anyway, and both finish.

writer to tail her for several days to get the full scoop. Because Terry had
entered her in advance on an official race application, as they were instructed
the year before, both he and Julia hoped for little or no interference.

As happened too often for the duo, things did not work out according to
plan. The race director said he had to uphold race tradition and what he
believed to be Connecticut AAU regulations prohibiting mixed-gender competition. Once again, Julia was refused a race number. "Okay," she said. "But
this time, I'm going to do the race anyway." She wouldn't stand on the sidelines again as a spectator. She aimed to run—with or without a race number.

When she jogged to the start line, Julia was surprised to discover two other
women there who intended to run. They had learned of her plans from the
newspaper articles and decided to join her in a show of support. These were
not just your average 1960s housewives. One runner was Chris McKenzie, an
experienced middle-distance runner from England. The other was Dianne
Lechausse, a dancer from Manchester, Connecticut. The women made hasty
introductions, formed a quick huddle, and decided to start together.

They were harassed from the outset. The race director recruited a small
militia of male volunteers to keep the women off the race course. He
instructed the men to join arms and drive the women from the starting line
onto the sidewalk. However, their efforts were no match for the three

quick-stepping women. The trio simply darted back onto the road at the back of the pack behind all the male runners. Although the race director charged after them, trying to talk them off the course, he was already too late. The starter's gun echoed through the air, cutting his arguments short. The runners stampeded down the road. For a moment, the cordon of race volunteers tried to block Julia, Chris, and Dianne again. But they failed.

"They were just a bunch of fat, old guys who couldn't move very fast," Julia recalls. "We just swerved around them and kept on running."

Liberated from the hassles of the start line, the three women settled into their respective paces and did what they were perfectly prepared to do: run. Along the way, they received warm support from the crowd, the largest in Manchester's 34-year history. Swarms of spectators gathered on the sidewalks to watch the race participants churn past. Local residents turned out in record numbers, because they didn't want to miss the spectacle of a woman (*now three women*) running in an otherwise all-male event.

"My wife and I have never seen this race before," commented one of the spectators. "But with the girl in it today, we sure weren't going to miss it."

Although running at a comfortable pace, Julia and Chris passed a handful of men on the course. Dianne, an inexperienced runner, fell behind early on. But Julia wasn't trying to compete; she was mostly focused on creating a lasting image of a female athlete finishing strong.

"After all the things that had been said or implied about me in the press, I wanted to present a good image at Manchester," she says. "I showed up wearing lipstick, my hair nicely brushed, and wearing a Smith College gym tunic with a skirt. I wasn't out to set any records. I just wanted to finish looking good and to show that women could run the race."

Julia felt confident the entire race, and she enjoyed the applause of the crowd. In particular, she remembers a tiny, older woman who stood on a street corner yelling, "You can do it! You can do it!" A mile from the finish, Chris turned to her, and said she was going to pick up the pace. She moved ahead of Julia but stopped short of the finish line, fearing AAU reprisals if she actually completed the course. Julia simply maintained her pace and composure, growing more excited as she approached a long-sought-after finish line—one that her heroes John Kelley and George Terry had crossed many times.

The last stretch proved almost overwhelming. "I wasn't sure where the exact finish was," she recalls, "and people were crowding into the street to

Chase, a Smith College sophomore, enjoys a quiet moment before warming up for the start of the 1961 Manchester Road Race.

look for me. The road got very narrow. I felt a bit like a scared, caged animal with the cage rattling and vibrating all around me."

She crossed the line in 33:40 for the 4.75-mile course, a pace of about 7:10 per mile, good for 128th place. "I was feeling just jubilant," Julia remembers. "I was doing cartwheels on the sidewalk. George was just as excited. He was giving me piggyback rides."

Ten runners came in behind Julia, among them Dianne, the dancer, who finished last in 41:12. The next day's *New York Times* reported: "All the women went the distance. Two of the men failed to finish."

Julia succeeded in her mission, she believes, because running teaches an inner strength. "Running puts you in touch with your primal self and your deepest resolve," she says. "You learn how to deal with pain and other obstacles. You realize that it's not important to do conventional things. You can do whatever feels worthwhile to you."

Julia continued running through the 1964 Olympic Trials, training for a time with the Los Angeles Track Club, where she logged up to 80 miles a week.

In December 1963, she attended the Western Hemisphere Marathon in Culver City, California, to encourage teammate Norm Higgins. Once there, she was delighted to see two women running—Merry Lepper and Lyn

Carman—and quickly turned her attention and support to them. Lyn would drop out, but Merry would become the first American woman to run a marathon, covering the distance in 3:37:07. Julia was one of the first to greet her at the finish line.

In 1964, Julia concentrated on the Olympic Track Trials again. At that summer's Trials, she improved her personal best in the 800 to 2:16, which was 30 seconds faster than her first 800-meter race in 1960. But by this point, the competition had grown much tougher. More women were given the opportunity to compete, and they responded by racing hard and pushing each other to even faster performances.

After serious injury in a car accident, Julia decided to put more emphasis on her academic life. She earned a PhD in zoology and taught for a time at Rutgers University and Barnard College. Then, midcareer, she switched to medical school and started a new journey in the field of psychiatry. In 1981, 20 years after her first Manchester Road Race finish, she completed the course again, finishing in 37:56.

Another 30 years flashed past, and women distance runners were no longer a curiosity. In fact, they numbered roughly 50 percent of all entrants in some road races. From the dawning days of 2011, Julia set her sights on running Manchester again, 50 years after her first historic finish. And she made it. This time she finished in 51:32, becoming the first woman known to have completed a road race on the 50th anniversary of her first finish in the event. (Others in this book may soon match Julia's feat, but they will all follow after her.) And she wore the same Smith College gym skirt she wore in 1961.

Like many of the other inspiring women in this book, Julia was moved to tears while watching Joan Benoit win the 1984 Olympic Marathon. She grew up in a family that believed in the march of political history and personal freedom, and that's what she saw in Joan's victory. "It was thrilling to see Joan's race that day," she remembers. "I walked around for hours afterward. I just couldn't settle down. It had such an impact on me.

"I felt that Joan had grabbed the relay baton from us, and raced it home the way we did from Wilma Rudolph in my day. Joan was so good about giving credit to the women who came before her. I appreciated that. We ran in the civil rights era, and sometimes we did feel a little like Rosa Parks. People tell me that I had great courage, but I mainly feel lucky that I had the chance to make a contribution."

Doris Brown leads the 1970 World Cross-Country Championships in Frederick, Maryland. She won the World Cross race five years in a row.

"Running lets you show what you can do. You never know how far you might go until you get outside your comfort zone. You have to reach beyond your grasp. That's where the real living begins."

DORIS BROWN

Born: September 17, 1942

MAJOR ACHIEVEMENTS

- Third place, 800 meters, 1960 U.S. Olympic Track Trials
- Indoor world record, one-mile, 1966
- Five consecutive victories, World Cross-Country Championships, 1967 through 1971
- Two Olympic teams, 1968 and 1972

BACK IN THE MID-1950S, most young female distance runners could only dream of competing for a girls track team. The teams were very few and far between. If you wanted to run, you could do it on your own. But how much fun would it be, especially if you were training to run long distance? Young Doris Severtsen was luckier than most. As a teen, she joined the Tacoma Mic-Macs, a Washington-State-based track team for girls. The Mic-Macs coach was a big supporter of girls' sports. Unfortunately, his good intentions couldn't compensate for his minimal knowledge of running, and particularly, nutrition. According to the coach's rationale, since running requires energy, and energy comes from food, then young runners should eat something immediately before their races.

"We'd be standing on the starting line," Doris recalls, "and Mr. McCrory would run over to feed us doughnuts or peanut butter or whatever he had."

Doris would gobble down McCrory's offering, blast off the starting line of the 400-meter race, cross the finish line, and then—predictably—throw up. Every time. Although her coach had much to learn about proper fueling, he did cultivate her track talent, tapping into a work ethic that Doris had developed as a young girl.

Doris grew up in a Scandinavian family from Gig Harbor, Washington, in the coastal Puget Sound region. Her father was a boat builder, carpenter, and handyman. He was always busy, with an ever-growing to-do list. His own around-the-clock labors meant he also expected everyone else to work hard, Doris included.

Doris's mother was likewise a no-nonsense Norwegian. The family lived simply and well by following a pragmatic approach to daily life. Chores came before anything else: Doris and her siblings were responsible for the animals, the garden, and bread baking—there wasn't much time, or inclination, for them to socialize with other kids, see movies, or go dancing. Their biggest celebrations were birthday parties and visits from the grandparents. Despite this strict upbringing, the family did enjoy music, and they encouraged Doris's love of the piano and French horn. Even more than playing her instruments, Doris cherished her time outdoors caring for the chickens and frolicking along the waterfront after school. "Sometimes, I'd see a bear on the beach," she recalls. "He'd race away in one direction, and I'd go the other way. I think I developed some good speed from those bear sightings."

But running for the Mic-Macs (and from bears) didn't completely satisfy Doris's yearning for competition. With no high-school girls track team, she could only watch the boys team practice from the sidelines. Occasionally, the coach allowed Doris to join practice for a few sprints, but nothing more. She never competed in a high-school track meet, getting only a taste of the experience when the coach invited her to ride on the team bus to a meet. "That was so exciting," she remembers. "It seemed like a really big deal to me then."

Although barred from competing in high school, Doris found that the summer meets on the Mic-Macs team helped improve her endurance. By 1960, while just 17, she ran the 800 meters fast enough to qualify for that year's Olympic Track Trials in Abilene, Texas. The year marked an important leap for women runners, as the women's 800 was finally included in the

Olympic schedule for the first time since 1928. Excitement ran high, and every young female middle-distance runner in the country wanted to qualify for the "new" event, the 800. Nothing could keep Doris from Texas; she and Coach McCrory took a train from Seattle, riding in coach, and sleeping while sitting up over the multiday journey. Despite arriving in Texas sleep-deprived and a little stiff, Doris delivered solid performances that advanced her through the qualifying rounds.

In the final, however, her inexperience trumped her talent. She ran too much of the race in the second and third lanes, elbows clashing with several of her rivals. She was still in contention coming off the last turn until another racer's errant elbow slammed into her rib cage, knocking the wind out of her. She finished third in 2:17.6; only the winner attained the Olympic qualifying time. Still, Doris managed to view the race in a positive light—as she did with the other disappointments that would come her way over her long and distinguished career.

"When you don't get what you want, you can let it drive you up or down," she notes. "The more heart and soul you put into it, the better your chances. Besides, the best things always take a while."

After the 1960 Olympic Trials, Doris returned to her home state to attend college at Seattle Pacific University. At SPU, the men's cross-country and track coach let Doris work out with his runners. But to prove herself worthy of the opportunity, she trained too hard and developed a series of injuries. "The guys were really good to me," she says. "But I was afraid if I didn't stay with them, they wouldn't want me around any longer, so I did way more than I should have."

To make matters worse, because Doris wasn't officially a member of the team, she couldn't be treated by the school's athletic trainers. Her injuries led to stagnating times in the few races available to her, and her poor performances led to frustration. Adding insult to injury, male distance runners who circled Green Lake, one of Doris's favorite training grounds, would harass her on her runs.

"They'd yell and throw things at me," she recalls. "Once, someone threw a football. Others would push me toward the water's edge. It was isolating

Brown received encouragement and training advice from Seattle Pacific coach Ken Foreman.

and alienating to be the only woman out there." She wondered if her running was worth all the effort she put into it. "Life was depressing for several years after 1960," she admits. "I slipped into a funk."

Fortunately, help soon arrived in the person of Ken Foreman, the Seattle Pacific coach. He had returned to SPU after a leave of absence to pursue an advanced degree in exercise physiology. Foreman launched the Falcon Track Club for noncollegiate athletes in the Seattle area, and he accepted Doris onto the team. He had rarely seen anyone with such dedication to her sport, and Doris thrived under his tutelage. "Ken helped athletes believe in themselves and treated everyone like they were capable of being an Olympian," Doris says. "As a result, we started to believe in ourselves. He always said, 'Action absorbs anxiety.' In other words, running gives you the opportunity to free yourself up."

Despite her newfound confidence, Doris had trouble putting it to good use in the spring of 1964. She had graduated from Seattle Pacific, taken a public schools teaching and coaching job, and gotten married. Now, with another Olympic Trials fast approaching, she found herself torn between teaching, coaching, training, and spending time with her husband. Her busy schedule only allowed her about five hours of sleep a night. She'd wake up at 5:30 a.m. for her first workout and keep going nonstop until dinnertime, 12 hours later. The pressures of her high-stress daily life and then an injury to her fragile foot were responsible for knocking her out of the 1964 Trials and bringing her Olympic dreams to an abrupt halt once again.

"It was such a frustrating year, because I did fine in the other meets all the way up to the Trials," she remembers. "When I got hurt, Ken and I didn't know what to do. I still wasn't allowed in the athletic trainer's room, so we just tried various ways of taping my foot. They didn't work."

With another Olympic opportunity missed, Doris and Foreman began looking for new horizons. One appeared in January 1966 when she was invited to Vancouver, Canada, for an indoor mile race—a rare distance opportunity offered to female runners. Canadian organizers were excited about the event and hoped that a young female Canadian runner would shatter the world record for the distance. Instead, that honor would go to Doris, who hit the tape first in 4:52.

"It was a big lift to win that race, and set the record," Doris says. "It proved what I had always thought—the longer the distance, the better I ran. It was very difficult for me to win 800-meter races, but the Vancouver Mile confirmed that I could win the longer races."

While Doris excelled at the longer distances, there were few such races for her to enter. She received her biggest opportunity yet when a new event surfaced in the spring of 1967. It was called the World Cross-Country Championships, and it included a women's division as well as the men's. The first race was held in Wales, and Doris received an invitation. A strong squad of British women were heavily favored, as they had considerable experience in tough, European-style cross-country racing.

Since Doris had never before competed in cross-country, Foreman advised her to start slow and follow the other runners. If she felt good near the end, he told her, she could unleash her kick and go for a top finish. The course in Wales included muddy cow pastures and narrow trails through the woods. Recent stormy weather had littered the course with broken tree branches. Doris, reminded of the windy, rainy days of her childhood on Puget Sound, couldn't have been happier. She completely disregarded her coach's instructions and zoomed to the front. There was no catching her. She ran wild and free to victory. "I couldn't help it," she recalls. "I felt so good, and the pace seemed easy."

Doris would repeat her World Cross-Country win over the next four years—in England, Scotland, the United States, and France. For five years in a row, she dominated the sport's toughest, longest race against the best women runners in the world, winning each time convincingly. She seemed to own the event, which required her particular combination of grit and endurance. She would likely have won six in a row if Amateur Athletic Union (AAU) officials hadn't forced her to enter the 1972 USA-USSR indoor meet, which was held the same weekend as the World Cross-Country Championships. In those days, AAU policies allowed officials to dictate where amateur runners were allowed to compete.

"That made me so mad," she says, uncharacteristically. "I was heart-broken. I didn't get the chance to keep my streak alive. It was the kind of thing that would never happen today, but it was the way we were treated at the time."

The distances in women's cross-country, Doris's specialty, ranged from 3 to 4 miles. On the track, however, the longest race for women continued to be the 800 meters. With the 1968 Olympics approaching, Doris buckled down and did her best to prepare. By now she was often running up to 80 miles a week in training, a prodigious amount for an 800-meter runner, male or female. The hard work paid off. At the U.S. Olympic Track Trials, she finished in a dead heat with Madeline Manning; both timed in 2:03.00. After studying the finish-line photo, the meet judges awarded the victory to Manning. But the judges' decision hardly mattered. Doris finally achieved her longtime goal. After two previous failures, she would be going to the Olympic Games for the first time.

Due to the high-altitude conditions they would face in Mexico City, site of the 1968 Games, Doris and others spent time preparing at an Olympic training camp in Los Alamos, New Mexico. Doris always found it difficult to cope with the challenge of altitude running, perhaps because she was born and raised at sea level. But she enjoyed the exotic new environment around Los Alamos and continued to log long runs, her favorite part of training.

At the Games, Doris qualified handily for the final and prepared herself for the most important race of her life. She was running strongly on the final curve when she and another runner bumped hard against each other. Before she knew it, Doris was thrown to the track. She bounced quickly to her feet and rallied in the final straight, but ran out of track. She finished fifth in 2:03.9. Madeline Manning won the gold in a world record time of 2:00.9. Doris refused to let her disappointment drag her down for long. "I swore to myself that I'd be back at the Olympics in four years, and that this time, I'd stay on my feet."

She did get back. Staying on her feet, though? That was another story.

By 1972, the International Olympic Committee had finally added the women's 1500-meter race to the track and field schedule, at long last opening the gates to the "metric mile" for women. Although Doris was 30 years old in 1972, older than most top American runners, she qualified for the Munich Olympics in the 1500. This time, she'd be competing in a race distance that was closer to her natural ability but still considerably shorter than the cross-country events at which she excelled. It proved a momentous Olympics for the United States, with Frank Shorter's marathon win and Dave Wottle's 800-meter victory. But Doris wasn't so lucky.

After confidently completing her warm-ups for the 1500-meter heats, she marched into the stadium close behind her teammates, *too* close. She didn't notice a small, protruding piece of track railing on the ground. Her foot struck it, and her ankle rolled inward, exploding with pain. Several German doctors rushed to treat her with a cortisone injection, but her injury was too severe for a quick fix. "I couldn't put any pressure on it," she says. "There was no way for me to run. Later, I learned that I had broken my ankle in five places."

Her Olympic race was over before it began. Worse, the ankle never healed properly, and her old speed and fluidity were gone forever. Doris continued running for the love of it. She turned her attention increasingly to her coaching duties at Seattle Pacific, where she assisted Ken Foreman. She also began working on various committees within the Amateur Athletic Union (the organization that eventually became USA Track and Field).

"I realized I'd probably never run at a high level again," she says, "but I believed my experience gave me a platform and responsibility to help other athletes in the challenges they faced. I knew what they wanted—to be treated fairly and to have the opportunity to compete well. I tried to cut through the bull of committee work to achieve that for others."

Before long, several of the runners Doris coached in college began venturing into marathons. One such group coaxed her into traveling to the 1976 Vancouver Marathon with them. "We had a hilarious trip," she recalls. "We drove up to Vancouver, and then all piled into one hotel room. We didn't know what we were doing. We didn't even know what marathoners were supposed to eat."

The next morning, they lined up on the road that circles Vancouver's Stanley Park. Doris did something different; she lined up on the dirt just beyond the road surface, almost as women marathoners a decade earlier had been forced to line up on sidewalks rather than the course itself. She chose this approach because she trained only in parks and on grass, and she didn't want to challenge her legs with 26 miles of asphalt. As she ran, spectators continually yelled: "Get on the road! It's shorter! It's a better surface!"

Doris ignored them and won the marathon in 2:47:35. It was her first 26-miler, and it came 15 years after her first Olympic Track Trials 800-meter. "The marathon was a really fine experience," Doris remembers. "It was a beautiful day, and I got to do what I loved best: run long and hard."

Doris hadn't even trained specifically for Vancouver, but few women in the world could match her performance. Six weeks earlier, Kim Merritt had run just 25 seconds faster to win the Boston Marathon. Once again, Doris proved that she possessed amazing endurance. "I never focused on getting ready for a marathon," she reflects. "I had to take care of so many other things at the college."

Within days, New York City Marathon race director Fred Lebow called, inviting Doris to the 1976 marathon. This was the year when the New York race toured all five boroughs for the first time, escaping the confines of Central Park. At first, Doris turned him down. Her Seattle Pacific cross-country team had a meet scheduled on Saturday, the day before the marathon, and she would not abandon her runners. There was no way she could race in New York early the next morning.

Lebow didn't relent. He needed famous and talented women runners to help promote the event, so he called Doris again and again. Eventually, she devised a crazy plan that would suit her goals and Lebow's as well. She would attend the Saturday cross-country race with her Seattle Pacific team, then later that day take a late-night flight from Seattle to New York City. Her plane would touch down at 6:00 a.m.—just enough time for her to get an hour's rest before boarding a bus to the marathon's starting line on Staten Island.

Despite the Saturday coaching schedule and overnight travel ordeal, Doris attempted to run with race favorite Miki Gorman. She matched Miki's pace for 15 miles until fatigue hit her. She faded to a second-place finish in a time of 2:53:02. In her typical, humble fashion, Doris apologized for not staying closer to Miki, though she never mentioned the extenuating factors behind her own race challenges.

"I regret that I couldn't stay with Miki a little longer," she says. "I wanted to help her run a good time. I never had any thought of winning for myself."

In 1984, Doris was named coach of the American women distance runners at the Los Angeles Olympic Games. She earned the honor partly because of her years as a competitive racer, but mainly for her dedication as a USA Track and Field volunteer working for athletes' rights and greater opportunities for women. "It was such a privilege to be coach of that team," Doris says. "If you can't get there as an athlete, being a coach is second-best."

As coach, Doris enjoyed a close-up view of Joan Benoit's marathon victory. "Joan was simply awesome. The day she won the first Olympic Marathon for women, I couldn't have been happier for anyone than I was for her."

In many ways, Joan's victory validated the principles that guided Doris's running and coaching through the decades. "Running lets you show what you can do," she says. "You never know how far you might go until you get outside your comfort zone. You have to reach beyond your grasp. That's where the real living begins."

Merry Lepper (left) and Lyn Carman train together in a park in Santa Barbara, California, while two of Carman's children play in the grass.

*"At that moment, I realized I had to finish.
If I didn't—if Lyn and I both dropped out—people
would say that women couldn't run the marathon.
They would say it was too long and hard for us.
They would tell us to stick to the shorter distances
and be content with what we could do."*

MERRY LEPPER

Born: December 31, 1942

MAJOR ACHIEVEMENT

First woman to run a marathon, the Western Hemisphere Marathon
in Culver City, California, December 16, 1963. Time—3:37:07

"C'MON, GET READY," WHISPERED Lyn Carman, Merry Lepper's friend
and training partner. "They're starting to line up." With that, Merry tossed
off the cotton sweatshirt she was wearing against the early-morning chill.
The two women edged out from behind the bushes where they were hiding
and jogged nervously to the street behind 67 male runners. Some of the men
bounced up and down on their toes; some reached downward to stretch
their hamstrings. But most of them stood still, conserving their energy. All
were waiting for the start of Southern California's annual Western
Hemisphere Marathon (also called the Culver City Marathon). The date was
December 16, 1963—less than a month after the assassination of President
John F. Kennedy. It was a troubling time for the nation and the world. Most
Americans, including Merry, felt uneasy. But she found an antidote for her
anxiety—running.

"I felt better when I ran," she recalls. "And the longer I ran, the stronger
I felt."

At the time, women who ran long distances were rare; those who ran the marathon, nonexistent. And it hadn't occurred to Merry to run one, either. She knew little about the history of women's running. But her friend Lyn Carman, married to an elite marathoner, had given the subject plenty of thought. In fact, Lyn was the one who dreamed of becoming the first woman to run a marathon. Merry, who was consistently at Lyn's side for most of her training, had come to Culver City only to help Lyn realize her goal. She had even rehearsed what she would do if they approached the finish line side by side. She would slow to a stop and let Lyn cross first. No question about it.

"Lyn earned it," Merry says. "She and her husband, Bob, had been training together for years. They were the serious runners."

Bob had even won Culver City once, in 1960, running 2:22:17—a world-class time. Together, the couple hatched the idea that Lyn could become the first female marathoner. That's what brought them—with Merry in tow—to the starting line of the 1963 Western Hemisphere Marathon. The morning of the marathon, Merry's day got off to a rough start. Not an early riser, she slept past her alarm and needed to scurry through her routine, grab her gear, and quickly bypass her morning chat with her mom and dad in order to make the carpool from Santa Barbara to Culver City. However, her parents noticed the frenzied way she got ready—and at such an early hour—and asked her what was going on. Merry didn't dare tell them the truth. She thought they'd worry too much or even try to talk her out of it.

"So I just told them that I was going to Los Angeles to run a race with the Carmans," she says. "That was a pretty typical activity for us."

Halfway to Los Angeles in the Carman's van, Merry realized she hadn't eaten any breakfast or packed snack foods, and she was ravenous. Luckily, Lyn had much more experience in these matters. Moreover, she was the mother of three young children. She cracked open a bag of candy bars, and Merry chose a Baby Ruth as her premarathon meal. Lyn was the clear leader in all their running adventures, while Merry was usually the easy-going follower.

Lyn and Merry had run other Southern California races with Bob Carman's road warriors. They weren't given race numbers (only "official" runners received them), and their names went missing from the national race results newsletter *Long Distance Log,* read voraciously by handfuls of ardent runners across the country. Women runners, like themselves, were almost totally ignored. But at least Lyn and Merry weren't constantly hassled by male runners and race officials to back down. They could line up and run behind the men, and many friendly Amateur Athletic Union (AAU) organizers even recorded their times for them. The general atmosphere at road races was casual and relaxed for all. Why get excited and heavy-handed about a sport that was virtually invisible to all but the most fervent practitioners?

Marathon morning in Culver City didn't feel so easygoing, and Merry noticed it right away. This was an altogether different kind of event. There were more organizers darting around with stopwatches and clipboards, conferring, comparing notes, trying to conduct the race in the most official manner possible.

"Everyone was edgier at Culver City," she recalls. "The other runners seemed a lot more anxious, too. There was no mistaking that the marathon was something bigger and more important than the other races we had run."

Bang! The gun sounded and the marathon started. A handful of front runners bolted off the starting line. The rest—those who wouldn't be competing for the laurel wreath and prizes—moved forward at an easygoing pace. Lyn brought up the rear, taking the first steps toward her historic goal. Merry ran at Lyn's side, as always. Their plan was unfolding exactly as they had envisioned it. But marathons rarely turn out as expected. They're too long, and too much can happen. Indeed, there's plenty of time and opportunity for things go wrong.

Merry's upbringing no doubt contributed to her enthusiasm for long-distance running. Her father served in the army, which meant her family moved often. In each new home, her father delved into the wonders of its unique environment.

"It seemed that every time my father got three or four days off, we went camping, regardless of the weather," she remembers. "We would do long hikes, and I enjoyed running in the wilderness. My father believed in roughing it. He thought we'd learn freedom and independence, and I think we did."

Wherever the family moved, Merry managed to make new friends by finding kids who played softball or kick the can. But after her introduction to horses when she was 12, she lost interest in pick-up games. She craved only the power and adrenaline rush that horseback riding could provide. For a while, she dreamed that she would one day become a jockey and ride her way to a Triple Crown victory. "The horses were just so beautiful," she remembers. "And their speed absolutely thrilled me."

Merry's romantic notions changed when she began reading about the serious injuries riders could incur on the track. And then it happened to her. When she was in ninth grade, a horse came crashing down on her foot. She had surgery and gradually recovered. But the foot never regained its full strength and flexibility.

"I suppose it might have been a blessing in disguise," she notes. "When I started running, I had to use a short, shuffling stride. Maybe that was a more efficient way to run."

After living in Ohio, Michigan, Wisconsin, Texas, Austria, Germany, and New Mexico, the Lepper family finally settled in San Bernardino, California. They resided there for most of Merry's high-school years. In San Bernardino, she found a small track club that occasionally traveled to AAU meets throughout Southern California. Her father encouraged her to work on her sprint speed, as he had once dreamed of running the 100 meters in the Olympics. His strategy succeeded . . . to a point. Merry could win the 50- or 100-meter races in small, local meets, but not when she advanced to the Los Angeles area competitions and had to face stronger, faster girls. "That was an awakening," she recalls. "It was depressing because I wasn't used to losing. But I simply couldn't keep up with them."

She was far more successful in the 200 meters. The extra 100 meters gave her just enough distance to eke out a win. Fewer girls competed in the 200, which, although only a half-lap, was considered a "killer" among racers. If you could succeed at the 100, the logic went, you didn't bother with the 200. Why exhaust yourself further?

Merry was clearly more suited to longer distances, and she wanted to try the 800-meter race, a distance some of the boys ran. She also wondered how she'd do in a fall event she had heard about, something called cross-country. To get in shape for cross-country meets, her male classmates would run as far as five miles in practice. Five miles! It seemed miraculous. But when she approached the coach with her idea, she was flatly refused. "I was told that it wasn't safe for girls to run five miles," she remembers. "I was limited to 200 meters, nothing more."

———

Still enthralled by her love for horses, and hoping to someday become a veterinarian, Merry began her college career at the University of Kentucky, in Lexington, the self-professed "horse capital of the world." But her move to Kentucky proved too great a shock to her system and sensibilities—especially when it came to her running. The university track was almost always locked, so Merry had to run big loops outside the cherished oval. Long, solo loops. "I never saw another person, male or female, running in Lexington," Merry says. "I wasn't aware of any running in Kentucky at all."

After a year, she returned home to attend San Bernardino Junior College. One afternoon while walking across campus, she heard a man and a woman—neither of them students—talking about running. She could scarcely believe it, but she thought the woman said, "I ran my five miles today in about 40 minutes."

A week later, Merry saw the same woman on another part of campus and mustered the courage to approach her. "I overheard you talking about running the other day," she said. "Could I run with you sometime?" Merry worried that the woman, whom she soon learned was named Lyn Carman, would brush her off. She'd heard about "the loneliness of the long-distance runner," and thought perhaps Lyn wouldn't want any company on the track. To her surprise and delight, Lyn was warm, friendly, and encouraging.

"We meet at the track at five every afternoon," Lyn told her. "You're welcome to join us any time you want."

Merry showed up the next afternoon. Clueless about what she should wear, she dressed in her regular school clothes instead of shorts and a T-shirt. "I must have looked like a real dork," she says.

At the track, she spotted Lyn jogging several laps with a small, raggedy group of guys. After the warm-up, everyone gathered around the man Merry had seen talking with Lyn. It turned out that he was Lyn's husband, Bob Carman, a physics instructor at the college and the group's coach. Dressed as she was, Merry nonetheless ran with the group for a mile or so.

Then she sat in the stands to watch the rest of the workout.

Merry understood enough about running to realize that she couldn't do everything the others did—not on her first day. But she observed every movement the team members made. They ran a considerable distance on the track, completed some fast strides, hopped and skipped for a while, and then finished with stretching exercises. Admittedly, Merry felt a little intimidated after watching. These people were real runners, serious about their training and execution. They knew what they were doing, especially Bob.

Merry felt like a total beginner, in comparison, and wasn't sure this was where she belonged. Still, she decided to return to the track the next afternoon, this time appropriately dressed. She tacked on a few laps more than the previous day, not trying to impress anyone, just doing her best. She worked to find a pace that she could maintain without completely exhausting herself and was glad other group members seemed to enjoy her presence on the track. They encouraged her to stick it out and build her endurance with them.

"They were so friendly, outgoing, and supportive—especially Lyn," Merry recalls. "We'd run around the track and in a nearby park. Sometimes, she brought her kids and their dog. We might cover five or six miles in an hour, or go a little farther and run for 90 minutes. We didn't have a fixed, set program, at least not one that I knew about. I was just tagging along with Lyn. It was social running."

When Merry's father learned of the increasing distances, he shook his head and wondered aloud about his daughter's new passion. He supported almost all the adventures she sought out, but believed in the then-common theories that women who ran long distances were endangering their health. "He kept telling me, 'Don't overdo it. I know someone who had an enlarged heart from too much running.'"

Merry respected her father's opinion, but Bob Carman—whom she came to know as a brilliant, knowledgeable mentor—convinced her otherwise. The first time she went to the Carmans' house for a post-workout gathering, she spotted a pile of Bob's library books. He was always reading something about long-distance running, math, or physics. Or all three at once.

"Bob was the most impressive person I'd ever met," she notes. "He was curious about everything and always trying to learn more." Merry, too, loved science and learning; she would eventually gain degrees in range management, ecology, zoology, and veterinary medicine.

In October and November of 1963, the group began to increase their mileage as they prepared for the annual end-of-the-year Western Hemisphere Marathon. On long runs stretching to 12 miles, 15 miles, and more, Merry realized for the first time that Lyn had set her sights on the marathon. She intended to be the first woman to complete the fabled 26.2-mile distance. In previous years, Lyn had watched Bob and friends run the three-lap course. This year, she aimed to do it herself. Merry had no such notions. She simply enjoyed the convivial, upbeat nature of the group and liked to gauge her improvement by the number of miles she could run. She didn't care about beating anyone else. "Lyn and I never competed," she notes. "We just built up our distance together. I wasn't interested in times. I never paid any attention to them."

Merry and Lyn scheduled most of their long runs for Sunday mornings, passing many churchgoers driving to and from their places of worship. They turned their heads quizzically at the sight of two women in shorts and T-shirts running on the road. And on more than one occasion, a male driver rolled down his window and inquired with genuine concern: "What are you ladies running from? Is someone chasing you? Do you need a ride, or would you like me to call the police?"

Lyn and Merry would just smile at each other and shake their heads no to the driver. Then they'd continue down the road for another 10 miles.

Even with a bright sun shining moments before the start of the 1963 Western Hemisphere Marathon, a cool breeze kept temperatures on the moderate side—perfect for a marathon. Merry wore white shorts and a light-green polo shirt, her most comfortable running attire. The early going should have been easy. After all, she only had to stick with Lyn, as she always did. But she glanced away for just a moment or two and somehow lost sight of her running partner. When she still couldn't spot Lyn a few minutes later, she figured her friend was feeling good, running strong, and hoping for a fast marathon time.

"It didn't bother me that I couldn't find Lyn," Merry recalls. "I figured I wouldn't see her again until the finish—assuming I made it that far. I didn't want to speed up and feel uncomfortable. When another runner said, 'C'mon along with me,' I fell in with him because he was going slow, too."

That worked well for a few miles. Then a car suddenly veered into Merry's path from a side street. Tires squealed as the vehicle nearly struck her. While Merry escaped a direct hit, she felt her heart racing and became light-headed. Trembling, she decided to sit on the sidewalk for several minutes to recover.

"It must've looked like I wasn't taking the marathon seriously," she remembers, "but I needed a few moments to collect myself."

Soon, she was up and running again, feeling very alone, but plugging onward. Always, she tried to hold a comfortable pace. She wasn't racing anyone or focusing on a particular time. She just wanted to reach the finish line to reunite with Lyn. At about the 16-mile mark, to her surprise, Merry caught sight of Lyn for the first time in two hours. "Oh, this is great," she thought. "Maybe now we can run together the way we always do." Merry floated up beside Lyn and greeted her warmly, happy and relieved to rejoin her running partner.

Unfortunately, Lyn wasn't feeling so euphoric. "I'm going to quit," she reported bluntly.

"What? Don't do that. I'll slow down if you want me to, and we can run together to the finish."

"No, I'm going to quit," Lyn insisted.

After a few more steps and several comments about how bad she felt, Lyn came to a complete stop. Merry couldn't believe what she was hearing and seeing. Lyn was supposed to be the first American woman marathoner. Now Merry was on her own, with all the pressure falling heavily on her shoulders to finish.

Years later, sports historian David Davis interviewed Merry about her experience in his book *Marathon Crasher*. "At that moment, I realized I had to finish," she told Davis. "If I didn't—if Lyn and I both dropped out—people would say that women couldn't run the marathon. They would say it was too long and hard for us. They would tell us to stick to the shorter distances and be content with what we could do."

For Merry, the marathon had morphed from a long run with a friend into a responsibility with far-reaching consequences. Her spirits lifted when she spotted an acquaintance, Julia Chase, who had attended the marathon primarily to support running-club teammate Norm Higgins. Two years earlier, Julia had crashed the five-mile Thanksgiving Day road race in Manchester, Connecticut. "Julia was in a van with a friend of hers, and they were cheering for all the runners," Merry recalls. "But they got especially excited when I passed one of the guys. They yelled extra loud for me at one point."

Merry reached the finish line in an unofficial 3:37:07, ahead of five fully registered men. More important, she made history by becoming the first American woman to run a marathon. "I wasn't even really tired at the end," she says. "I guess I was a little road-weary because I was more used to running in parks and on grass. But it seemed pretty easy."

Although unprecedented, Merry's achievement went unreported at first. A week passed before the San Bernardino paper picked up the story. It began:

> Instead of doing her Christmas shopping, an attractive 20-year-old San Bernardino Valley College co-ed ran a different sort of errand. She ran in the Culver City Marathon—all 26 miles, 385 yards of it—and is believed to be the first American woman ever to finish a marathon.

The next semester, Merry transferred colleges but couldn't find a running group anything like Lyn and Bob Carman's. She went on to attain multiple advanced degrees and to build her career. Along the way, she ran whenever she could, but never again with focus and intensity. While she celebrated Joan Benoit's victory in the 1984 Olympic Marathon, she felt wistful, too.

"I wonder what would have happened if there had been a women's marathon in the 1960s?" she says. "We certainly would have trained harder with a big goal in front of us. The way it was, I always wanted to improve, but I didn't have any real targets to aim for and get excited about. Even at Culver City, I wasn't trying to win or run a particular time. After Lyn dropped out, there was only one reason to keep going—to prove that a woman could do it."

Wearing a pair of her brother's Bermuda shorts over a black bathing suit, Roberta Gibb finishes the 1966 Boston Marathon in 3:21:40.

"I was happy to call into question a repressive structure that prevented women from reaching their goals at that time. It was much the same then with doctors, lawyers, scientists, writers, and other fields. People thought women were incapable of doing these things. But how do you know unless you first give women the chance? That was the point I wanted to make."

ROBERTA "BOBBI" GIBB

Born: November 2, 1942

MAJOR ACHIEVEMENTS

- First woman to run the Boston Marathon, 1966
- First female Boston finisher three years in a row, 1966–1968

ROBERTA GIBB BOUGHT HER first pair of running shoes—boys shoes, by Adidas—for $6 the day before she boarded a bus in San Diego for the long trip to Boston. She rode across the country in a cramped seat for three days and four nights, with only an occasional stop for the bus to refuel and for passengers to grab a quick bite of food.

She finally reached her parents' home outside Boston on Monday, April 18, 1966, the day before the famous annual marathon. She had just 17 hours to rest, relax, and mentally prepare for her date with destiny. Ravenously hungry after the long trip, she wolfed down a big home-cooked roast beef dinner.

Roberta, nicknamed "Bobbi," was just 23. She didn't know that women weren't allowed to run the Boston Marathon. When she had written to the Boston Athletic Association (BAA) two months prior to request an entry form, she was shocked to receive a return letter denying her permission to run. The letter said, in effect, that it's against the rules for women to run any distance longer than 1.5 miles. Besides, women can't run the marathon distance. It's too long for them.

Bobbi's dreams were completely deflated. She remembered her excitement watching the marathon two years earlier—how it looked like a parade, and how the whole city came together to celebrate it as a traditional rite of springtime in Boston. It never occurred to her that the Boston Marathon was restricted—closed to half the human race. "I was infuriated by the BAA letter," she recalls. "Why did people think women were incapable of so many things? The angrier I got, the more it became a feminist statement for me. It had started as simply something I thought was natural, beautiful, and eternal. I was very shy and wasn't looking for publicity, but at that moment, I knew I had to run Boston to show what women could do."

Although Bobbi understood little of the official world of running and marathons, she knew she could cover prodigious distances on foot. She often ran for hours on the San Diego beaches, oblivious to the passage of time, simply luxuriating in the soft sand below her bare feet and the rhythmic sound of the waves.

One afternoon, without realizing it, she crossed over into Mexico. When she turned around to come back, she was spotted and stopped by Mexican border guards.

"What do you think you're doing?" they asked.

"I'm just running," she responded.

But, as far as the guards were concerned, this was a highly suspicious answer. No one "just ran" to Mexico, especially not a woman in her early twenties. They suspected her of leaving the country for nefarious reasons and held her for several hours for questioning. Luckily, Bobbi was able to make a few calls to friends who vouched for both her character and her strange beach-running habit. On future long runs along the beach, she was careful to stay north of the border.

She returned to Boston for the 1966 Marathon. Bobbi's mother drove her to the start in Hopkinton. "Good luck," she chirped. But, in truth, neither parent thought much of Bobbi's marathon scheme. Her mother displayed enough interest and support to provide transportation, while her father spent the day in Cambridge, attending meetings. "He thought I was delusional," Bobbi recalls.

With several hours remaining before the noontime start in Hopkinton, she was gripped with doubt and fear. She didn't know what to do or where to position herself, so she wandered around the Town Green, adjacent to the actual starting line. She also explored the first half-mile of the course. She wore a one-piece black bathing suit under a hooded sweatshirt and her brother's Bermuda shorts. The sweatshirt was meant for warmth, not to camouflage her. But she did worry about being discovered, and what might be done.

"I didn't know how the men would react if they saw me," she says. "What if they started pushing and shoving and bullying me? I was even more afraid of the policemen. I thought they might arrest me and throw me in jail."

Today, Bobbi's comments sound almost ludicrous. But in 1966, they were entirely warranted. She had no way of judging how she'd be received and was particularly worried that local police, all men, would react angrily to the sight of her. For a time, she kept moving around the Town Green, growing excited as the pace of activities quickened. Hopkinton seemed almost bursting at the seams with fife-and-drum corps, hot dog stands, balloons, frolicsome children, fried dough, and the milling crowd of spectators, not to mention the 500 or so male runners.

Bobbi's nervous energy and her mother's big roast-beef dinner caused her stomach to begin rumbling. Eventually she spotted some blooming forsythia bushes about 100 yards in front of the start line—the perfect place to hide and try to calm her nerves before jumping into the race. She crouched down behind the bushes. When the gun went off at noon and runners began to move past her, she'd be ready to blend into the crowd of them.

Bobbi was born in a hospital elevator, and she stayed in motion throughout her childhood—always doing things on her own time. "When I was four years old, I had fallen in love with horses," she recalls. "I would pretend I could run like a horse. I would whinny and gallop. I got in a lot of miles as a horse."

Why did she start running? She always seemed to be chasing answers. The daughter of two college graduates, a chemist and a schoolteacher, Bobbi was encouraged to be curious about all things, particularly the marvels of the natural world. Running through her backyard in Winchester, Massachusetts, she was fascinated by the budding leaves of spring and even more by their multihued colors in fall.

"I felt transported by the beauty and patterns of everything I saw," she says. "I would study the sunbeams of light through our big chestnut tree. At the beach, my father asked why there were ripples in the sand, and I spent hours trying to figure it out."

She rarely wore dresses, as they were ill-suited for her adventures. Bobbi never had the thought that she wanted "to get married, or to follow all the conventions of the time." She lived in the moment instead. Her days weren't spent thinking about what it took to become a "proper" young lady. Instead, she played games with neighborhood friends and soaked up life around her by taking long walks and runs with her dog. Soon enough, other families were asking her to exercise their dogs. She often trotted into the woods with a half-dozen canines in tow.

When she ran, Bobbi never measured distances or timed herself. She just ran for the pure pleasure of it—in thick, heavy boots during winter blizzards or a Gloucester fisherman's slicker during nor'easters. Weather wasn't an obstacle. To her, it was just another sign of nature's infinite variety and power.

Everyone who saw her run noticed her natural grace. One time, at a big Thanksgiving family gathering, she and her young cousins played "chase" games for hours. Later, her uncle told her that she seemed to float when she ran. "You have a gift for running," he said.

In college, Bobbi met a male student who was on the cross-country team. They became (literally) fast friends, accompanying each other on long runs around Boston. Three miles became five miles, five miles became eight, and their mileage continued to grow. Although Bobbi usually ran to express herself, she noticed that she could cover long distances easily. However, the thought that distance running might be a competitive sport completely eluded her. At least it did until April 1964, when she heard one of her father's coworkers talking about the upcoming Boston Marathon. "What's that?" she asked, having never heard of the annual Patriots' Day race.

He replied that it was a race covering 26.2 miles from Hopkinton, Massachusetts, to downtown Boston.

"What? How can anyone run 26.2 miles? That's impossible," she said.

To believe it, she had to see it. So, on Marathon day 1964, Bobbi and her dad staked out a prime spot in the middle of the course and waited for the runners to approach. As they churned by, Bobbi experienced a transcendent moment.

"I felt I had discovered an ancient, lost, yet civilized world of runners," she says. "They were in sync with the most primitive human traits. They seemed so natural, so graceful, like animals. That afternoon something inside me decided that I was going to run the Boston Marathon someday. It was like an instinctual edict from my soul."

Bobbi was so taken by the marathoners that she didn't notice that none of the participants were women. To her, they were just runners, identical in the way they pumped their arms and lifted their legs, sneering in the face of their pain from blisters and fatigue, refusing to quit. That summer, she took a coast-to-coast camping trip in her family's VW bus with only her dog as a copilot. At each stop, she pitched a tent and then took off running. The Great Plains, the Rockies, the Black Hills. Each offered a new kind of challenge and opportunity—a new exploration. If a distant hill was 15 or 20 miles away, that's how far she ran.

"I combined running and thinking," she explains. "I immersed myself in the present moment, listened to the wind in my ears, took in all the amazing sights around me, and wondered where all of it, myself included, had come from."

She planned to run Boston the next spring, 1965, but severely sprained an ankle while crossing an icy Boston intersection in March. She and her father again watched from the sidelines, though Bobbi felt her inspiration and motivation soar even higher than the April before.

In the fall, she traveled north to Woodstock, Vermont, to run, improbably enough, in a three-day, 100-mile horse race. Although the horses were faster than her, Bobbi was able to catch up to many of them at noon when riders and animals took time to rest and eat lunch. With no support, food, or fluids, Bobbi covered 40 miles the first day, slept overnight in a barn, and then ran another 25 miles the second day. She had to quit when she developed severe knee pain.

"That race probably wasn't the smartest thing I've ever done," she observes, "but I learned that I had plenty of endurance for covering long distances."

———

In April, 1966, even after the long bus ride East from San Diego and an overly large dinner, Bobbi felt ready to go the distance. Crouched in the bushes, she waited patiently until she heard the starter's gun and watched runners stream down the road in front of her. Once most of them passed, she stepped out from the forsythia bush, walked along the roadside for a few seconds, then took off down the middle of Route 135.

For the first time in the history of the Boston Marathon, the world's most famous marathon, a woman was running in the pack. Bobbi found it a huge relief to be moving at last, but she still wondered what trouble might lie ahead. What would happen when another runner, or many other runners, discovered that a woman had crashed their all-male party? Then, a mile or two down the road, she learned the answer. The rhythmic sound of runners' shoes tapping the pavement was broken by a loud voice that snapped her back to reality.

"Hey, is that a girl?"

Bobbi turned in the direction of the voice, smiled as sweetly as she knew how, and nodded in the affirmative. Suddenly, a chorus of raised voices echoed:

"Look over there. There's a girl running with us."

"Geez, there's a girl running the Boston Marathon."

"Atta, girlie, you can do it."

No one sounded angry. In fact, the men seemed totally delighted to have her on the road with them. Several said, "I wish my wife were a runner like you and would run with me." She could barely believe her ears.

"I had been afraid they might try to push me off the road," she says. "Instead, to my great relief, they were all really friendly."

Still running in her hooded sweatshirt, she began to overheat. She told her newfound running buddies that she wanted to toss it aside, but was worried about what might happen when every spectator and policeman realized she was a woman. Her fellow marathoners calmed her fears. "Don't worry, we won't let anyone do anything to you," they said. "It's a public road, and we'll take care of you."

Once journalists on the press truck caught wind of Bobbi's presence in the marathon, reports began to circulate on the biggest Boston radio stations. Spectators flocked to the course, eager to witness the unexpected event. And still, no one threatened her. Even policemen patrolling the course smiled and offered their support. "Girl, there are a bunch of guys just ahead of you up that away. See if you can catch them."

When word spread to the women of Wellesley College that a woman was running the Boston Marathon, a tidal wave of students rushed to the course in support. They might not have been runners or even athletes, but they knew to shriek and let loose with cheers when Bobbi came into view.

"I heard the sound coming from a distance," she recalls, "and then the decibel level kept getting more and more gigantic until it completely enveloped me."

Encouragement poured out to Bobbi from all sources. Several were almost saintly, particularly one from a woman holding her two children, who began to sing "Ave Maria" when Bobbi came into view. Best of all, Bobbi felt good. The bloated feeling in her stomach subsided, and she was able to run smooth, fast, and comfortable. Her spirits were lifted by the support she felt from fellow runners and spectators alike.

"I learned later that I was probably under a three-hour pace much of the way even though I was being very careful to hold back and go slower than my normal training pace. By this time, I realized I had to finish strong. If I didn't, or didn't finish at all, my marathon would send out the exact opposite message from what I wanted."

Bobbi was enjoying a great run, but few marathons are free of rough patches—and that day was no exception. Heartbreak Hill proved every bit as difficult as she had heard it would be. Her stride shortened, her legs began to stiffen, and she felt a jolting pain in her hips and lower back. Worse, her new shoes began to blister her feet. With three miles to go, she hit The Wall—the infamous point in a marathon where many runners find themselves lightheaded, energy-depleted, and struggling to continue.

"My pace slowed dramatically," she recalls. "I was barely going faster than a walk, and I wanted to stop so badly to take my shoes off. I wasn't used to running so far on pavement in thin soles. I was used to running on dirt in nurse's shoes. So my feet were killing me at the end."

Each mile seemed longer and more difficult than the previous one, and "the last mile felt worse than the preceding eight." Bobbi knew she was get-ting close to the finish line at the towering Prudential Center—when the building came into her sight, it was the only thing that kept her going. She figured there'd be almost no one there, the winners having finished an hour earlier. She could stop quietly, buy a soda to slake her thirst, and go her pri-vate way. Bobbi turned the final corner from Hereford Street onto Ring Road (which no longer exists) and continued hobbling toward the towering Prudential Center at the finish line. "What the—"

To her surprise, the sidewalks were jammed with cheering crowds. The road itself narrowed down, due to a crush of photographers and TV cam-eras. Dozens of newspaper reporters crowded around the finish line with their pens and notepads ready for a quote. No one was leaving until the first Boston Marathon woman appeared.

As Bobbi crossed the finish line, someone threw a blanket over her shoulders and led her to a smattering of dignitaries. One, Massachusetts Governor John Volpe, who actually lived in her hometown of Winchester, congratulated her while cameras clicked and snapped. Next, she was led to a small interview room where reporters showered her with questions. Who was she? Why did she run? Was she trying to break through the gender barrier? Bobbi answered each question patiently, choosing her words with care.

"I told them that I simply loved to run," she remembers, "and that I didn't run the marathon to threaten anyone. I did it because I wanted to change the perception that women couldn't do it. I said I thought women could be feminine and strong and athletic at the same time."

The following day, newspaper headlines resounded with stories about Bobbi. Her tale combined several themes that could punch up newspaper sales: She was a new face, she had accomplished something unprecedented, and she was young and attractive enough to be considered sexy. Who wouldn't want to read about this strangely alluring individual? The biggest headline declared, "Hub Bride First Gal to Run Marathon." Another said: "Marathon's Course Just a Bridal Path"—both referencing Bobbi's marriage two months earlier to her college sweetheart, Will Bingay. One story even began: "A blonde 23-year-old beauty . . ."

While the newspapers mostly ridiculed Bobbi's achievement, the Boston Athletic Association (BAA) downright denounced it. Will Cloney, BAA pres-

Police and a supportive male runner escort Gibb from the
1966 Boston Marathon finish line.

ident, issued a press release: "Mrs. Bingay did not run in yesterday's marathon. There is no such thing as a marathon for a woman. She may have run
in a road race, but she did not race in the marathon."

Cloney's statement was challenged by a marathoner, Alton Chamberlin,
who had run at Bobbi's side much of the way, finishing just ahead of her.
He told the press that she not only covered the entire distance but also that
"she didn't look half as bad as some of the men." Indeed, Bobbi had beaten
two-thirds of the men in the field and recorded an unofficial time of

Gibb returned to win the 1967 Boston Marathon (shown here) and the 1968 Boston, giving her three victories in a row.

3:21:40—which would be a Boston Qualifier today. It was also the fastest time ever run by a female marathoner, not that many had been recorded previously.

Many years later, Bobbi recalled her 1966 marathon philosophically: "It was an odyssey completed," she says. "I was happy to call into question a repressive structure that prevented women from reaching their goals at that time. It was much the same then with doctors, lawyers, scientists, writers, and other fields. People thought women were incapable of doing these things. But how do you know unless you first give women the chance? That was the point I wanted to make."

Bobbi came back to run Boston in 1967 (3:27:17) and 1968 (3:40), finishing as the top female racer each time. In effect, she was undefeated during her prime racing years—three Boston starts, and three Boston wins. Yet, none would be acknowledged at the time by the BAA. After 1968, Bobbi redirected her attention to attending medical school for a time, then receiving a law degree, and finally becoming a sculptor. "I still loved running and continued running almost every day," she notes. "But it didn't hold the same place in my schedule."

In 1984, on the occasion of the first U.S. Olympic Marathon Trials for women, Bobbi was commissioned to sculpt the figurines awarded to the top three finishers. She traveled to the Trials and had the opportunity to meet and congratulate the three Olympians—Joan Benoit, Julie Brown, and Julie Isphording—after their triumphant efforts. Several months later, along with the entire world, she watched Joan break the tape in the Los Angeles Coliseum. "It was wonderful to meet the women at the Trials and talk running with them," Bobbi says. "And it was so thrilling to watch Joanie win. I thought about all the women who organized to get the event into the Olympics. I was the seed, but I'm not an organizer."

In 1996, on the occasion of the 100th Boston Marathon, a new group of Boston Athletic Association race organizers apologized for past wrongs by naming Bobbi the official women's winner of the 1966, 1967, and 1968 Boston Marathons. The group also gave her a traditional winner's medal, with her name and all three dates on it. She and Sara Mae Berman (first Boston woman finisher in the Boston Marathon from 1969 through 1971) were recognized for their wins at a public ceremony. "That was a wonderful day," Bobbi remembers. "I've never had a better day. I didn't have the least bit of anger over the past. I did my part, and now millions of women are running marathons—exactly what I had hoped for."

Eight years after her first Boston Marathon in 1967, Kathrine Switzer hits the 1975 finish line in a personal best time of 2:51:37.

"I think the Olympic Marathon was in many ways as important as giving women the vote. Everyone had come to accept what women could do in the social and intellectual realms, but it took the Olympic Marathon to show the entire world how physical and powerful women could be."

KATHRINE SWITZER

Born: January 5, 1947

› MAJOR ACHIEVEMENTS ‹

- Second woman to run the Boston Marathon (1967)
- Winner, 1974 New York City Marathon
- Director, Avon Running Global Women's Circuit

IT'S SAFE TO SAY that during her long and storied career, Kathrine Switzer received more press coverage than any other female runner. The first article ever written about her began: "After Kathy Switzer pumped out her legs at a track meet, she pumped her accordion in a beauty pageant." She was always leading the way, often on several fronts. Indeed, at age 19, while a freshman at Lynchburg College in Virginia, Kathrine ran in her first track meet and participated in her first beauty pageant—on the same day. The track meet went well. It launched Kathrine toward a career in running. The beauty pageant? Let's just say she didn't go straight to the Miss America contest.

On the track, Kathrine ran a strong 5:58 mile for her team. She achieved this despite the considerable pressure of a large, curious crowd who had gathered at the track to gawk at the only girl on an all-male track team. When it came time for Kathrine to swap her spikes for a pair of heels, her feet were already aching in pain. Her racing spikes, which were two sizes too small, had tortured her feet throughout the four-lap race. And the foot pain continued when it came time for the pageant, as she squeezed her already distressed toes into a pair of high-heeled dress shoes.

"The stiletto heels were the death knell to my toenails," she wrote in her memoir *Marathon Woman*. "Later, they turned black and fell off. I'd never seen anything like this on my own body—I thought I had gangrene or something!"

The next fall, 1966, she transferred to Syracuse University in upstate New York to study at the renowned Newhouse School of Public Communications, with a focus on sports writing. Kathrine asked permission, which was granted, to run as an unofficial member of the men's cross-country team. Not knowing exactly what her membership would entail at such a big, serious-about-sports university, she took a taxi to the golf course for her first practice, dressed in slacks and a loose blouse. The coach paid no attention to Kathrine's attire. He simply said, "Run five miles around the golf course." She glanced down at her casual clothing, completely inappropriate for a running workout, but did not back down. She ran beside the long fairways and around the putting greens until she had managed to tally up five miles. The next day, she returned in gym shorts and a T-shirt.

Kathrine mostly trained with a short, excitable 50-year-old named Arnie Briggs, who served as a volunteer coach. He was a motor mouth. When he ran, he talked nonstop. This was fine with Kathrine, who gasped for breath while struggling to keep up. Mostly Arnie talked about the amazing history of the Boston Marathon. He had run it 15 times, once finishing in the top 10. After cross-country season ended, Kathrine and Arnie kept running together. Almost every afternoon, they ran six or eight or ten miles on the roads surrounding campus. Arnie enjoyed longer distances as it gave him more time to talk.

"He'd coach me every step of the way," Kathrine recalls fondly. "Stuff like, 'Lower your arms. Pretend you're putting your hands in your pockets.' I couldn't get in a word. Then, he'd babble on about the Boston Marathon and how great it was." Finally, she snapped. On one run, she turned to look directly into her training partner's face. "Oh, damn it, Arnie! Let's quit talking about the Boston Marathon," she said. "Let's just run the damn thing!"

Arnie stopped short in his tracks. He whirled and returned her stare. This was serious stuff. She was talking about his most-cherished athletic event. "Oh, no," he declared. "Twenty-six miles is a lot more than ten miles. A woman can't run the Boston Marathon."

Kathrine challenged him instantly. "How do you know that?" she asked. "What if I show you I can do 26 miles in practice?"

Arnie pondered the question for a few moments, then responded, "If you can run 26 miles with me in practice, we'll run the Boston Marathon together."

So, one morning in March 1967, having already completed several 18-mile workouts together, Kathrine and Arnie set out on the appointed 26-mile training run. Kathrine breezed through it. Still, she felt a nagging doubt. What if their training route was short? What if she and Arnie had only covered 24 or 25 miles? She didn't like that idea. If she was going to enter the Boston Marathon, she wanted to have complete confidence that she could complete all 26.2 miles.

"Arnie, we should run an extra five-mile loop just to be sure," she suggested at the end of their 26-mile workout. He found the proposal completely unappealing. But Kathrine insisted, and off they went. At the end of the extra five miles, which gave them a total of 31 miles, Kathrine felt strong and exultant. Arnie was having a tough time, and his legs wobbled with fatigue.

"We did it, Arnie! We did it!" Kathrine remembers shouting to him. "We're going to Boston!" Arnie, the nonstop talker, couldn't open his mouth. He looked as white as a sheet, all the blood having drained from his head. Seconds later, he fainted. Luckily, Kathrine was there to catch him in her arms.

Kathrine grew up in Chicago and Vienna, Virginia, second child and only daughter to an army major and guidance-counselor mother. The men in her extended family were big—her father was 6-foot-5—powerful and adventurous.

"They worked hard, led clean lives, and had great determination," Kathrine says. "They believed that the harder you worked on something, the more successful you'd be."

Her mother was less adventure-driven, but more intellectual, and more interested in maintaining her appearance and dressing professionally while balancing work and her home. She was a *supermom* before the term was even invented. More than anything, she preached self-reliance to her daughter. "She made sure I understood that I should never let myself rely on a guy for support," Kathrine says. "I had to make it on my own."

Kathrine's family encouraged her to strike a balance between grit and girliness. As a kid, she enjoyed participating in neighborhood games as well as playing indoors with her dolls. Entering high school, she wanted to try out for cheerleading like all the other popular girls. Her father disapproved.

"You shouldn't be cheering for others," he said. "You should do a sport where people are cheering for you."

Kathrine liked the idea, but what sport would that be? The only sport for high-school girls was field hockey, and Kathrine struggled at trying to master the stick skills. Making the varsity team seemed like a long shot. But then her father offered some sage advice: "Don't worry so much about the technique stuff," he counseled. "You just have to get in better shape than everyone else by running a mile a day."

A mile? The distance seemed impossibly long. But Kathrine and her father calculated that she could cover a mile by running seven laps around their house and big yard. The next day, she gave it a try. She felt silly, awkward, out of breath, and overheated. Somehow, she finished the seven laps anyway. She kept up a daily seven-lap routine, and that September, she made the varsity field hockey team.

"It worked just the way my dad said it would," she recalls. "I didn't have many skills, but no one could match me running up and down the field. So I learned an important lesson: Running isn't just about running. It's about the sense of empowerment you get from going the distance. That empowerment can help you succeed in so many other activities."

Five years later, Boston Marathon day in 1967 dawned cold and rainy. But the dreary weather didn't bother Kathrine, Arnie Briggs, or their several friends who traveled to the city with them. They had all trained through a Syracuse winter in far worse conditions. Besides, they were actually enjoying themselves at the starting area in Hopkinton, as Kathrine's very presence was creating a mild sensation. None of the other runners had ever seen a woman standing on the Boston Marathon start line. Most seemed pleased. A few of them said, "Hey, a girl. That's great. I wish my wife would run with me." And the wives, standing nearby, would said, "Hey, a girl. Could I get a picture of you with my husband?" It was very similar to the reception

Switzer runs smoothly through the early miles of the 1967 Boston Marathon, having no clue about the coming altercation, and how it will change her life.

Roberta Gibb had received the year before, proving that the era's male marathoners (and their families) were openly welcoming to women runners, even though the world of male officialdom was not.

Arnie stuck to Kathrine's side, basking in the attention. "I trained her," he said to anyone who cared to listen. "She's ready to go the distance."

With the noon start time growing close, the Syracuse group moved toward the runners' corral. To enter the corrals, racers needed to show their race numbers. Kathrine had pinned hers on a shirt that she wore under a thicker hooded sweatshirt. She lifted the outer layer to reveal her number—261—to race president Will Cloney. Luckily, Cloney never glanced up at her face, he simply herded her into the corral, and moved on to the next runner in line.

While Roberta Gibb had run unofficially the year before without a race number, Kathrine's official race application was accepted because she used the initials K. V. instead of her full name. As a budding writer, she chose to follow the steps of hip young authors like J. D. Salinger and E. E. Cummings. Kathrine was also an Amateur Athletic Union (AAU) cardholder, and had asked Arnie to pick up her number in the Hopkinton High School gymnasium. After all the tense moments at the start line, wondering if she would be caught and rejected for wearing an official number, Kathrine was thrilled when the marathon finally got under way.

"It was such a release to begin running," she recalls. "We were laughing and having a wonderful time. When I warmed up a little, I pulled off my hooded sweatshirt. Suddenly, more of the men recognized that I was a woman. They were great. They'd call out, 'We're with you' and 'Go all the way.' I had no inkling that this was going to turn into a nightmare."

Near the four-mile mark, Kathrine sensed a commotion behind her. The press truck was slowly working its way through the field. As soon as several photographers spotted Kathrine, they began snapping shots of her and simultaneously shouting questions her way. Moments later, she heard the rapid *slap-slap* of hard leather shoes on the road. Whirling around, she spotted an enraged man with a snarling mouth bearing down on her.

"Get the hell out of my race, and give me that number!" he shouted. It was Jock Semple, a fiery Scotsman who was the unofficial race director at Boston for many years.

"I was so surprised and frightened that I slightly wet my pants," Kathrine recalls.

At that moment, Kathrine's boyfriend, Tom, intervened. He was a burly hammer thrower on the Syracuse track team and was running alongside Kathrine and Arnie. Tom slammed a huge body block on Semple and sent him flying off the side of the road. The next thing Kathrine heard was Arnie's voice, sounding as terrified as she was. "Run like hell!" he commanded. For the following 20 miles, as the fear, shock, and adrenaline slowly drained from her body, Kathrine mulled over the meaning of the out-

In the most important women's running photo of all time, Boston Marathon official Jock Semple tries to bulldoze Switzer out of the 1967 Boston Marathon. He failed, and she completed the distance.

rageous attack. At first, she felt angry at Jock, and violated. But those feelings eventually faded. "You can't run long distances and stay mad for long," she says.

Then Kathrine began wondering why there weren't more women in the marathon with her, allies in the fight for equality. What was wrong with them? The answer came to her quickly. Unlike many women, Kathrine realized she was among a lucky few with a support system of parents who believed in fairness, an experienced running coach, and friends to run at her side. "I was so fortunate to have all the gifts of my life," she says. "But I began to think that if I had so many blessings, I also had a responsibility to bring opportunities to other women. I wanted to create events and awareness about feats women were capable of."

Kathrine finished the 1967 Boston Marathon in 4 hours and 20 minutes—almost an hour behind Roberta Gibb. But her photos were splashed across newspapers around the globe the next morning, a clear example of the old adage, "A picture is worth a thousand words." The photo showed a startled woman runner, head jerked around backward, facing assault from an angry balding man, Semple. To this day, it remains the most famous and most impactful photo in the history of women's running. It also set Kathrine on a path toward a lifelong career. First, however, she had more running to do.

———————

The 1967 Jock Semple photo made her famous, but Kathrine Switzer wanted to be known as an athlete, not just a footnote in history. She was determined to improve on her first marathon time, so she decided to devote herself to training—for years, if necessary. Unfortunately, she would miss the next two Bostons because she wasn't in top shape, and she didn't want to race again until she felt ready. Among other things, her marriage (to Tom, the hammer thrower) was not going well. It drained her energy and ended in divorce. Before she ran Boston again in 1970, she followed an intensive 18-month training buildup to prepare. Her effort paid off: She lowered her time by almost 50 minutes—to 3:34. It was a huge leap forward, though she still finished last among the five women who ran. The pioneer women marathoners weren't just courageous—they were fast, as well.

Kathrine was determined, without a doubt. She just wasn't a great race-day performer, as a number of race officials and reporters enjoyed pointing out. "I got extremely upset at some of the comments," she admits. "Jock Semple said he could walk the Boston Marathon faster than I ran it. Others said I was a 'no-talent' runner. Okay, I realized I would never be one of the best. But I believed that hard work would pay off, and I was very driven."

So she trained even harder. In 1972, when women finally gained official status at Boston, Kathrine finished third in 3:29:51, behind Nina Kuscsik and Elaine Pederson. Afterward, she began working with the New York Road Runners Club (NYRRC) to organize events on a grand scale, beginning with a women-only race in Central Park. When NYRRC race director Fred Lebow trotted out several Playboy bunnies to promote the race, she smiled tightly and said nothing. "Fred was hilarious and off-the-wall," she remembers. "We knew he was just trying to get more publicity for women's running. It was a very heady time. Title IX was about to be passed."

That summer Kathrine attended the 1972 Munich Olympic Games as a freelance journalist. She watched Frank Shorter's transformative victory in the men's marathon, and, strangely, never considered the lack of an equivalent women's race. "We were so happy to have official status at Boston that year, and then Title IX, and the Olympic 1500 meters," she says. "No one was thinking about an Olympic Marathon for women." Not yet, anyway.

Back in New York, Kathrine increased her training to 100 miles a week. She woke up at 5:30 a.m. for her first run, worked a nine-hour day, and ran another hour in the evening. On several weekends, she ran 27-milers—more than even elite marathoners generally attempt. "I wanted to see how far a 'no-talent' runner could go," she recalls. "I never got bored. Running has always been a creative process for me. And on Sunday mornings, I never felt I needed to be in church when I could get so much closer to God by running through the natural world."

Again, the training paid off. She improved her marathon PR (personal record) to 3:01:39 at Boston in April 1974, and in September, she pushed through extremely hot and humid conditions to win the New York City Marathon in 3:07:49. The weather conditions weren't her only obstacle that day. A week before the race, a mugger grabbed her as she ran along the East River in Manhattan.

"Give me your money; I'm going to cut you," he hissed, with an arm around her neck and a knife to her throat. As he dragged her toward a small grove of trees, Kathrine squirmed to free an arm, reached for her pepper spray, and shot him in the face. It worked. He let go of her and dashed off.

She had escaped immediate danger, but it took much longer to recover emotionally. She could force herself to go out for runs, but she always worried about a mugger around the next corner. Finally, Kathrine willed him out of existence. "Night after night, I invited him to appear, and night after night, I fought him, maimed him, and killed him," she recalls. "I always won. I'm not sure what a psychiatrist would make of this grotesque fantasy, but we deal with our demons as best we can."

During the winter of 1974, still hoping for more marathon improvement, Kathrine pushed her training to as much as 115 miles a week. Her weight dropped to an all-time low of 120 pounds. "I was almost skinny for the first time in my life," she says. "A friend asked me if I had a strategy for the marathon. I told her, 'I'm going to run the hell out of this race.'"

And when the starter's gun went off at the 1975 Boston Marathon, she did just that, running hard from the start. Some spectators yelled, "You're first, woman!" Although that turned out to be a mistake, Kathrine realized how strong she was running. Her ultimate goal was personal improvement, not her finish position. The Wellesley students cheered insanely as she ran past. "I felt my eyes well up," she recalls. "I even pumped my fist in the air several times. I couldn't help it. I wanted them to know that, yes, we are powerful women, and I was doing this for all of us."

After Heartbreak Hill, the race became more difficult for Kathrine. It always did at that point. She had to turn inward, and grind it out. "I went back to concentrating," she says. "It was hard—my body felt great, but my brain was getting tired."

At the finish, she felt certain she had broken 3 hours. Perhaps she had even beaten 2:56? "What did I run? What did I run?" she asked the timers. The reply: "You ran 2:51." Her official time was 2:51:37, good for second place.

"I felt light—very, very light, and free, as if a huge weight had been lifted," she recalls. "I knew I had flatlined my training and my racing that day. I would never have to turn back years later and wonder, 'What if?'"

Feeling that she had achieved her marathon potential, and beginning to suffer from foot injuries, Kathrine focused on her burgeoning career in sports marketing. One weekend in 1977, an Avon executive asked her to review a proposal for a women's marathon in Atlanta. Kathrine thought the concept was great, but she found the proposal to be underwhelming. She felt the time was right for something bigger and better. "I decided to write up my dream race, to create the proposal of a lifetime," she recalls.

Atlanta was just the beginning. Her dream race would start as an international women's marathon, then spread to dozens of countries where Avon products were sold. Her core mission was no longer about organizing one race, it was about convincing the International Olympic Committee to add a women's marathon to the Olympic Games.

To do so, Kathrine would need to organize women's marathons in at least 25 countries on three continents. Not an easy project, but she knew Avon had a big enough international presence to pull it off. Her vision was ambitious and unlikely to succeed, but she wanted to take aim at the stars. To her astonishment, Avon accepted her proposal and hired her to oversee the program. For the next several years, she lived out of a suitcase, flying around the world to stage brand-new women's races in countries that never had them before. It was an exciting time—sometimes frustrating, always a bit scary.

"I was in so many corporate meetings where I was the only woman present," she says. "I could see the men sizing me up: 'Okay, lady, impress us. Show us what you've got.' That's very intimidating. You get cold feet. But then I would tell myself, 'This is nothing compared to having Jock Semple practically jump on your back.'"

In 1980, Kathrine and her associates compiled the Avon Women's Running Report for submission to the International Olympic Committee (IOC). The report chronicled Avon's success in 25 countries on five continents—more than were required by the Olympic charter. Just as important, with help from respected marathon statistician and sports medicine expert Dr. David Martin, Kathrine was able to show that marathon running didn't physically affect women any differently than it did men. There were no health-related issues. The IOC revealed its decision in Los Angeles in February 1981. Kathrine was in the hotel meeting room at 6:30 p.m. for the announcement, holding hands tightly with an Avon colleague.

"The women's marathon will be added to the Olympic schedule for the Los Angeles Games," the IOC spokesperson said. "This was not an easy victory for the women, but it is a very important one."

Three years later, Kathrine joined the ABC TV network as a commentator during the worldwide broadcast of the first Olympic Marathon for women. When runner #361 surged to the front at three miles, Kathrine told viewers that Joan Benoit had made a reckless move—it was too dangerous to break away early in an Olympic Marathon with the world's best runners lurking close behind. "Joan is taking a big risk against the great talents like Ingrid Kristiansen, who I pick to win, and Grete Waitz," she noted. But over the next dozen miles, Kathrine began to recant. "I realized that rather than hedging her bets, Joan was running for all or nothing. She is a take-no-prisoners runner, and this was her day. Eventually, her victory will be seen as one of the great, classic marathon efforts of all time."

As Joan ran through the tunnel and onto the Olympic track amid thunderous cheers, Kathrine marveled at the moment.

"That race fulfilled all my dreams," she says. "In fact, I think the Olympic Marathon was in many ways as important as giving women the vote. Everyone had come to accept what women could do in the social and intellectual realms, but it took the Olympic Marathon to show the entire world how physical and powerful women could be."

Sara Mae Berman wins the women's New England Cross-Country Championships of 1968, well ahead of the pack, as she often was.

"I liked the way that running is different for girls than ice skating, where you have to be pretty, or swimming, where no one sees you sweating under the water, or equestrian events that are so very genteel. Running takes a lot of hard effort and sweat, and you're wearing clothes that aren't much more than underwear. I didn't run to promote myself, but to promote women's running."

SARA MAE BERMAN

Born: **May 14, 1936**

> **MAJOR ACHIEVEMENTS**

First woman, Boston Marathon, 1969 through 1971

SARA MAE BERMAN WAS probably the first woman in the United States who traveled to a road race with her husband (a runner), three kids, a babysitter, and plans to enter the race herself. She had attended many races previously to watch her husband, Larry, run while she took care of the kids. But for this one—a 5-miler in Marlboro, Massachusetts, in 1964—she wanted to step onto the starting line herself. That meant the jam-packed family car had to hold a sixth person, the babysitter.

Marlboro was not just Sara Mae's first road race—it was also one where she had a specific time goal. She had started running seriously several years earlier with Larry on the track at MIT. He would be doing various kinds of speed work, while she was struggling to complete four laps—a mile. When she succeeded, Larry told her it was time to run farther—five miles. Sara Mae was astonished by Larry's outrageous target.

"I didn't know anything about competing with yourself, and trying to improve," she recalls. "All the concepts around distance and pace were new to me. They were completely foreign."

But she plunged ahead anyway, and eventually managed 20 laps on the MIT track—five miles. It seemed the ultimate achievement. "No," said Larry. "Now you have to run the five miles faster." He suggested a goal time of less than 40 minutes.

That goal proved tough to achieve. Sara Mae tried repeatedly, but failed. So Larry, an aeronautical engineer who enjoyed solving technical problems, decided that she should begin doing interval workouts like 12 x 200 meters. Sara Mae did these, but still couldn't break 40 minutes. That's when Larry realized she needed a change of scenery. From personal experience, he knew that runners often managed to go much faster in actual races than in training. A race was the next step for Sara Mae. So the family packed the car, picked up the babysitter, and headed for Marlboro. Sara Mae wouldn't be allowed to register for the race, or receive an official number—that was prohibited by Amateur Athletic Union (AAU) regulations. But she bore no grudges.

"I couldn't be angry with guys like Jock Semple and Bob Campbell," she notes. "They were friends I saw almost every weekend at different races. They were always very nice to me, but they also believed they had to uphold the rules of the time."

When the men crowded onto the road for the race start, Sara Mae stood on the sidewalk immediately adjacent to them. Some of the men noticed that she was wearing her cheap, makeshift shorts and shirt from Filene's Bargain Basement. Several asked: "Hey, are you going to run with us?"

Sara Mae nodded quietly. She was more the strong, silent type than the flamboyant protestor. She didn't want to make waves. Besides, she had never done this before. Until she actually completed the race, she had no idea how things would turn out. She was very happy about her reception. No one seemed angry to have a woman in the race with them. "The guys were all very pleasant and very pleased," she recalls. "They said things like, 'You're welcome here. The roads are public. No one can keep you off them.'"

After the start, Sara jogged onto the road and fell in with the back-of-the-packers. Soon she learned one of the great truths of road running: With changing scenery and companionship, the miles pass more easily than on the track. "All through the race, I would see other runners and spectators, and they were so encouraging," she says. "They kept saying, 'You're looking good, you can pick it up.' So that's what I tried to do."

Sara Mae crossed the finish line in 38:37—well under her goal of 40 minutes. Unfortunately, history would not record her valiant effort. Women were prohibited from road races, so neither the race results nor media reports reflected her presence. She was like a ghostly spirit: Only Larry, Sara Mae, and a handful of respectful Boston-area male runners knew what she accomplished.

Sara Mae never expected to be an athlete or to compete in any sports. She was born in the Bronx, New York, and moved with her family to New Hampshire when she was four. The family owned a small but successful clothing company that specialized at first in sweaters, and then in khaki pants during World War II. Her father was a football fan, especially of Harvard football, and her mother claimed to have been a swimmer in her youth. But Sara Mae doesn't remember them as active athletes, not at all. "I was a proper little Jewish girl, and my parents were watchers, not doers," she says.

When Sara Mae was nine, her mother decided she should experience a life with more cultural enrichment. Every Saturday morning, they drove to downtown Boston, where Sara Mae attended a series of classes in piano, art, and ballet. She enjoyed the music practice and came to be a reasonably good pianist—but the ballet was something else. "Let's just say I was not gifted in ballet," she says.

After six months, Sara Mae's mother allowed her to go alone on the trains and subways to Boston. Sometimes, she continued onward to New York City, where relatives would meet her. Sara Mae calls this her time of "structured independence." She learned how to do things on her own, but always with her family's support. Sara Mae met Larry while both were still high-school students. From the beginning, she felt more relaxed with Larry than with anyone else she had dated.

"He could hold an actual conversation," she says. "He wasn't all fidgety and nervous like the other boys—it wasn't strained. We didn't have to dig for subjects to talk about. We just felt so natural together."

It also didn't hurt that her parents adored him. Larry was a smart kid who attended the elite Phillips Exeter Academy in Exeter, New Hampshire.

He had a bright future and was the kind of man you would want your daughter to marry.

That eventually happened but the two waited until they had graduated from college—Larry from MIT and Sara Mae from the Rhode Island School of Design in Providence. They had their first two children in 1957 and 1958 and lived in several places in Providence and Boston, settling into a conventional family life much like any young couple at the time. Except that Larry, a former captain of the MIT cross-country team, began to enter New England road races. He liked the way that running kept him in good shape, and he thought it important for every person (including his wife) to cultivate the body as well as the mind.

One day, before heading to a nearby park where he did much of his training, Larry asked Sara Mae if she wanted to join him. He mentioned that he had just read an article theorizing that an individual's fitness and body condition at age 30 was likely to remain that way for the rest of one's life. This caused Sara Mae to pause and ponder. She hadn't reached 30 yet, but she could see it coming in a few years. So she asked herself these questions: Are you happy with your shape right now? Will you be content to stay the same for the rest of your life? In both cases, the answer was no.

That propelled Sara Mae to join Larry for his next workout in the park. They did a little warm-up, some stretching, and lined up beside each other on a cinder path. Larry didn't give Sara Mae any instruction, so she leaned forward tensely as she had seen track stars do on TV.

"One, two, three . . . Go!" Larry said.

Sara Mae blasted forward like a sprinter, leaving Larry in the dust. This lasted for about 50 yards. Then it was all over. She collapsed at the side of the path, her chest heaving, her lungs desperately begging for air. On her next visit to the park with Larry, Sara Mae started slower and managed to cover 100 yards or more. It was the start of a long, arduous process. But at least she had begun.

By 1965, Larry and Sara Mae had moved to Cambridge, Massachusetts, where they still live today. In Cambridge, they began to organize groundbreaking cross-country races for women. They believed that this was the best way to entice girls and women to run longer distances. To encourage younger, slower runners, they "handicapped" the races so inexperienced runners got a head start. This meant that Sara Mae, the most serious runner in most races, could never win. She was always chasing after runners who had a big head start. Her best finish was third.

"I was never a self-promoter, but the Cambridge races taught me a lot," Sara Mae says. "I'd call in the results to newspapers, because we wanted people to read about what women runners were doing. In the process, I became more comfortable and better at talking to reporters and other people about our goals."

Thinking they should take the struggle to a higher level, the Bermans attended several national Amateur Athletic Union (AAU) conventions. They argued that the rules should be changed to allow women to run farther than 1.25 miles. But AAU kingpins weren't receptive. "They just laughed at us," says Sara Mae. "Worse, they said we were exploiting young girls by having them run longer races. Nobody said that about boys moving up to greater distances—only about girls and women. The top men in the AAU had an image of where women belonged, and that was in the kitchen."

Larry ran his first Boston Marathon in 1965. Sara Mae dropped him off at the start, and then sped to the finish with their three kids in tow. While she was waiting for Larry, a strange thought flitted through her mind: Maybe she should run the Boston Marathon. No woman had ever done this, but Sara Mae felt the time was right. She dropped the idea quickly when she considered how difficult it would be to train correctly while mothering three young children. Seeing Larry at the finish confirmed that the marathon was different, and much harder, than the every-weekend New England road races. He looked terrible. Despite finishing in a fine 2:54, he was pale, stooped-over, stiff-legged, and looked as though each mile had added a year to his age.

Sara Mae knew that this would never do for a woman finisher at Boston. If a woman runner looked like this, the press would attack ferociously. There would be more stories about her haggard appearance than about her triumphal achievement.

It had happened before, after all. At the 1928 Olympics, several women runners collapsed after the 800-meter race. Major newspapers expressed their disgust that women were being encouraged to attempt such debilitating events. While men received praise for do-or-die determination, the same behavior by women was seen as completely inappropriate. The Olympic

Committee dropped the 800 from the women's Olympic schedule until 1960. Many decades later, analyses of the 1928 race footage revealed that the newspaper reports at the time had significantly distorted the events.

The year after Larry's first Boston Marathon, Roberta "Bobbi" Gibb became the first woman to run the Boston Marathon in 1966. While Gibb ran the following two Bostons and was joined by Kathrine Switzer and others, Sara Mae spent all three of those years on the sidelines. She was tempted to enter, but she set high standards for herself—an approach learned from Larry—and decided not to run a marathon until she felt fully trained to run a *strong* marathon. "I might have been a little sad that I wasn't the first woman at Boston, but mostly, I felt pleased and proud of Bobbi and Kathrine," she says. "I knew I wasn't ready yet. I didn't want to run a marathon until I knew I could feel good and look decent doing it."

In 1969, Sara Mae was ready. She had amassed the training, endurance, and road-racing experience necessary to run smart and fast for 26.2 miles. She entered her first Boston Marathon and won handily in 3:22:46. At age 32, she was the oldest-ever woman to run and win Boston.

She won again the next two years, joining Bobbi Gibb as an early three-peater in the Boston Marathon. She also improved Gibb's best time (3:21:25 in 1966) to a new course record (3:05:08 in 1970). Yes, Sara Mae waited a long time to begin her marathon career, but when she did, she got it right. Of course, at the time, Sara Mae received no official acknowledgment for her accomplishments.

Like Gibb, she was still considered a nonentrant. She might have covered every single step of the historic Hopkinton to Boston course, but according to race organizers, she hadn't actually run the Boston Marathon. It took a long time for Gibb and Sara Mae to receive the recognition they so obviously deserved. That came about in 1996 at the 100th Boston Marathon when Boston Athletic Association officials finally made right on the past by awarding Gibb and Berman medals to signify their victories.

Berman makes little of her first Boston finish in 1969. The truth is, the day was warm, and she didn't run as fast as she had hoped. The 1969 Boston attracted two other women runners—Nina Kuscsik and Elaine Pederson—but Sara Mae never saw either of them. However, she did see and hear the women of Wellesley College cheering from the roadside. They greeted her with a roar. But Sara Mae was concentrating so hard on her personal quest that she only recalls thinking: "Easy for you ladies to yell like that, just standing on the sidelines. But not so easy out here where I'm doing all the work."

She also remembers that the male marathoners around her were completely supportive. "I don't remember a single nasty comment," she says. "There was more a sense of community and camaraderie. The truth is, I don't think I ever felt safer or more secure than when running road races. I was always surrounded by men who were like me, and understood and encouraged me."

At the finish, Sara Mae was surprised by the lack of media attention. In 1966 and 1967, Bobbi Gibb and Kathrine Switzer had produced tidal waves of press clippings. But by 1969, no one seemed very interested in Sara Mae's story. She thought that reporters found her less glamorous than Bobbi and Kathrine. One journalist asked, "Why did you do it?" She took this as an affront, as if he were implying that she must have had an ulterior motive. Perhaps she craved the attention or wanted to draw attention to a "cause." Sara Mae cut him off with a simple, brusque response: "Because I wanted to see how fast I could go."

In 1970, she trained harder than ever—up to 100 miles a week, with frequent mile-repeats on the Harvard indoor track. Larry did the same. Both aimed to set personal records at Boston.

The day dawned unexpectedly cold, windy, and rainy. After the usual charade in Hopkinton—Larry lining up with all the male runners in the starting corral, Sara Mae on the sidewalk—they set off on their individual pursuits. Sara Mae hoped to beat Roberta Gibb's course record, 3:21:25. "I felt good and strong most of the race," she says, "and it was helpful to be more familiar with the course after the year before. The only problem was the cold. I was cold much of the way."

She began begging spectators for gloves, and someone finally offered her a pair of white gardening gloves. Problem was, her hands were too frozen to pull them on. She had to reach down with her mouth, and use her teeth to yank the gloves up to her wrists. She received a big emotional boost when Larry showed up in Kenmore Square with a mile to go. He had finished in a sensational 2:38:03, and now he was telling her she could reach her goal, too.

"You can do it," he said. "Only a mile to go. Just concentrate on holding your pace." Sara Mae reached the finish in 3:05:08, a huge personal record

Larry Berman finished the 1970 Boston Marathon in 2:38:11, then accompanied his wife, Sara Mae, to her second-straight Boston win. She set a new course record, 3:05:07.

and course record—one that would stand until Miki Gorman ran in 1974. There were five women finishers, but once again she had seen none of them during the race.

That changed in 1971 when Nina Kuscsik glided past Sara Mae at the 22-mile mark. Sara Mae knew that Nina was an experienced marathoner, so this represented a serious challenge. "Nina went past me with a couple of guys from New York," she recalls. "I didn't want to let her beat me, so somehow I found the resolve to speed up a little and pass her back. That was one of the first times I actually raced another woman, but we never had any animosity with each other. We just all tried our hardest, and figured the winner would be the one who had trained best or had the most talent."

Once back in front, Sara Mae held on grittily to win the 1971 Boston Marathon in 3:08:30, almost as fast as the previous year. Kuscsik followed in 3:09. It was the first time two women runners finished so close together in a major marathon. Now, like Bobbi Gibb before her, Sara Mae Berman was a three-time winner of the Boston Marathon. Just as important, she had achieved the kind of serious, outstanding times that had been her intent, and Larry's, from the beginning of her athletic and road-racing career. She didn't run Boston as early as she could have. Instead, she waited until she was tough, experienced, and well-trained.

In 1972, the Boston Marathon finally began to accept women entries. Sara Mae's reaction: "It's about time." She entered, despite having the flu, and finished fifth in 3:48:30. Nina Kuscsik won that first official women's race at Boston in 3:10:26. It was her fourth Boston finish.

That same year, Sara Mae and Larry formed the Cambridge Sports Union, an amateur running club that has been a running, skiing, and orienteering stronghold in Boston since its establishment. Sara Mae continued running marathons through the Avon International Marathon of 1978 in Atlanta, Georgia, a celebration event that she didn't want to miss.

"All I ever wanted was the chance to run and improve," Sara Mae says about her years in running. "At first I would finish near the back of New England road races, but after a while, I moved up to the middle. I felt I was part of a women's running movement that eventually couldn't be ignored. I didn't know when the change would come, but I knew it would.

"I liked the way that running is different for girls than ice skating, where you have to be pretty, or swimming, where no one sees you sweating under the water, or equestrian events that are so very genteel. Running takes a lot of hard effort and sweat, and you're wearing clothes that aren't much more than underwear. I didn't run to promote myself, but to promote women's running."

Judy Ikenberry (201) goes out fast to lead the 1974 International Women's Marathon in Waldniel, Germany. She finished seventh.

"Most of life isn't glamorous. People aren't watching and applauding. You're doing the dishes, cleaning the bathroom, or running hilly 18-milers. No one gives you a trophy for those things. But you have to get through them as part of your daily life and your daily progress toward running goals."

JUDY IKENBERRY

Born: September 3, 1942

- Fifth place, Olympic Track Trials 800 meters, 1960
- Winner, first National Marathon Championship, 1974

JUDY SHAPIRO WAS THE youngest and least experienced 800-meter runner at the 1960 Olympic Track Trials in Abilene, Texas. The 17-year-old arrived in such a whirlwind of chaos that it's easy to imagine her confusion. She had entered only a handful of track races in Southern California—and those only a month or two prior to arriving in Texas that summer.

But her mother, an energetic soul, had decided to fully support her daughter's new passion. She drove Judy 1,000 miles for that year's National Championships in Corpus Christi, Texas, and then to the Olympic Trials in Abilene. For good measure, she carted along several siblings and Judy's young coach, Dennis Ikenberry. Ikenberry, a physics student and 400-meter runner, appreciated the logic and order of training systems for runners. He was the perfect fit for Judy, who needed that type of guidance. She was more a free spirit in overdrive.

"I wasn't good at any school sports, because my eyes were so bad," she recalls. "Plus, I was so hyperactive, I was nearly out of control much of the time. I felt like I was bouncing off the walls."

Still, she had enjoyed success in several track meets, especially in the 800. No one else wanted to run that event. Two laps? It sounded like scaling Everest to other female runners—but not to Judy. She enjoyed the challenge. Judy only had one problem: She was terrible at setting a proper pace. She always seemed to start too fast, causing her to stagger the second lap as her lungs heaved and her legs nearly buckled. Dennis was appalled by Judy's bad pacing at the National Championships in Corpus Christi. She not only ran too fast the first lap but also ran most of the race in the second lane. Afterward, she recalls, he made her walk an entire lap again with him.

"He was trying to drill me about the extra distance I had covered," she remembers. "He figured this was a good way to make sure that I understood the principle and would never forget it. He was always an outstanding teacher in that way."

While Dennis worried about track tactics, Judy's mom found her own outlet. Appalled by the horrid food and dormitory quarters provided to the female runners, she began lecturing every Amateur Athletic Union and Olympic Committee official she could corner. She hand delivered formal complaints in writing. But the officials advised her that women should feel privileged just to be allowed into the Olympic Trials. Judy shared a similar skepticism of the officials. She was convinced they kept a list of the protesters, and then took their revenge. When she lined up for the first of three heats in the Olympic Trials 800, she looked across the line and saw a disproportionate number of the fastest competitors.

"I'm sure they put the best of us together in the first heat," she says. "They wanted all us bad eggs to eliminate each other and go home."

Still a month short of her 18th birthday, Judy made the cut. She advanced to the final of the Olympic Trials 800, the first held in the United States since 1928, and by far the most important race of her life. She knew this was the time to get everything right. Unfortunately, that didn't make executing the 800-meter final any easier. Judy fell into her usual trap. Despite Dennis's coaching, she shot to the front on the first lap. She figured she had no chance of actually doing well but wanted her mother and Dennis to be proud of her, at least for a lap. On the second lap, she faded, eventually finishing fifth. She felt no sense of loss or defeat. She simply wasn't ready to consider herself a winner.

"I thought the others were much better than me," she recalls. "I never expected to beat anyone. I was more worried that my mother and Dennis might be disappointed. They seemed to care more than I did."

For the first time, however, she started to realize that running had introduced something new into her life. She had tried other activities in high school but never excelled at anything. Running appealed to her, and she seemed to be good at it.

"It gave me something I did well, maybe even excellent," she remembers. "I had been a good dancer, but not great. And in dancing, they judge you by the way you look and hold positions. In running, it was just me, the other girls, and the clock. No judgments. I liked that."

Judy was born in Brooklyn, New York, the daughter of left-leaning parents who subscribed to socialist newspapers and believed in economic fairness and equality for all races, sects, and genders. When Judy was barely a year old, the family moved to Southern California. Her two older brothers had serious asthma, and doctors advised that they would live more healthfully in a clean, dry-air environment.

The Shapiros landed in Sunland-Tujunga, California, northeast of Los Angeles. Her father had an aeronautics engineering job with the California Institute of Technology, and the family soon settled into the sun-filled California lifestyle—until the dark cloud of McCarthyism intruded on their lives. Suddenly, people everywhere were being investigated to ensure they weren't tied to the Communist party.

Although Judy's father was not affiliated with Communism (he was completely cleared of all suspicions), there was no denying the unusual newspapers that arrived on their stoop each morning. Even though he was advised to cancel them, he refused on principle. He and his wife felt that they should be allowed to read the periodicals of their choice, particularly since they didn't engage in any illegal activities. Unfortunately, he soon lost his job and was forced to work in a plastics manufacturing business to support the family. "He was never really the same after that," Judy recalls. "He lost his energy and never felt like playing with us anymore. It was a miserable job, and he seemed angry much of the time. That was a scary time when people were being blacklisted from their occupations."

Despite the desperate times, Judy felt that she learned many important lessons from her parents. They gave what they could to anyone in need, her mother often preparing large group dinners for neighborhood kids. "If someone puts their hand out, you give them something," her father preached. "They wouldn't be asking like that if they weren't desperate."

Other kids her age rebelled against their mothers and fathers. They fought everything, especially the curfews that were imposed. Judy felt no need to wrangle with her parents. She considered them to have the highest moral standards of anyone she knew. They wouldn't impose a certain policy on her unless they absolutely believed it in her best interest. "I would have slit my wrists before I disobeyed a curfew or anything like that," she says. "I would never have dreamed of violating the trust my parents had in me."

When doctors diagnosed Judy with scoliosis—a curvature of the spine— her mother signed her up for ballet lessons. Judy continued taking classes for a half-dozen years, and they helped build her poise, as well as her back and leg strength. But ballet dancing also involved comparing yourself with the girls around you—and Judy didn't like what she saw.

"I thought I wasn't pretty enough," she remembers. "Everyone wanted to be like Marilyn Monroe, and I certainly wasn't like that—I was dark-haired and skinny. My mother was always trying to praise me, but I didn't believe her. I figured she was just trying to make me feel better."

In school classes, she often assumed the role of class clown. She was more inclined to talk and make jokes than to sit and listen. Her teachers complained to her parents: "We can't get Judy to shut up."

Judy admits she didn't seem to have a normal filter like everyone else. She would make sharp comments about her classmates and often get in trouble. "I didn't distinguish between appropriate and inappropriate thoughts," she recalls. "You might say I had diarrhea of the mouth. I just seemed to let it all out."

Judy tried various activities in high school, hoping to find one that fit with her personality and limited talents. Basketball showed the most prom-ise, with its furious action up and down the court. But not being able to play full court, because they were girls, made her lose interest. "It was so frus-trating that they wouldn't let us run from one end to the other," Judy remembers. "I was just getting going, and then we had to stop and turn around."

Although she only performed a small part in one high-school play, *The King and I*, the adrenaline associated with live theater performances struck a nerve. The costumes seemed so glamorous, and the audience sat in rapt attention just a few feet from the stage. "I loved being up there, playing a part with everyone watching," she says.

She was always ready to try something new. One day, a girlfriend suggested that they attend a track practice at a nearby community college. Judy said, "Sure." Everyone else at practice was much older. And they were doing such bizarre activities: jumping, throwing, hurdling. Judy tried them all and finished next to last in everything.

"I don't know why I liked the track practice so much, especially when I was so bad at everything," Judy recalls. "But for some reason, I enjoyed it. I was so easily distracted when I was young. I popped from one activity to another. Running gave me something to concentrate on. It was so physical, it forced me to channel my energy."

Judy's friend lost interest after the first day, but Judy told her mother that she wanted to keep going. When her mother realized that Judy was serious and determined, she decided to give her whatever assistance she could, including a coach. That's when she located Dennis Ikenberry at Occidental College in Los Angeles, where he was on the track team. Dennis soon began giving Judy workouts and tried his best to convince her not to go all out in the first lap of her races—she had to learn to pace herself. Several months later, Judy and her whole gang piled into the Shapiro family station wagon and headed for Texas. With little knowledge of track history, and none concerning the women's 800, they set out with just one purpose—to help Judy discover if she could excel at her newly adopted sport.

After graduating from high school and placing fifth in the 1960 Olympic Trials, Judy enrolled at the University of California, Riverside, and continued training under Dennis's tutelage. When he enrolled in an academic graduate program at Riverside the next year, they spent even more time together. Soon, Judy couldn't figure out which she enjoyed more: running for Dennis or simply being with him. The two brought out the best in each

Ikenberry's parents typically drove long distances, complete with multiple family members and in-car sleepovers, to get Judy to important track meets.

other, on and off the track, with his sense for calm and logic balancing out her emotion and energy.

Since there were few road races for women, Judy found it more thrilling to compete in the several indoor track meets that came to Los Angeles each winter. They gave her the same rush of excitement she felt as a kid in the school play. With the bright lights overhead, the boards thumping to each runner's stride, and the closeness of cheering crowds, indoor meets had much of the same drama and electricity as a stage production. "I always felt great when I raced indoors," Judy remembers. "The small track was good for short runners like me, but I mainly enjoyed the enthusiasm of the crowds. I think I had a desire to be famous, or at least recognized and respected. Indoors, I felt I got that."

Together, she and Dennis devised a long-term training plan that would culminate in 1964, the year of the next Olympic Track Trials. The two also decided they would get married at the Trials in New York. But their plans were derailed when Judy developed an injury. They canceled their trip to New York and got married in California. On their honeymoon, they hiked in the High Sierras, covering 12 to 17 miles a day. Judy's endurance kept increasing.

In the mid-1960s, Southern California road running experienced its first mini-boom. Judy began training occasionally with Lyn and Bob Carman, who lived near California State University, San Bernardino, where Judy and Dennis had moved. Other days, she joined a local group called the Rialto Runners (RR). The RR had a surprising number of women interested in covering longer distances. Weekend runs stretched to 10, 12, and 14 miles.

"We'd run several hours at a comfortable pace, and no one seemed to have any problem with the distance," Judy recalls. "We had a couple of men in our group, and they loved having us around. The only problem was guys in cars honking their horns at us, and sometimes throwing beer cans. When things got bad, we steered our runs off the roads and into various parks."

For a female endurance runner, the mile was the next obvious distance after the 800. However, women were not allowed to run the mile event in official races. Meanwhile, on the men's side, the distance was exploding, fueled by interest in Jim Ryun's sensational high-school and open performances. Every track fan in the United States followed the mile. But women had no opportunity to run it.

Finally, Dennis crafted a plan to give Judy a chance. She would enter a women's 800 and just keep running for another two laps beyond the 800 finish line. It proved to be a chaos-producing idea. When Judy continued running past the race's end, male officials swarmed onto the track to shoo her off. This spurred Dennis into action. He raced onto the track yelling at the officials to let Judy continue.

When they didn't listen, this sparked an argument and a shoving match in the middle of the track. Judy wasn't involved—she was still running hard—but she could see and hear the altercation. And she found it highly upsetting. She felt that she must have been doing something wrong—something bad—and that all the raised voices and finger pointing were her fault. All her life, Judy had been a people-pleaser, trying to make others feel good. This time, people were angry, and she was the center of the controversy.

Ikenberry stands beside the track at the University of California-Riverside, where she did much of her training in the 1960s and 1970s.

"I came around the track and saw Dennis and the officials yelling at each other," she recalls. "I was so scared, I was crying the last lap." But she finished. She always finished. She proved that she could run four laps as readily as she could run two.

In the fall of 1967, Judy and Lyn Carman received a completely unexpected invitation. The director of the Las Vegas Marathon thought he could get his race some extra publicity by inviting a couple of women runners to participate. This was six months after Jock Semple had attacked Kathrine Switzer on the Boston Marathon course, which sparked worldwide media coverage. The Las Vegas race director offered the Ikenberrys and Carmans driving expenses, a couple of nights in a swank Las Vegas hotel, and $20 a day in meal money. Both couples found it impossible to reject this opportunity. They had never heard of anything like it. Not only were track and road running entirely amateur sports but they weren't even famous runners in the sport.

"It seemed incredible that someone would pay us to come to his race," Judy remembers. "And the meal money sounded generous back then. The whole trip was a lark. Dennis and I didn't know anything about marathons except that they weren't to be taken seriously. Track was the serious sport. That was what we always trained for."

On marathon morning, Judy and Lyn encountered the real world of women distance runners. They may have been invited to the race, and even treated nicely by the promoter, but they weren't truly welcome at the start line. That area was controlled by Amateur Athletic Union (AAU) types, and women couldn't run officially. Judy and Lyn were shunted off to the sidewalk behind the small crowd of onlookers that had gathered to watch the skinny, thin-clad runners. The two women looked even more out of place in Las Vegas than the handfuls of other women runners similarly forced to start on sidewalks in other American cities. At the starter's gun, Judy and Lyn simply ran along the sidewalk for 100 yards, and then crept onto the road behind the men marathoners. No one paid much attention to them during the race except for their husbands, who dispensed water at several key points.

"It was a warm, windy day, and we needed the refreshments," Judy says of her first marathon. "Other than that, I only remember that the race seemed really long. I was so glad to finally get close to the end. I thought, 'Okay, that was interesting, but I'll be glad to have it done and behind me.'"

Despite the lack of support from race officials, Judy and Lyn finished strongly and with respectable times: 3:40:51 for Judy and 3:47:50 for Lyn.

––––––

In the late 1960s, Judy and Dennis adopted two young children and moved to Salt Lake City, Utah. The transplant didn't take. They found the culture too restrictive and moved back to San Bernardino in 1971. Even with two kids to care for, to be followed in several years by a biological daughter, Judy returned to her running as an athletic outlet and stress-reducer. She and Dennis decided to close the door on her track days. It was time to focus on longer distances.

Dennis, the student-scholar, read everything he could find about the burgeoning sport of marathon running. He was drawn, in particular, to the philosophy of New Zealand's Arthur Lydiard, who believed even half-milers should train like marathoners for part of the year. Dennis adopted Lydiard's program for Judy, pushing her weekly mileage up to 100 miles, then dropping it back to 70 when she developed anemia.

"Dennis was the perfect coach for me," she says. "He was always tinkering, always willing to change his mind. That's how he got absolutely the max out of me."

In 1973, Judy won the Mission Bay Marathon in San Diego in 3:00:05. The next year, she won it again, improving to 2:54:08. She had now started three marathons, going back to the one in Las Vegas, and she had won all three. But the big ones still lay ahead.

"At first, I had no idea where I was going in the marathon," Judy admits. "Then at some point you start to see a more sharply defined vista in front of you. I saw that I was at Point A, and I wanted to get to Point B. The first time I broke three hours was a big deal for me. It showed me that I was one of the top women runners in the country."

Judy didn't race often, preferring to do long buildups and recoveries with each of her marathons. "I always found that life is a lot like training for a marathon," she says. "Most of life isn't glamorous. People aren't watching and applauding. You're doing the dishes, cleaning the bathroom, or running hilly 18-milers. No one gives you a trophy for those things. But you have to get through them as part of your daily life and your daily progress toward running goals."

The month of February 1974 produced a clear and important target—the first National Championship for women. The race in San Mateo, California, attracted a strong contingent of entrants hoping to become the USA's first official national champ in the women's marathon. The breakthrough honor went to Judy, who captured first place in her fourth marathon in a row with a time of 2:55:18.

"Since it was an AAU Championship, it was a no-brainer for me and Dennis," she says. "A few other women were more interested in the Boston Marathon two months later, but we came from the AAU mold where championships were the most important competitions. Maybe you had to have been a runner for 20 years like me, but I really appreciated the significance of the first national championship for women. It meant a lot to me."

Five months later, in September 1974, Judy traveled to Waldniel, West Germany, for the first of Dr. Ernst van Aaken's International Women's Marathons. He had been promoting women's endurance abilities for many years and now realized that he could draw attention to women's potential by staging a major event in his hometown. A tireless enthusiast with a medical degree that added authority to his claims about women's strength, Dr. van Aaken played a pivotal role in the history of women's marathoning.

Because Judy had won all four of her previous marathons, she was considered one of the race favorites. Unluckily, she came down with a hip injury just before the marathon. Dr. van Aaken himself treated her, but the discomfort remained. Moreover, Dennis was unable to make the trip. As a result, Judy repeated an old pattern—starting too fast. "I think I was just too hyped up," she recalls. "I wanted to win so badly that I got too excited and went out too fast. I did love leading. It was so nice to be out front. But it didn't last."

She faded over the second 13 miles, finishing seventh in 2:58:47. Judy ran two more sub-three-hour marathons in her career, the last at Houston in 1979. That was also the year she and Dennis launched Race Central, which grew into one of the largest road-race timing companies in the United States.

In May 1984, the day before the first U.S. Olympic Marathon Trials in Olympia, Washington, Judy jogged the entire 26.2-mile course with several friends, who were also pioneer women runners. "We spent the whole distance chatting about such a long list of things," she recalls. "One of our group said, 'We could go a whole lot faster if we didn't talk so much.' But we weren't there to run fast. We were there to celebrate the event and the roles we had played.

"In my competitive days, it had never crossed my mind that I could run in an Olympic Marathon. The idea was so far from our thoughts then that it never crystallized in our minds. We were just runners chasing whatever opportunities we had. Running also gave me more control over my life. It leveled me off. I didn't need drugs. I could just run for an hour, and then life didn't seem so crazy."

Mary Decker (492) wins the 1500-meter race to complete her "Decker Double" in the 1983 Helsinki World Championships.

"I just seemed to have an Olympic jinx. But I feel good about all the other contributions I made. I didn't have women to emulate when I started. People who saw me out running in the early 1970s reacted like I had three heads or something. Today's high-school and college girls have a lot of opportunities. A lot of us who came before them made these a reality."

MARY DECKER

Born: August 4, 1958

MAJOR ACHIEVEMENTS

- Marathon, age 12, 3:09:47, 1971
- American records, every distance from 800 meters to 10,000 meters
- Winner, "Decker Double," first Track and Field World Championships, Helsinki, 1983

IN HER competitive prime, Mary Decker established herself as the greatest distance runner, male or female, in American history. With her powerful-yet-graceful stride, she left most of her competitors far behind. Mary always made it look easy, even when setting American records, which she did 36 times, indoors and outdoors. But her talent came with a cruel twist. She was fragile and often injured. As a result, she never managed to achieve the great Olympic dreams she formed as a young teenager. At one point in her career, Mary held every American record for distances from 800 meters to 10,000 meters. She exhibited an unparalleled combination of speed and endurance. She probably could have held the marathon record as well. In fact, she came close in her only 26-miler, despite being only 12 years old.

Mary ran her one and only marathon just three days after she first heard about the event. She was 12 years old, barely reached five feet in height, and weighed 89 pounds. She had been cooling down after a midweek afternoon workout with her fellow Long Beach Striders, and as the runners jogged slowly, she picked out fragments of conversation about something called a marathon. There seemed to be one coming up over the weekend, and a number of her older, male teammates were planning to enter.

"What's a marathon?" Mary asked, completely clueless.

The others filled in the grim details.

"That sounds like fun," she said. "I think I'll enter."

Her coach, Don DeNoon, tried to talk her out of it. "No, I really want to do it," she insisted with what came to be her trademark fearlessness.

That Sunday morning in May 1971, Mary entered the Palos Verdes Marathon. It was a typical marathon—that is, the course followed asphalt roadways and covered 26.2 miles. But Mary had never run even 13 miles and had done all her training on parklands or beaches, never the roads. These details didn't deter her, though the race didn't go entirely as she might have hoped.

For one thing, Palos Verdes presented a hilly and challenging route on a coastal peninsula southwest of Los Angeles. For another, runners and spectators kept telling her to drink this sickly sweet orange "ade," which contained extra sugar for added energy. It sounded like a good idea, but she found the taste revolting. She kept sipping only because the other runners insisted that she must. For years afterward, she couldn't stomach the thought of drinking anything that tasted similar to the "ade."

As Mary ran, she received encouragement from some of the male runners—dads of the girls on her Long Beach team. They seemed excited to have her in the race. Of course, the distance and hard road surface eventually took their toll. Also, the ocean breezes buffeted her tiny frame. She had to work extra hard when running into the windy blasts. "The last six miles were pretty tough," she admits.

Still, despite her age and inexperience, Mary was the first female finisher. She crossed the line in 3:09:47. At the time, the world and American record for the marathon was 3:01:42. (Marathon historians believe the Palos Verdes course was probably a quarter-mile short, though it is much tougher than most marathons.) It was obvious to all that "Little Mary Decker," as she soon became known, was a runner of exceptional, almost incomprehensible, talent.

After the marathon, Mary took no recovery period. She jumped right back into her track practices. A week later, she ran four races in a track meet in San Diego, culminating with her first-ever 2-mile run on the track. Something went wrong in that last event. She felt intense stomach pains and couldn't finish. That was weird, she thought, that she could run 26 miles but not 2?

At home, her mother could do nothing to ease her daughter's physical distress. Eventually, they headed to a hospital emergency room, where doctors told them that Mary needed an immediate appendectomy. There was no time to hold off. Her appendix had reached the point of bursting.

"Have you been under a lot of stress?" an inquiring physician asked her.

"No, nothing unusual," Mary replied.

Mary had begun running only two years earlier, shortly after her family moved to Southern California. Before that, she lived in New Jersey, where she enjoyed outdoor games but also sewing and other indoor craft projects. No tomboy, she didn't try to join the boys in their baseball and football games. But she quickly realized she could run fast. No one ever caught her in any of the school or neighborhood "chase" games, but she could catch others. This upset the boys—she could actually run them down from behind.

"They stopped asking me to play," she recalls. "They really didn't like that I could catch them."

In Southern California, Mary and her best friend, Sue, participated in almost every activity offered by the local parks department. One week, they learned about an upcoming cross-country race. Neither had any idea what that meant, but they showed up at the Huntington Beach event anyway. When they arrived, they were lined up with other girls 9 to 11 for a ³/₄-mile scamper through undulating hills. Mary took off fast, went straight to the front, and won by a large margin. Sue dropped out.

"I had never run anything nearly that far, so it seemed like a long way," Mary recalls. "But it was fun to do it, and fun to win."

A local coach asked if she would like to do more running with his team, the Long Beach Comets.

"I guess so," she said.

Soon, she was training three days a week with the Comets, mainly for the 100, 400, and long jump. A fourth day was required for fund-raising at a local supermarket, which was actually the toughest part for Mary. She was shy and didn't like approaching strangers to ask for a donation. Her running proved better. Although she showed little prowess in the 100, she often won anything longer. She quickly realized that the farther the distance she raced, the better she did.

At 12, she began running the mile from time to time and soon broke five minutes. Everyone else seemed to think that that was a big deal. Mary had no history or context to evaluate her time. "Five minutes didn't mean anything to me," she recalls. "I almost never ran for times. I don't have a good head for them. The only thing I thought about was getting to the finish line first."

Before long, Mary was traveling around California and Arizona with her Long Beach team, and then far beyond the Western United States. In 1973, just before her 15th birthday, she was selected to join a U.S. international team to tour Europe, the Soviet Union, and parts of Africa. Mary was so young that her mother at first resisted the idea that she take such a long trip, but relented after receiving assurances that Mary would have a chaperone and curfew at all times.

The trip was a life-changer. It opened Mary to her own potential, the world of elite athletics, and the kind of runner she would try to become. In many ways, she felt like a young princess in a world of more mature athletes. Several of the older male distance runners looked after her as if she were their young sister. They worried that Mary was training too hard and long by following the meticulous program she had brought along from her California coach. She wasn't just the youngest runner on the team but also the last to finish her workouts, and the last to board the team bus back to the hotel.

Mary herself barely noticed. "I never felt pushed or exploited," she notes. "I just liked to run fast. It came so natural to me. I didn't have to try hard; it just happened. The speed always came easily."

She also liked the idea of running strong and confident. She couldn't find any role models among the other American women, but she did with an impressive New Zealander, John Walker. Walker held the world record in the mile and was renowned for his brash, charismatic front-running. That

"Little Mary" Decker, 15, sets a new meet record in winning the National Indoor Championship 800-meter in 1974.

struck Mary as the right way to run. "I didn't have any women runners I could emulate," Mary says. "They all seemed too girly to me. I wanted to be tougher than that—more like John Walker."

Even the famous Nike star Steve Prefontaine (Pre, for short) was one of those concerned by Mary's arduous training. He seemed to see a bit of himself in her—the way she always pushed to the front and tried to destroy the competition. But he also believed she needed to be more careful in training to ensure a long, healthy career.

"That fall, Pre called about once a week," Mary remembers. "He wanted to be sure I would preserve my talent. He made me feel like I was his half-sister. He and I developed this connection. When I watched him race, I felt that I had the same instincts inside me. When we talked, it was like he expressed thoughts that I was already having with myself."

Mary's meteoric rise to fast times and stardom seemed almost destined for a subsequent fall. Sure enough, she hit some hard times in the mid-1970s, when she grew 6 inches and added 15 pounds. It was almost like living in a new body, and this one didn't function so well. For several years, she endured sharp pains in her shins. She was forced to give up regular running. Her parents divorced during this period—another emotional blow.

"I had grown accustomed to using running for therapy," she acknowledges. "It made me feel whole. When I got injured, I lost that outlet." She struggled on.

In 1976, Mary moved to Boulder, Colorado, and worked in the retail running store owned by Frank Shorter, the 1972 Olympic gold medalist in the marathon. It was an Olympic year again, and Boulder's many elite runners were dedicating their lives to the Olympic Trials and Olympic Games. But not Mary. The ever-present shin pain had reduced her running to almost nothing. The store was mostly a happy place, full of young, hard-training runners with big aspirations. If Mary could have joined them for workouts, it might have proved the perfect environment. But her shin injury precluded this, making life even more frustrating. At the end of the retail day, the other employees would suit up for their evening run.

"We can let Mary close the store for us," she remembers them saying, "and I was left there alone. I was the nonrunner. I felt almost as if I didn't exist."

In the spring of 1977, Mary was finally able to start training again, and she made some good progress. She always got back into shape quickly. Predictably, her shin pains soon flared up, forcing her to stop yet again. However, this time Mary heard about another runner with the same problem and a surgical procedure that had cured him. She elected to have the same surgery and was relieved to find it worked like a miracle.

Her pain disappeared at last, and Mary ran strongly the next several years. She had high hopes for the 1980 Olympic Games, the ultimate challenge. She set many new records along the way, and won the 1979 Pan American Games 1500-meter competition. She had missed the two previous Olympics, deemed too young by U.S. officials in 1972, and injured in 1976. Maybe the third time would prove the charm? She poured everything she had into the effort.

At the 1980 Olympic Track Trials, Mary won the 1500 by a whopping two seconds. No other American runner was in her league, and she looked ready to take on the world in the Moscow Olympics. But President Jimmy Carter saw it another way. He declared that the U.S. would boycott the Moscow Games due to the Soviet Union's invasion of Afghanistan. "We athletes talked about it all the time," Mary remembers. "I don't remember anyone who thought it was a good idea or that it would have any influence on the Soviets. I was still young, just 22, and I felt that I would have other Olympic chances. But I felt bad for the athletes who wouldn't be around in another four years. We were angry, but there was nothing we could do about it." She had no choice but to look forward. Always forward.

Mary turned her attention to the next big, worldwide track meet—the first ever World Championships of track and field scheduled for Helsinki, Finland, in 1983. It was the perfect location for the perfect track meet. Unlike the Olympics, overgrown with dozens of sports that many people barely knew or understood, the track and field World Championships would focus just on track.

Track and field is perhaps the most historic of all Olympic sports, dating back to the first modern Olympics of 1896 and the original Olympics in Greece. While women didn't compete in those ancient Games, they certainly did now. Women's running opportunities were expanding rapidly in the United States, 11 years after the passage of Title IX (a federal law prohibiting discrimination on the basis of sex) in 1972. The rest of the world, especially Eastern Bloc countries, were more than keeping up, fueled by intense training and rampant use of performance-enhancing drugs.

Mary was excited and ready. "We all had the same feeling—that Helsinki was going to be a pure track championship," she recalls. "In some ways, it was better than the Olympics. There were no politics, no boycotts. Everyone would be there. Everyone wanted to perform their best."

Mary decided to run both the 1500 meters and the 3000 meters. But no one gave her a chance for a high placing. The Soviets and East Germans dominated women's distance running, grabbing 8 of the top 10 rankings in the 1500 in 1982. Mary ranked 9th. And the Eastern Bloc countries were just as strong in the 3000. But Mary refused to give in. She believed this was her time, at last, and her place to shine. "No one thought I could beat the Russians because they were so tough and had great speed at the end," Mary remembers. "I decided not to play games with them. I just wanted to take it out hard at the start, and run hard all the way."

Her plan worked to perfection, though Mary was hunted and haunted every step of the way. The 3000 came first, and the Soviet Union's Tatyana Kazankina dogged Mary for seven of the seven-and-a-half laps before exploding into her kick on the final curve. Mary, with a longer, more fluid stride, also started sprinting on the curve. She refused to let her Soviet rival pass, matching acceleration with acceleration. It was a gritty race to the tape, and Mary got there first, winning the impossible gold medal.

"It was fun, win or lose," she told *Sports Illustrated* magazine, "because it's a nice feeling to come off the last turn with runners there. It's supposed to be a competition. I didn't tense up at the end. I took a deep breath, relaxed, and went for it."

Several days later, Mary returned for the 1500-meter final. Much of the race looked like a replay of the 3000. Mary led, and the Soviets pursued her. The last half-lap got feisty, almost combative. The Soviet Zamira Zaitseva bumped Mary several times, surged ahead of her, and then cut in too sharply.

"She moved in so suddenly, she blocked me," Mary says. "I had to slow down, I had no place to go. That pissed me off. I thought, 'That's cheating.'"

Somehow Mary channeled the anger directly to her pumping legs, moving up beside Zaitseva with 50 meters to go. She had a motto for the way she aimed to finish: "At the end, make like a sprinter." She drove her arms and legs as hard as she could, inching slightly ahead of her rival. At the finish line, Zaitseva threw herself forward in an attempt to literally fly past Mary. It didn't work. She ended up a sprawling, twisted wreck on the track, while Mary claimed another gold medal.

Everyone called it the Decker Double, and it made headlines around the world. An American woman had beaten the untouchable Eastern Bloc runners, not just once, but twice. The Olympics were a mere year away—in Los Angeles. They would be held virtually in Mary's backyard, where she had run her earliest record-breaking efforts more than a decade earlier. What a story line! The headlines would read: "Little Mary Comes Home."

But for the time being, Mary focused on her hard-gained victories in Helsinki. "I lost a lot of space when Zaitseva cut in front of me," she said. "I can't say I'm happy about that. But that's international competition, and that's what I have to get used to."

Her words proved more prophetic than she could have known.

In a perfect athletic world, Mary would have gone into hiding for the next 12 months to concentrate exclusively on her Olympic training. She would have emerged from time to time for a test race, and then have disappeared again. Her world-class track career had now spanned three Olympics, but she had yet to reach a single Olympic start line. It was time for an all-or-nothing approach of total dedication.

That proved impossible. The Decker Double remained a topic of excited discussion, women's sports were enjoying an ascendant period, and Mary was the hometown hero in Los Angeles. Everyone wanted to interview her for a pre-Olympic story, and she felt obliged to say yes to everyone. It was the best way to help promote women's running at this important juncture, but it came at a cost to Mary. The constant demands stole time from her training and piled anxiety onto her mental state.

"There was pressure like never before," she admits, "not just from the media, but from myself. I wanted to advance the sport of track and field and the cause of women's sports."

Soon, she had an even bigger foe—her usual dance with injuries flared up again like a recurring nightmare. She lost training time and entered the 1984 U.S. Olympic Track Trials knowing that she wasn't in top shape. There, she won the 3000, but lost the 1500, forcing her and coach Dick Brown to change their Olympic plans. They decided not to go for the "double" again. Instead, Mary would run only the 3000. It was much more important that she focus on one great effort rather than risking two mediocre ones. Because the Soviets and most of the Eastern Bloc countries were boycotting the 1984 Los Angeles Olympics, she didn't have to worry about them. That left primarily the Romanians and a new face on the world stage, the pixie Zola Budd.

Zola had been born in South Africa, a country barred from the Olympics because of its apartheid racial policy. But after Zola broke Mary's 5000-meter world record in January 1984, her father and a British newspaper engineered her move to England. Suddenly, she was eligible to run for Great Britain and could compete against Mary, her idol. At home in South Africa, Zola had festooned her bedroom walls with posters of Mary.

As the Games approached, Mary's fitness improved. She felt stronger, more prepared. She had done this many times before. She knew how to gather her mental and physical powers, and how to throw them into one supreme race. "I never quit on myself, not even with all the injuries," she says. "I always came back positive and tenacious."

But her coach suggested a change of tactics. Why not rest for a few laps in the middle of the 3000? "That turned out to be the biggest mistake of my life, to let someone else lead," Mary remembers. "I always ran my own race at my own pace. But we thought maybe with the Olympic pressure, we should play it a little safe."

In the climactic Olympic 3000-meter final, Mary led for several laps in her usual manner, and then let several runners come alongside her, including Zola. The other runners were outside Mary, so they had to run harder and faster to maintain their position. Mary remained in control without having to force every stride from the front. On the one hand, it seemed an aggressive strategy. On the other hand, it wasn't Mary's usual way of racing, and things got crowded.

Zola held her ground on the outside for nearly two laps, then got edgy and moved a half-stride ahead. She didn't have a clean lead, however, so she didn't cut inside. The race would take about 8 minutes and 40 seconds. After 5 minutes, Mary and Zola brushed each other several times. Nothing unusual. International races always included a few elbow jabs and leg bumps.

Then something more serious happened. To this day, no one is quite sure what. Legs tangled, and Mary pitched almost headfirst onto the grass infield of the track. She tried to bounce back up and rejoin the race but encountered such searing hip pain that she couldn't get to her feet. Eventually, she was carried off on a stretcher.

Zola, who had just turned 18, held the lead for another lap, with boos raining down on her from the huge stadium filled with American fans. Then she slowed to a near jog, her eyes filling with tears. Romania's Maricica Puica won the gold medal; Zola finished seventh. After the race, struggling with her own disappointment, Zola tried to make a consoling comment to Mary. But Mary brushed off her apology with a wave and a cutting, "Don't bother." The incident was widely cited as bad sportsmanship on the part of Mary, distraught that her Olympic dreams were once again thwarted. Later, she wrote an apology letter to Zola, and received a warm note in return.

"I believe I handled the situation with dignity," Mary says. "I didn't call her a name or anything. I just said, 'Don't bother apologizing. It won't help.' It's too bad neither of us had the race we wanted. At least she stayed on her feet."

They raced again the next summer in a much ballyhooed rematch in England, with Mary winning easily. In fact, 1985 was her best year ever. She ranked number one in the world in both the 1500 and 3000, and improved

The much anticipated Mary Decker–Zola Budd (151) race in the 1984 Olympics ended badly for both when their legs tangled. Decker fell to the infield, while a distraught Budd faded badly.

her 3000-meter time to 8:25.6, more than 10 seconds faster than the winning time in the previous year's Olympics. But Mary's Olympic aspirations were never realized, not even when she made the U.S. team again in 1988. By then, her fastest running years had passed.

"I just seemed to have an Olympic jinx," she concludes. "But I feel good about all the other contributions I made. I didn't have women to emulate when I started. People who saw me out running in the early 1970s reacted like I had three heads or something. Today's high-school and college girls have a lot of opportunities. A lot of us who came before them made these a reality."

Nina Kuscsik wins the historic 1972 Boston Marathon—the first to allow women to enter and wear official race numbers.

"I never found running to be boring, the way some people say. I simply loved the freedom that running gave me, and the rhythm of the movement. Most of the time, I never planned where my mind would go. I let it run free. I might look up and see three clouds in the sky. That would make me think of my three children."

NINA KUSCSIK

Born: January 2, 1939

> MAJOR ACHIEVEMENTS

- First official women's winner of the Boston Marathon, 1972
- Winner, New York City Marathon, 1972 and 1973

ON AN otherwise quiet Saturday morning in 1969, the police in Huntington Station, New York, received an unusual report from headquarters. "Be on the alert for a crazy, one-armed woman running through the streets," they heard over the police radio. "She's bleeding, so she might be hurt. She's either injured from an accident or running away from something." Much of the description turned out to be accurate, though the police assumptions were all wrong.

The "crazy" woman was 30-year-old Nina Kuscsik. It was the day before Easter, and she had decided she needed to log another 20-miler to get ready for her first Boston Marathon. Even before beginning her day-before-Easter run, Nina felt conflicted. She knew that all across Long Island other suburban women of her age were fixing big holiday meals, spring cleaning their houses, or taking the kids shopping for new clothes.

"It was what everyone else did to get ready for Easter," she says. "It was hard to be someone doing something else, particularly something no one understood." After all, she, too, was married and the mother of several young children.

Nonetheless, Nina pushed aside the social pressure, rose early for her long run, and tried to choose something to wear against the chilly, rainy weather. She settled on a white, cotton sweatshirt that read "St. John's University" across the front in red lettering. She also had to deal with a cast on one arm, the result of a strained shoulder ligament. The cast forced her to run with a strange arm carriage. She would have looked unusual enough on a good-weather day. In the rain, she appeared like a dazed and bedraggled homeless woman.

No wonder someone reported her to the police. By the time a patrolman found her, Nina had covered almost 18 miles. She was looping back toward her house en route to the full, confidence-building 20-miler. But the patrol car pulled up ahead of her and flagged her down. She jogged over to the policeman.

"What are you doing?" he asked.

Nina explained herself as best as she could. She was training for a marathon, a big race was coming up in Boston, and so on. The patrolman didn't appear to understand a thing she was saying. When he told her about the description of a crazy injured woman, she looked down at herself.

"My cast was soaked and heavy, so I was supporting it under the waistband of my sweatpants," she remembers. "And the red 'St. John's University' lettering was running from all the rain."

All in all, Nina looked very much like the woman described in the police report. Fortunately, the cop accepted her explanation, though he wouldn't let her finish the workout. He ushered her into his car and drove her home.

"I was devastated," she recalls. "Here I was feeling guilty already because I wasn't preparing for Easter, and then I couldn't even finish my long run."

Two weeks later, she drove to Boston with several running friends from Brooklyn. While the men went to the Hopkinton High School gymnasium to pick up their numbers, Nina waited quietly outside, determined not to create a disturbance. She didn't see another woman runner anywhere. At the starting line, she slipped into the big mass of runners and found her friends.

The three of them started together, but that didn't last long. While Nina was less experienced than the guys, they were older and slower than she was, and so she soon found herself moving ahead. "I felt bad, pulling away and leaving them behind, but we all had different paces," she recalls.

Well-trained despite her disappointing pre-Easter run, Nina covered the course at a pace she found comfortable. As she approached the finish line in downtown Boston, she fell in with a male runner, and memorized his bib number. She knew she wouldn't receive an official time or place but figured she could determine her finish position by looking up his. She did this the next day when the Boston newspapers traditionally published the bib numbers, names, and times of all finishers. After all, there weren't that many. Nina searched down the columns of small type until she saw the number she had memorized. As it turned out, she had crossed the line in 3:46, making her the third woman finisher—after Sara Mae Berman and Elaine Pederson—in the 1969 Boston Marathon. She never saw Sara Mae or Elaine, but there was no mistaking her (unofficial, of course) third-place effort.

"That first Boston was a terrific experience," Nina recalls. "Even without a number, I felt welcome on the course. The fans were nice to everyone. I remember picking up orange slices from them along the way.

"But I never imagined that I'd run another marathon. I didn't even have time to think about it. The next day, back on Long Island, I started a big project repapering my kitchen. That took all week. I was happy that I had finished Boston, but I didn't think any more about it."

Not immediately, perhaps. But the enthusiasm soon returned. Nina ran Boston again in 1970 and 1971, improving her time to 3:12:16, then 3:09. She was the second woman finisher both years.

Nina grew up on a bustling block in Brooklyn, New York, with an older and younger sister and a brother nine years younger. Every spare moment, the siblings filled neighborhood streets and parks with their games: kickball, stickball, volleyball, and other fast-paced activities. "I don't remember that we had a lot of restrictions placed on us," Nina says. "We had to go indoors for supper when my mother called, but the rest of the time, we were free to play."

Neither her mother nor father participated in sports, but her father had sufficient interest in cycling to buy the children bikes when they were old enough. One of these bikes led to Nina's earliest running experience. In May 1954, when she was 15, she heard about Roger Bannister's historic first sub-4-minute mile. It was a big, worldwide story on radio and in the newspapers. Nina decided she wanted to get a sense of exactly how fast Bannister had run.

To do this, she had to find a local track. There was a track two miles from her home. She rode her bike there, scrambled over the fence, and timed herself for one lap. "I ran the quarter-mile as fast as I could," she remembers. "It took me 85 seconds. I was so impressed that Bannister could run a lap 25 seconds faster than I had done, and keep going at the same pace for three more laps."

Soon, her older sister introduced her to speed skating, which was popular at their local roller-skating rink. Nina proved so talented that she won New York state championships in 1960, both on roller skates and on ice skates, over distances of 1 mile to 1.5 miles. One day, she attended a roller skate "marathon," purely as a spectator. It didn't look very appealing. "The track was 16 laps to the mile," she recalls, "and they had to go round and round for 26 miles. There were so many turns, and it took so long. It didn't look like anything I would ever want to do."

But the more Nina thought about it, the more she believed a long bicycle race might prove interesting and challenging. She began entering 30-mile bike races in Central Park. Her parents worried about her safety, because the bikes didn't have brakes. But Nina had few doubts. She simply loved the thrill of competition. "They let the men race longer distances than we women did," she says. "But they treated us very well, very fairly. We had our own events and our own prizes."

She tried her hand at basketball, too. But her experiences on the court led to shoulder injuries that required a cast and a sling. Her options for sports seemed limited until she noticed a book in a store window, *Jogging,* by Bill Bowerman. She almost laughed when she saw the photos inside. In New Zealand, 60- and 70-year-old women were trotting around running tracks with bonnets on their heads. She'd never seen a sport that looked so silly. But she had another thought as well: She wanted to give it a try.

In the early 1970s, Nina probably ran more marathons than any other woman. She became a fixture in Central Park road races, including the first two New York City Marathons in 1970 and 1971. Race director Fred Lebow used Nina and Kathrine Switzer to get publicity for his virtually unknown event. A male runner was just a kook in a small crowd, but a woman was a "story."

Leading up to the inaugural 1970 New York City Marathon, Nina was both a race entrant and a volunteer. The night before the marathon, she stayed up late making sandwiches—more than 100 of them—for the finishers. Days earlier, she had caught a cold. She took the starting line exhausted and sick, making it just to the 15-mile mark before dropping out. "That was disappointing," she admits. "I felt that my DNF [did not finish] reflected badly on all women runners back then. But I had too much pressure on me, and I got sick. I told myself there would be other races to run."

Her next race would be the most exciting. In 1971, Fred Lebow predicted the first-ever sub-3-hour marathon by a woman at the New York City Marathon. Many may have favored the lanky Beth Bonner, who at just 19 had set a new world record of 3:01:42 several months earlier, but Lebow believed that Nina, 32 at the time, could also break 3 hours. He had two of the world's fastest women in his race, and he wasn't shy about telling everyone, or about predicting a sub-3-hour winning time. Lebow proved an apt prognosticator. Beth won in 2:55:22, her second world record of the year, and Nina finished less than a minute behind in 2:56:04. Nina couldn't have been happier.

"I never had the goal of beating Beth," she remembers. "I was only trying to do my best. If I had a strong race and someone else just happened to run faster, that was fine with me."

That fall, Nina also attended the annual convention of the Amateur Athletic Union (AAU). Advised by her friend Aldo Scandurra—head of men's long-distance running—Nina hoped to bring change to the fussy, outdated rules imposed on women. AAU rules stated that only "certain women" could run races longer than 5-K. What did that mean?

"No one knew," Nina explains. "I thought the AAU was supposed to help athletes. Instead, the rules were hindering us."

You couldn't apply logic to your arguments with the AAU. That never worked. The organization seemed more interested in upholding tradition and its no-women-allowed way of doing things rather than adapting to the times. But in 1971 Nina and others convinced the AAU to give an inch or two. It was decided that women could run the marathon, and the 1972 Boston

Marathon promptly announced that it would give women official race numbers for the first time. This was a crucial change in attitude, as the rest of the road-running world generally followed whatever the Boston Marathon did.

However, the good news came with a ridiculous requirement from Boston's organizers: Women would have to meet the same qualifying standard as men—3:30 and under. Only six women managed to hit this standard and qualify as official runners at the 1972 Boston. Not only that, but AAU regulations also decreed that women had to be segregated from men at the starting line, either by time or with a separate start area. Race executive Will Cloney chose the latter, and scratched a women's starting line on the sidewalk with a crayon.

"We stood there for a moment," Nina remembers, "and then we simply merged onto the road with the men and started wherever we wanted."

Nina hoped to improve on her 2:56 from New York, and she felt great for half the distance. Then she developed diarrhea. She was a registered nurse and knew how to treat her condition. However, there wasn't much you could do while racing in the Boston Marathon. And not just any Boston Marathon, but the first to officially recognize women, featuring her as a star performer. Nina was so worried about how she looked, and what some telling photos might reveal, that she could barely concentrate on her performance.

"It was the first and only time this happened to me," she remembers. "On the course, there was lots of cheering when I came up to people, but none when I passed. I figured they could see my problem. When I finished, I was glad they gave me a big blanket that I could wrap around myself."

At the press conference, someone asked what she had proved with her marathon win. "I proved that I, and all women, have a lot of guts," she recalls saying. "And then I realized what I had said, but it was too late. Fortunately, I don't think anyone noticed."

She stands forever in the record books as the first official women's winner at the world's oldest, most historic marathon—Boston.

Year: 1972. Winner: Nina Kuscsik. Time: 3:10:26.

The 1970s were a heady decade for women in sports, business, and beyond. Nina also made headlines at the 1972 New York City Marathon. Race officials, once again complying with the AAU rule of a segregated start, chose the option of a separate start time. The women were sched-

Angry about a rule requiring women to start at a different time than the men, Kuscsik helped organize a sit-down strike at the start of the 1972 New York City Marathon. She is second from the right, on the road.

uled to start 10 minutes before the men. In response, Nina proposed a protest. When the starter's gun signaled the start of the women's race, the runners didn't surge forward. Instead, they sat down cross-legged on the pavement and lifted large, hand-scrawled signs. One read: "Hey, AAU, This Is 1972. Wake Up." Another: "The AAU Is Archaic." Spectators and the male runners cheered lustily. After 10 minutes, just before the men's start, the women stood up, and joined them.

Nina won the marathon in 3:08:42. The pre-race "sit-down strike" received large-scale coverage, especially photos showing the women's protest signs. Finally, stories highlighted the struggles female runners faced in road racing—officials would not treat them the same as men. Several months later, Nina attended the AAU convention again and found that opposition to women's running had evaporated. The former rules were all stricken. "That was essentially the end of discrimination against women in road racing," she says.

Well, not entirely. There was still no Olympic Marathon for women. Just three weeks earlier, Nina had visited friends Jane and Gary Muhrcke (winner of the 1970 NYC Marathon) to watch the 1972 Munich Olympic Marathon on TV. That day, American Frank Shorter cruised to an impressive victory. "To see Frank Shorter take the lead, and then to win, that was really exciting," Nina recalls.

Nina had won both Boston and New York City in 1972, plus five other marathons that year. She was among the top women marathoners in the world, and the most prolific. However, she had no global stage—no Olympics—on which to test her talent. She was forced to live vicariously through Frank and her male marathon brethren.

In 1976, Nina delivered a talk on the history of women's marathon running at a landmark sports medicine conference sponsored by the New York Academy of Sciences. "Like our male counterparts, we sometimes wonder what cravings keep us out on the road," she said to an international gathering of running and physiology experts. "We find there is an admirable interdependence of our mental, emotional, and physical energies. We've concluded that marathon running is a truly human and healthy endeavor."

At the meeting, the hundreds of assembled medical experts gave unanimous approval to a resolution supporting an Olympic Marathon for women. It read as follows: "Current research including that presented at this conference demonstrates that female athletes adapt to marathon training and benefit from it in virtually the same way male athletes do. There exists no persuasive scientific or medical evidence that marathon running is contraindicated for the trained female athlete. Therefore, be it resolved that it is the considered judgment of the participants of this conference that a women's marathon event as well as other long-distance races for women be included in the Olympics program forthwith."

The next year, at age 38 and eight years after her first Boston Marathon appearance, Nina recorded the two best performances of her life. She was a single parent by this time, raising three children and working as a hospital nurse. She continued following the same training program she had used for many years, running about 70 miles a week, including one speed workout and one long run. "I never found running to be boring, the way some people say," Nina notes. "I simply loved the freedom that running gave me, and the rhythm of the movement. Most of the time, I never planned where my mind would go. I let it run free. I might look up and see three clouds in the sky. That would make me think of my three children."

In October 1977, she ran a 2:50:22 to finish third in the Twin Cities Marathon. Two weeks later, she entered a 50-miler in hilly Central Park. She figured she needed a mental strategy to run strong for the full distance, and concocted one you won't read about in any sports psychology textbook. "I pretended to talk to a different girlfriend during every loop of the Park," she says. "First I'd call one, and we'd talk about recent shopping trips. Next, I might chat with another friend about movies we had seen. Then how things were going at work, then cute guys we had bumped into recently, and so on. This helped me pass the time and stay on pace." The strategy worked well enough for her to set a new world record for women, 6:35:53.

In 1984, Nina witnessed Joan Benoit's victories in both the Olympic Trials and the Olympic Games. She and a friend followed the marathon from several locations along the course in Los Angeles. The first point was almost exactly where Joan made her breakaway move at the 5-K water tables. "We wanted to jump up and down and cheer for her," Nina remembers. "But we thought it would be smarter not to. It was still so early in the marathon. We didn't want to get her overly excited."

From there, she hurried to the Coliseum, not wanting to miss the moment when the first woman marathoner would break the tape in her Olympic gold medal race. Nina had been deeply involved in the efforts to create this opportunity. That's what came to mind as she watched Joan circle the track far ahead of her competitors. "I knew I was watching history," she says. "And it was special to see an American, Joan Benoit, on the track in an American Olympics. I felt this was an important statement about fairness in sports for all women."

Nina might have been an Olympic marathoner herself, but the opportunity arrived 5 to 10 years too late for her. Still, she says she has no regrets. In fact, she seems to be one of those rare people who always lives in the present, always finds something of importance to engage with, and always giggles over the strange and wonderful life she has led. "Running for myself and working for other women's rights in running has been very fulfilling," she explains. "The people I've met and the places I've traveled to have been the biggest reward. Running exposed me to a world I might never have known. More important, the sport accepted me as a total person— athletically, socially, and intellectually."

Twenty years after making her first Olympic team in 1972, Francie Larrieu places third the 1992 Olympic Marathon Trials, qualifying for her fifth Olympic Games.

"I did some of my best running during an era of bra burning and Billie-Jean-King-versus-Bobby-Riggs tennis matches, and I supported everything the women's movement was doing. But I didn't seek out a symbolic or leadership role. I found that I could only do one thing really well, and had room for only that cause in my life—women's running. It made me strong, tough, independent, and goal-oriented."

FRANCIE LARRIEU

Born: November 23, 1952

MAJOR ACHIEVEMENTS

- Member, five U.S. Olympic teams, the most for any American male or female distance runner, 1972, 1976, 1980, 1988, and 1992
- Fifth place, First Olympic 10,000 meters, 1988

FRANCIE LARRIEU began her running career with a big, fat lie. Here's the story behind that lie.

When Francie was 12, she took an interest in running and quickly wanted to do more. She asked her parents if they could find her a coach. They supported her aspirations and began exploring options among friends and making phone calls. They found a coach with a good program and solid reputation at the Santa Clara Valley Track Club.

But before allowing Francie to join the club, her parents proposed two preconditions. First, they insisted that Francie sit down with them to discuss the family-wide implications that her track club membership would have. There was a substantial driving distance to the practices, and her mother would have to do it, wait at practice, and drive home late.

This would steal precious hours from her normal family responsibilities, including everything from cleaning to cooking. Her mom was willing, but only if Francie assured her parents of her genuine interest in running. This couldn't be a lark. It had to be something Francie would take seriously. The family discussion took place. "I understood the point they were making, and I told them, 'Yes, this is something I'm really interested in,'" Francie recalls. She may have been just 12, but she had learned to see the big picture.

She passed step one. Next, her parents explained step two. They weren't going to call the coach themselves and conduct all the conversations. That was Francie's job. They handed her the phone and the coach's number. "You have to step up and talk directly with the coach, right from the beginning," they explained. Francie wanted to prove her independence, so she dialed the phone number with no hesitation. Coach Preston Doss answered. He and Francie chatted a bit, and then he asked her the key question: "Can you run 800 meters in under three minutes?" At the time, in the mid-1960s, the 800 was the longest track distance women were allowed to run.

Francie responded quickly, betraying no doubts. "Sure," she said. "I can do that. I can run faster than three minutes." That was the lie. Francie didn't even know how far 800 meters was—and she certainly didn't know if she could cover the distance in 3 minutes. But she didn't let that distract her. She answered strong and confident, and Doss believed her.

Francie satisfied her parents' demands and now (with the help of a confident fib), her newfound coach as well. It was the beginning of an amazing track and road-running career. Francie would eventually qualify for five U.S. Olympic Teams—more than any other American distance runner, male or female. She would run Olympic races that extended from 1500 meters to the marathon—no other American runner has ever exhibited such an incredible range. She achieved her best Olympic performance in the first women's 10,000-meter race at Seoul in 1988. There, she trailed three East European women at a time when Eastern Bloc athletes followed a (then-undetectable) doping regimen. Otherwise, Francie might very well have attained her longtime goal—an Olympic medal.

Francie grew up the sixth of nine children in a modest home in Palo Alto, California. The place was cramped, so she always had to share a bedroom with several sisters. Her parents worked as many jobs as they could find to make ends meet, and family discipline was tight at times. There were strict rules governing who could leave the house, and when. Palo Alto was not then the high-priced housing mecca it is now. Given the lack of extra cash for travel and vacations, the Larrieu children spent most of their time outdoors, playing street games, or hiking in the hills around Stanford University. "I remember racing around the bases in kickball," Francie says. "And our hide-and-seek games had gigantic boundaries. We covered a lot of ground. During the week, I biked three miles to school every day."

In the annual fitness testing at school, Francie was always the fastest girl and among the fastest overall, boys included. Several of her siblings were also quite talented. In fact, she she had an older brother, Ron, who was one of the United States's best distance runners. Not that Francie ever paid much attention to Ron. He was 15 years older than she; he seemed to belong to another world.

That held true until the day in sixth grade, in 1964, when she was startled out of a reverie by hearing her name—Larrieu—mentioned by a teacher. The teacher was explaining how Francie's big brother would be flying to Tokyo to compete with other Americans in something called the Olympic Games. "I didn't know much about the Olympics at that point," Francie admits. "But when one of my teachers began talking about the Games and my brother in the same breath, I thought, *'Gosh, they must be something special.'* That was one of the incidents that first made me set a goal of becoming an Olympian."

A few years later, she attended one of Ron's track meets in Los Angeles. Again, she wasn't particularly impressed with his running. Ron seemed to be just one of the hundreds of men running around in circles, covering varied distances. It was the women's two-lap race that grabbed Francie's attention. Women were allowed to run in track meets? Now, that looked like something exciting and challenging.

Aside from her brother Ron, Francie had few athletic models. Her dad played a strong tennis game, but her mother was totally housebound. At the time, few mothers were active, certainly not ones with nine children. All weekend long, Francie's mother labored to prepare meals for the coming week. Most were pasta-based because it was inexpensive. But she made sure to cook liver at least once a week for Francie, as liver was then widely considered a health-and-strength food. The extra effort didn't produce good results. Francie despised liver; it was her least-favorite food. When her mom wasn't looking, she fed it to the dog.

Although her parents were not college graduates themselves, both stressed the importance of a good education and tried to expose their children to as many opportunities as possible. If the kids showed interest in a particular activity, well, there was always a way. "We couldn't afford private tennis lessons," Francie says, "but we got lessons at Parks and Rec. We couldn't take private piano lessons, but we got lessons from the girl next door who did take private classes. My parents supported anything we showed genuine interest in."

From day one at Preston Doss's track practices, Francie dove into the program wholeheartedly, running near endless numbers of 100-yard sprints. A year later, she transitioned to Augie Argabright's San Jose Cindergals program. Argabright was a passionate student of distance-running theory, and he melded the two primary training methods—slow, over-distance training and fast, interval training—into a system that made sense for him and his athletes. Francie thrived, and she improved at an incredible pace.

By 1968, not yet 16 years old, she was selected to compete in a USA international meet in Stuttgart, Germany. She would run the 1500 meters, where she had a best time of 4:28. It was sensational for an American girl her age, but not for the mature European women she would be facing. There were only three other runners in the race—a Soviet, an Italian, and an American, Doris Brown—and all were far older and faster than Francie. She admits she was scared. "I was so nervous," she remembers. "I thought, '*Oh, my goodness, what have I gotten myself into?*'"

Francie needed a plan. Common sense suggested that she should run at her own pace and simply hope for a modest improvement. But she rejected this approach. She had traveled all the way to Germany, after all. Why jog along by herself? With a combination of grit and grandiosity, she chose to run aggressively. "I decided to attach myself to the others and not let them drop me," she says.

This strategy could have been a disaster, but it proved an illuminating lesson. It also yielded a dream result. Francie finished last, yes, but much closer than expected to her rivals. And her time was 4:16.8, an impressive leap forward, and an American age-group record that lasted for many years. More important, it changed the way she regarded herself among top-ranked women middle-distance runners. "It was the first time I realized that I might have the potential to race with the best runners in the world," she notes.

The next summer, Francie learned a completely different kind of lesson. While traveling with a group of U.S. runners on an international tour, she discovered that a number of her male teammates found her attractive. They attempted to ply her with alcohol and get physical. Fortunately, several older, married members of the team stepped in to stop the advances. "Those two international trips matured me more than anything else in my life," she says. "I saw people and places and behavior that I hadn't known before."

The trips also helped Francie adopt an entirely new attitude during her final year of high school. She realized that she didn't need to worry about becoming more popular or joining more high-school cliques. Instead, she could focus her attention on pursuing her personal goals. "I felt freer," she recalls. "I stopped trying to be someone I wasn't, and concentrated more on being me and pursuing the things I wanted to do. It was so much more enjoyable." And she kept running faster and faster.

Through much of the 1970s, Francie ruled the American distance scene for women. In 1972, she had her first chance to make it to the Olympics—in the new women's event, the 1500 meters. This would be eight years after her brother Ron had participated in the 1964 Olympics. She felt the pressure. "At the Trials, the women's 1500 meters was the very last event," she remembers. "It was hard waiting so long while everyone else was nailing their spot on the team. I was confident, but you never know what's going to happen."

Francie won the Trials race, and she joined the USA team that would compete in the Munich Olympics. "It was the most incredible feeling to qualify for the Olympics," she says. "You think about them for so long, and finally, the day comes when you know you are actually going. Then, to step on the track at the opening ceremonies with a full stadium roaring, it's just so spectacular. You think, '*Oh, my God, I'm really part of the Olympics.*'"

After the peak, the crash. The Munich Games were nearly canceled when Palestinian terrorists attacked and killed Israeli athletes. Francie felt scared, confused, and isolated—about what you would expect for a 19-year-old who was all alone, without family or a coach. She couldn't even figure out how to get updates on the horrendous sequence of events. "We didn't have anything like CNN back then," she notes. "We had to go to the media center and listen to Jim McKay's reports for ABC television."

The Olympics continued, but on a delayed schedule. Francie ran her semifinal, but failed to qualify for the final. Her joyous, then tumultuous Olympics were quickly over. "You run as many competitions as I have, and there are a lot of 'should have, could have, and would haves' among them," she says. "In Munich, I felt distracted, alone, and unsupported. It wasn't my day."

Nearly 25 years later, while watching the movie *Fire on the Track* about Steve Prefontaine, she realized for the first time that he had received much more support in Munich than she had. In particular, Prefontaine's college coach Bill Bowerman, also the Olympic head coach, counseled him through the maelstrom. The movie left a bitter taste. "Before *Fire on the Track*, it had never occurred to me that I had been denied anything in my track career, because I always went after what I wanted," Francie says. "But then I saw how Pre had much more support in Munich than I did, not to mention that he was recruited to college and never had to pay a dime, while I had to pay for my college education. The film really upset me because I always thought my path to the Olympics was about the same as everyone else's. Apparently, that wasn't true."

A few years later, the legendary Prefontaine played a role in another drama involving Francie. At the time, she was running in East Coast and West Coast indoor meets on successive evenings. Many nights, the organizers would time her at two distances, 1500 meters and the mile, so she could set two records in one race. In February of 1975, Francie achieved a "double triple": two meets, two days, three world records. One of those was a 4:29 indoor mile. Prefontaine also won his event in the same meet. Afterward, he said, "I admire Francie tremendously. But the fact is, I can run six 4:29 miles in a row."

The cutting comment didn't go unnoticed. The *New York Times* soon published a rebuke from Francie Kraker Goodridge, a top American miler who had been on the 1972 Olympic Team with Francie. She argued that it is silly, and wrong, to compare men's and women's times due to "biomechanical, physiological, sociological, and psychological differences." In summary:

"Sports at all ages and all levels has been highly encouraged and promoted among males. Until this kind of involvement is achieved among females, comparisons of the relative performances of men and women will be pointless."

Francie agreed, but didn't commit herself to the fray. "I never, not from my first day in track, had any interest in competing against men or comparing myself with men," she notes. "I saw my brother Ron run in that long-ago San Jose track meet, but it was the 800-meter women's winner, Marie Mulder, who got me so excited. After her, I wanted to race against and beat the best women in the United States. I never cared about what the boys and men were running."

In 1976, Francie qualified for her second Olympic team. She had hopes for a strong performance at the Montreal Games but came down with a case of the famous "Olympic virus." (This kind of thing happens frequently at the Olympics, due to the athletes congregating together from all corners of the world. They often bring with them various viruses that athletes from other countries have never encountered.) Again, she failed to advance from the semifinals. "It was a big disappointment," she says. "It's very hard to go home and face your friends. They all want to know what place you finished, but they don't understand the way the Olympics work. They can't grasp why you weren't running in the final."

Francie paid little attention to another runner with the same problem—Norway's Grete Waitz, just 22 at the time, a year younger than Francie. Grete had great endurance, but not enough speed for the metric-mile distance. Norway's track fans couldn't understand why she won races at home, and even set world records, but couldn't win a medal at the Olympics. They whispered that she was a "choker." The emotional environment was so bad for Grete that she considered quitting the sport. Instead, she moved up to the marathon and discovered her natural distance. A decade later, Francie would follow a similar path.

But first, Francie prepared for what she had always imagined would be her prime Olympic years—1980 and 1984. She would take her strong performances in the 1970s and build upon them with greater experience and more physical maturity. In the early 1980s, she figured, she would hit her peak. It didn't work out exactly that way.

In 1980, the United States boycotted the Moscow Olympics. Francie had made her third straight U.S. Olympic team at 1500 meters, but no Americans competed in Moscow. Instead, they got an honorary trip to the White House. "We got paraded around Washington," Francie remembers, "but we all knew that that was no substitute for actually competing in the Olympics. I felt especially bad for the athletes who never qualified for another Games."

In the buildup to 1984, when the Olympic Games were held in Los Angeles, Francie found herself running in the long shadow of Mary Decker. This was a new and unsettling prospect. She suffered from a loss of confidence, then a loss of joy for running. "I worried too much about others," she admits. "That doesn't work. You need to keep a positive attitude and keep your focus on the only thing you can control—yourself, and your own workouts and races. You also have to keep running for fun. Otherwise, what's the point?"

She hoped to run in the first Olympic 3000 meters for women. Only problem: She didn't qualify at the U.S. Track Trials. Francie was off her game, lacking the necessary concentration she needed to push herself, and instead focusing on her place among the competition. "I was counting places while we ran," she says. "That's never a good thing." She ended up finishing fifth, not high enough to qualify.

Having failed to make her fourth straight U.S. Olympic team, Francie followed the big events in Los Angeles as a spectator. While Mary Decker and Zola Budd tangled legs in the 3000, and Joan Benoit racked up a sensational marathon victory, Francie sat and watched. Benoit's powerful run proved a revelation. "Joan was just totally, completely amazing," Francie says. "She ran away from all the queens of marathoning—Grete Waitz, Ingrid Kristiansen, Rosa Mota, Lorraine Moller. I knew immediately that her win represented a big leap forward for women in road racing. She popularized it for all of us."

In January 1986, Francie was ready to follow directly in Benoit's footsteps. She entered her first marathon, Houston, and finished second with a fast debut time of 2:33:37. As the 1988 Seoul Olympics came into view, she considered specializing in the 26.2-mile race. But Seoul also

Larrieu charges from the start line in the 1987 World Championships 10,000 meter race.

offered the first-ever 10,000 meters for women, and Francie opted for that distance instead. It was a good choice. Everything came together, and she enjoyed an Olympic experience without massacres or viruses. She placed fifth in that first women's 10,000, placing behind one British runner and three Eastern Bloc rivals who were likely participants in the massive doping programs of their countries. In different circumstances, Francie might have stood on the Olympic podium, a silver medal around her neck.

"I didn't come home with the medal I always wanted," she reflects. "But I walked off the track knowing I had left everything I had out there in the race. It was an exciting competition, and I was the first American to finish. You're always competing for one spot or another."

Four years later, Francie committed herself to the marathon distance and made her fifth Olympic team. More memorably, she was chosen by a vote of her Olympic teammates to carry the U.S. flag into the 1992 Barcelona Olympics opening ceremonies. She grew nervous, however, as the day grew

At the 1992 Barcelona Olympics, Larrieu's U.S. teammates selected her to carry the American flag.

closer and closer, because no American Olympic officials introduced themselves to organize a rehearsal or at least give her some instructions. She wondered if a big, heavy American flag might prove too much for her slim arms and shoulders to support.

No one said a word. She simply stood at the front of the U.S. contingent as it formed outside the stadium and followed all the other teams as they marched inside. As Francie strode through the tunnel, an American flag materialized as if out of nowhere. Moments later, a TV cameraman looked her way and said, "You're on live TV to the entire United States."

She found the flag of reasonable weight and carried it with pride in both country and self. The 1992 Barcelona Olympics came 20 years after her first, the Munich Games of 1972. She had enjoyed and achieved so much, and risen to a level where she was considered the dean of all U.S. Olympians. This was the most emotional moment of her long running career, and a good time to give thanks. "I still get tears in my eyes when I think about it now," she says. "It was an incredible honor to carry the flag in Barcelona."

A week later, Francie ran the Olympic Marathon in Barcelona, the third different distance race she completed in her Olympic career: 1500 meters, 10,000 meters, and the marathon. The previous year at the London Marathon, she had improved her marathon best to 2:27:35. In Barcelona, the early pace was slow for 20 kilometers. Then the eventual winner, Valentina Yegorova, made a strong break that carried her to victory. Francie couldn't respond, concerned about the heat and a long uphill grind near the end.

"Hindsight is always 20-20," she notes. "I didn't run a particularly fast time, but it was a very hard race, and I gave it my all." She finished 12th in 2:41:09. It was her last Olympic race.

At times during Francie's two decades of track and road running, others wanted to use her as a symbol. They saw her as a constant, shining light to women waging advancement battles on many different fronts. She remembers how Gloria Steinem and *Ms. Magazine* featured her in a campaign before one of her big indoor meets in New York. It didn't feel right.

"I did some of my best running during an era of bra burning and Billie-Jean-King-versus-Bobby-Riggs tennis matches, and I supported everything the women's movement was doing," Francie recalls. "But I didn't seek out a symbolic or leadership role. I found that I could only do one thing really well, and had room for only that cause in my life—women's running. It made me strong, tough, independent, and goal-oriented. I wouldn't trade those days for anything."

A shy teen at Indianapolis High School in the mid-1960s, Cheryl Bridges blossomed with her high-school and college cross-country successes. A few years later, she set a marathon world record.

"The Olympic people said women couldn't run longer distances, but that was only because they never gave us the chance. That made me angry. Still, even without the Olympics, running gave me the chance to figure myself out."

CHERYL BRIDGES

Born: December 25, 1947

- Member, five U.S. World Cross-Country teams
- First woman to break 2:50 in a marathon and set a world record, 2:49:40, at the Western Hemisphere Marathon, 1971

IN HIGH school, all Cheryl Pedlow wanted was to disappear. Or, if that wasn't possible, at least to shrink down to a much smaller size than her 5-foot-8 height. She was shy and didn't want to attract any attention from her fellow students at massive Central High School in Indianapolis, Indiana.

Even more important, she hoped to fade into the background at home to escape her stepfather's verbal and sexual abuse. If she could turn herself into a skinny, scrawny, sticklike figure, she thought he would lose all interest in her. "I didn't want to add another pound that might make me more voluptuous and attract him to me more often," she remembers.

Unfortunately, her hopes to slim down didn't work. Instead, she found herself developing in the other direction, adding pounds, especially around her hips. She needed a plan but didn't know what to do, until one Sunday morning when she was skimming the newspaper. Her eyes fell on an article about Bill Bowerman, the famous track coach at the University of Oregon. Bowerman had just returned from a visit to New Zealand, where he was astonished to discover middle-aged men (and women) jogging around local running tracks.

A visionary New Zealand coach named Arthur Lydiard was preaching that such activity could lead to weight loss, heart health, and renewed vigor. In the United States at that time, only young men ran, and they ran to compete. No women ran. No one ran for his or her health. The idea of running to exercise and lose weight intrigued Cheryl. She wanted to try it.

"I was so shy and very much a loner then," she recalls. "But I was a member of the Girl Scouts, and I did like outdoor activities. I thought maybe I could go to the track and finish a lap."

Of course, Cheryl didn't want anyone else to see her attempt this new activity, "jogging." That would be far too embarrassing. So late one fall afternoon—well after the band, the football team, and the cross-country team had left the practice fields—she snuck onto the track. It was getting dark, she noted with pleasure. The darkness wrapped her in a cocoon that prying eyes couldn't penetrate. "I really wanted to be invisible," she recalls. "That was so important."

Those first few steps in the dark were difficult. "My lungs hurt. My legs hurt. It wasn't the least bit fun. And the worst thing of all was the shoes—the Keds sneakers we all wore then. They were terrible. They hurt so much." She thought someone had maybe fictionalized the tales from New Zealand. Yet Cheryl didn't quit after her first attempt at running laps on the track. She was desperate to lose weight and escape her stepfather's attentions. So she returned to the track every night. One lap, two laps, three laps. All alone. All in secret.

In time, the physical effort became easier. But, more significantly, something magical began to happen as she glided along the track's straightaways and curves. "I would have conversations with myself, and think in different ways," she says. "I could tell someone off without saying a single word to them. Or maybe role play a situation where I was stuck. It became like therapy. And when I finished a run, I felt so much better. I felt like I had accomplished something."

The next fall, a friendly teacher saw Cheryl doing laps and suggested she run with the boys on the cross-country team. Cheryl liked the idea of a change of scenery and other runners to pull her along. So she bundled up in the same gray, hooded sweat suits the boy wore—protection against the chilly weather—and tagged along far behind the pack. She had no intention of entering boys' races. She remained as quiet and nonconfrontational as ever.

Nevertheless, someone noticed, and her unprecedented activity was reported to the Board of Education. The board decided the matter was worthy of debate—a girl running on the high-school track? No one knew what to make of it. After much discussion, including a comment from one board member who deemed her activity "inappropriate," the board put Cheryl's athletic future to a vote.

The verdict: Cheryl could continue running on the high school's extensive campus, but she had to stay away from the boys. Far away. She would not be allowed on the track or any part of campus where the boys practiced. "They said I might prove a 'distraction' because I had long blonde hair," she remembers. "So I did what they said. I didn't want to stir up anything. At that time, we were all raised to be 'good girls' who quietly followed whatever the authorities told us to do."

Cheryl doesn't say much about her childhood—not because she's unwilling to talk about it, but because she believes she has repressed many of the details. She does note that her mother suffered from a mental illness. She remarried when Cheryl was just two.

At first, Cheryl's stepfather seemed to deny her existence. On holidays, like Christmas and Easter, he would buy presents for his other children but not for Cheryl. The more he continued to ignore her, the quicker she came to understand that he considered her worthless—until she became a teenager. Then, he suddenly took an interest in her, too much so. In her mid-teens, Cheryl sought refuge in running. She survived her stepfather's advances by staying away from home whenever possible and by throwing her energy into track and cross-country.

In 1965, as a junior in high school, she joined the Hoosier Track Club, an Amateur Athletic Union (AAU) team. She tried all the usual events, beginning with the sprints. If you had success in the sprints, she figured, why would you ever run any farther? Cheryl tried to sprint using the starting blocks, but she was too tall and lanky. "I basically fell on my face," she recalls, "so I tried a standing start. That didn't work, either. I just didn't have the speed. So the coaches kept pushing me into longer and longer distances."

The longest distance available to her was 800 meters. "It gave me a goal—a task to complete—and I liked that." She even kept running during the oppressively hot and humid Indianapolis summer months when everyone else quit. "The training in July and August wasn't so great," she says, "but I was determined. And I was good at tackling challenges. I literally ran toward them, not away."

She soon learned that her personality and her passion were better suited to running cross-country, with its hills and distance, rather than track. She did many hard workouts with coach Larry Bridges. He would lead, and she would follow. He'd pick up the pace to test her. She'd begin to feel the burn, the pain, and the mental anguish. Still, she'd match him, relying on Larry's words that these grueling runs would give her the grit and toughness to serve her well in races. "I was always motivated to be in control of my own life, and these workouts showed me what I could do," she remembers. "I also found that I loved being out there in the environment. It didn't bother me to have wind, cold, and rain in my face."

In the fall of 1965, while Cheryl was still at Indianapolis High, she and Coach Bridges drove to the AAU Women's Cross-Country National Championships in Cambridge, Massachusetts. While high-school teams didn't have cross-country races for girls, the AAU was beginning to allow women to run cross-country races, provided they didn't exceed 2.5 miles. The opportunity to enter an important women's race thrilled Cheryl. But it also terrified her. How could she, an inexperienced Midwestern girl, a teenager no less, compete against the best runners in the country?

"We got out of the car on race day in Massachusetts, and I remember thinking how scary it was," she says. "I didn't know what I was supposed to do next. For just a moment, I thought about telling Larry, 'This isn't such a good idea. I want to go home. Maybe we should just pick up and leave.'"

She fought the nervousness and went to the start line with one thought: "*Run your own race. Don't worry about the start, where everyone will go out way too fast. Run your own pace. Keep it steady. You'll catch them later.*"

Her strategy worked. It was hard at first, as the other runners bolted from the line in a furious rush, pulling well ahead of her. Her own breathing became raspy and laborious. But then things settled down. Cheryl found herself relaxing into a rhythm. She concentrated on maintaining her position in the field. It was too soon, she knew, to worry about catching anyone. That happened in the last mile. "It was fun picking them off one at time," she remembers. "And it was exciting, too. I had no idea I could move up that much."

She was an unknown 17-year-old from Indianapolis running far away from home. Yet, in her first national meet against the best distance-running women in the United States, Cheryl finished seventh—not bad for a novice with a case of butterflies in her gut. The race inspired her to dream about distant horizons. "I began to see that I could tackle more than I had imagined," she says.

Several days later, her achievement was noted at a Central High assembly intended to kick off the basketball season. Basketball is a big deal in Indiana, practically the state religion. Cheryl had no idea that anyone had learned about the cross-country results. But then she heard her name announced over the loudspeaker. She was asked to stand in front of the entire student body. Despite the fact that few, if any, students understood cross-country racing, they looked her way and applauded. "I was very surprised by the announcement, and also surprised that I liked standing up and getting a little attention," she recalls.

Cheryl spent the next three years at Indiana State University, graduating a full year ahead of her classmates. At the time, ISU offered scholarships to Indiana high-school students "with special talents." Since Cheryl had a unique talent to outrun just about any other female, she earned the ISU scholarship and in effect, became the first female to receive an athletic scholarship in the United States.

Yet, scholarship or no, Indiana State didn't have a women's cross-country team. Cheryl had to compete against local high-school boys in their meets. The coaches were mostly agreeable, as long as she followed two rules that they established. First, she had to prove that she was a serious athlete. Her record attested to that. Second, she had to give the boys a five-second head start before she began running. That way, no one could claim that she was an official entrant in the races. She just happened to be running in the same place at almost the same time.

Cheryl liked the way these "handicap races" worked out. She had to give chase to the boys—a sort of carrot dangled in front of her—and she prided herself on never finishing behind more than a handful of them. Before and after the races, she always remembered to turn on the charm.

"I tried to be very gracious and ladylike all the time," she recalls. "It was an era when female athletes, especially the ones from Russia, were often portrayed as muscular and masculine."

Still, she heard dismissive talk everywhere. Sports and running weren't the kind of activities most young woman wanted to pursue. There could be negative effects. She even had a boyfriend once who warned, "You'd better be careful, or no one will want to go out with you."

To which she responded, "Oh, yeah, well, what are you doing with me?" He didn't last much longer.

In the spring of 1969, Cheryl qualified for the World Cross-Country Championships. She would eventually make this prestigious team five times. The 1969 championship race was held in Edinburgh, Scotland, over a difficult course in nasty conditions. Cheryl recalls it as "a killer, killer course—hilly, muddy, and filled with ruts, a soggy, soggy mess." Still, she finished fourth. She crossed the finish line just a stride behind the bronze medal winner, and loved every step of the race.

"It was a strength-runner's course, which really played to my style," she remembers. "We went up, we went down; it was as muddy as could be. A really tough course. I loved that sort of thing—the challenge of it."

The competition wasn't as draining as the financial aspects. The U.S. men had their expenses paid by the AAU or by a branch of the military. The women had to pay their own way, begging from their local clubs, fund-raising with bake sales, and so forth—or dipping into their own pockets.

"Financially, making the international teams was a double whammy," Cheryl points out. "First, you had to pay your own way. Second, you were docked pay for the days you missed from work." This happened to her several times over the years she spent teaching and coaching.

A few months later, Cheryl heard about the Association for Intercollegiate Athletics for Women (AIAW) Track Championships, to be held in Texas. Years later, the AIAW would be absorbed into what is now the National Collegiate Athletic Association (NCAA). Although Indiana State didn't have a team, Cheryl and several college friends who were eager to compete found a car and drove to Texas together. Some teams at the AIAW meet entered as many as 20 athletes. But with Cheryl winning the 800 and

Bridges displays her strength and power in a 1969 cross-country race in Michigan.

mile, and running on a relay team, Indiana State earned enough points to finish second in the overall standings.

"It was great, and we had a ball," Cheryl recalls. "It was a pure adventure, the kind that doesn't exist much any longer."

The next year, 1970, Cheryl moved to San Luis Obispo, California, where Larry Bridges, then her husband, earned a coaching job at California Polytechnic

State University. Cheryl also worked all day as a public school physical education teacher, and she began to wonder if her serious running days had come to an end. After all, she was 23 now—old by her terms. It seemed the appropriate time to step aside and let younger girls take her place. Few women ran distance races at all, and virtually none continued racing after their high-school and college days.

It was the time to start nesting—to settle down into the role of the good wife. On the other hand, the California weather was intoxicating to her. "After the often-depressing weather back in the Midwest, especially the winters, I felt like a kid in a candy store when I got to California," Cheryl recalls. "We could train year-round, and there were many more racing opportunities than I was accustomed to."

Instead of quitting, she fell into training with the men on her husband's cross-country team at Cal Poly. "It took my body several years to catch up with the training, but they were such a supportive group," she says. "We understood each other. We were going through the same ups and downs. Gradually, I got fitter and fitter."

After cross-country season, many of the central California runners headed to Los Angeles for the annual Western Hemisphere Marathon in Culver City. In December 1970, Cheryl joined them. Everyone thought the end-of-year timing was perfect. If you needed a long recovery after the marathon, no problem. "I was already doing longer weekend runs with the guys," she remembers. "We called it 'The Church of the Sunday Run' because we saw so many other people going to church while we were running. I often think we got closer to God on our runs than they did in church. Anyway, I was always up for another challenge, so when we began discussing the marathon, I thought, 'Why not? It's just one more wild-and-crazy thing to do.'"

That seemed to be Cheryl's specialty—tackling new events, even when she knew little about the challenges. Cheryl cruised through the first 10 miles in 58 minutes—way too fast. At 15 miles, she still felt okay. But as she approached 20 miles? Not so much. "Everything quit working at that point," she says. "It was a death march. I didn't want to walk, but if I hadn't done some walking, I probably would not have finished."

She had to slow and walk a few times, but she finished. Not only that, she ended up being the top female finisher in her first marathon, in 3:14:45. Best of all, she knew she could run much faster. "I realized almost right away that I would want to run another marathon," she says, "because I knew I could run better with smarter pacing."

The next year, she recruited a new coach, Bill Dellinger, from the University of Oregon. He admitted that he had never coached a woman before but didn't see any reason why he couldn't draw up an appropriate training plan. They exchanged letters and phone calls every couple of weeks. Cheryl quickly noted a key difference in the day-to-day workouts. Dellinger, like his mentor Bill Bowerman, believed in a training regimen that alternated hard-day efforts with easy-day recoveries. Cheryl had almost never run truly easy days, just moderate days. "Under Dellinger's program, I felt silly some days when I got suited up for nothing but a slow 30-minute run," she recalls. "But the hard days were often harder than I had done before."

She experimented with 100-mile weeks, but then dropped back to 60 or 70. That seemed to be her sweet spot. In November, she finished third in the National Cross-Country Championships. Several weeks later, she headed for the Western Hemisphere Marathon again. "More than anything else, I wanted to finish the sucker strong, unlike the year before," she says. "I also believed that I was ready to do something special."

First order of business: Don't start too fast. She passed 10 miles in 61 minutes—considerably slower than the previous year—but still fast. The rest of the way, she concentrated on holding pace without letting her mind dwell on the miles still to run, the side aches, and the leg-muscle fatigue. She recalled something she had learned in a recent sports psychology course. "We talked about people who can walk on coals," she recalls. "They took their minds away from where they were. I tried the same in the marathon. When it got tough, I refocused my mind someplace else. Soon enough, the bad patch passed."

Although Cheryl slowed some during the late miles, it was nothing like the previous year. She did, however, encounter one new, unexpected and unpleasant obstacle. At 22 miles, she caught a male runner who didn't want to be passed by a woman. He shouldered Cheryl one way. Then, when she tried to scoot past on his other side, he nearly plowed her onto the sidewalk. Cheryl finally got past the big bruiser only after several other male runners came to her aid and blocked the guy. "He was so different from all the other

Better known for her cross-country and marathon prowess, Bridges also competed occasionally on the track. Here, in the Naturite uniform, she runs a 10,000-meter race in Eugene, Oregon, in 1976. Another First Lady, Jackie Hansen, is just outside Bridges on the track.

men who were rooting for me," she remembers. "I was taken aback by his behavior."

Once past the obnoxious runner, Cheryl enjoyed clear sailing. In fact, she broke the tape in 2:49:40, a new women's world record and the first sub-2:50 marathon by a woman. "I ran within myself the whole way," she says. "I didn't want to walk or to hurt as bad as the year before, and I succeeded on both counts."

Cheryl's new world record attracted scant attention. Few reporters followed the sport of marathon running. In truth, Cheryl didn't think it such a big deal herself. "Basically, it was just a test," she says. "It was just an opportunity to spread my wings and challenge myself. And it turned out to be a wonderful, wonderful day."

The next year, 1972, was an Olympic year, and would include the women's

1500 meters for the first time. But there would be nothing longer—no 5000, no 10,000, no marathon. The 1500 wasn't a realistic goal for Cheryl. "I just didn't have the kind of leg speed that could gobble up the track," she says. "It took me forever to break five minutes in the mile. I was more of a strength runner, a hill runner. I was good at cross-country and probably would have been good in the steeplechase, too, but that event was a long way off for women." (The women's 3000-meter steeplechase wasn't added to the Olympic schedule until 2008.)

Cheryl spent the summer of 1972 training for the Marathon Marathon in Terre Haute, Indiana, where she had attended college. On race day, August 12, the weather was sweltering. It covered the city in a blanket of hot, humid air—a marathoner's worst nightmare. "The humidity was so thick, it looked like fog," Cheryl recalls. "The temperature climbed up into the nineties. It couldn't have been a worse day for running. I felt like death warmed over." Yet she finished in 2:55:43. "In better weather, I'm sure I could have run 10 minutes faster," she says.

A month later, American Frank Shorter won the Olympic Marathon in Munich. It marked a turning point for running in the United States. Many believe it launched the running boom that has continued unabated to the present. Cheryl watched Shorter's Olympic victory on television, transfixed. She couldn't help but think about what might have been. What if she had the chance to run an Olympic distance race? "It just seemed unfair, because the reasons were all wrong," she notes. "The Olympics people said women couldn't run longer distances, but that was only because they never gave us the chance to try. That made me so angry. Still, even without the Olympics, running gave me the chance to figure myself out. It served me well in all aspects of my life."

She saw her victories humbly, but still as important stepping stones for female athletes today. "I was in the first wave of feminists who wanted to change women's role in society, but I didn't know how. The big issues seemed so much bigger than my small existence. Then running came along, and I saw it as a place where I could make a difference, both as an individual and for other women, too."

Joan Ullyot dressed as lightly as possible for the steamy 1976 Boston Marathon, known as "the run for the hoses." She finished 14th in 3:15:57.

"These guys writing the articles at that time simply didn't know what they were talking about. So what if someone misses a few periods? Who wants them? . . . And if sagging breasts is such a problem, why wasn't anyone writing about sagging testicles? They hang a lot looser than breasts."

JOAN ULLYOT

Born: July 1, 1940

MAJOR ACHIEVEMENTS

- Transition from a "creampuff" MD into a many-time sub-three-hour marathoner with a best time of 2:47:39

- Author, 1976, *Women's Running*, the first book to allay myths about women's running and to outline its many benefits

JOAN ULLYOT didn't have an unscheduled moment in her day. She was a busy young woman, a recent graduate from Harvard Medical School, married to a surgeon, with a young child to care for. She planned every minute of every day and had no patience for interruptions. Her packed schedule couldn't tolerate the unexpected. But one particular Monday afternoon in 1969, Joan's tolerance was tested.

She had carried her son to a nearby grocery store in Boston for her weekly shopping trip. After buying what she needed, Joan tried to retrace her steps home. It didn't work. They were met by a police barricade. What was going on? Joan had no clue. But she grew angry over the unexpected delay. Peering around, she could see that people were lined up on both sides of the road, as if waiting for a parade. Then, she began to notice what had apparently drawn their attention. A few skinny and thinly clad men trotted past. Joan couldn't imagine what they were doing.

"They were wearing these little shorts," she remembers. "I looked at them and thought, '*How weird.*' I'd never seen anything like that, certainly not in public."

Standing at the side of the road, waiting for the police to let her pass, Joan heard a few spectators talking about something called the Boston Marathon. She had never heard of the Boston Marathon, didn't know where the runners had come from, where they were headed, or how far they had run. Or, more important, why? With her analytical mind, the "why" question nagged her. Why were the men doing this silly thing in public? But the thought passed quickly as Joan's attention turned to the cold milk in her grocery bag and the heavy young boy in her arm. She wanted to get both of them back to her apartment as soon as possible. Damn these Boston marathoners for disrupting her perfectly planned agenda!

Flash forward five years to 1974. Dr. Joan Ullyot is standing on the Boston Marathon start line in Hopkinton, Massachusetts, roughly 26 miles west of Boston. She had been building up her strength and endurance for three years, preparing herself for the prestigious race. She was a keen student, trained to become an expert in all that she tackled—she read all she could find on marathon lore, from the legend of Pheidippides to the muscle damage caused by downhill running.

A runner couldn't be much better prepared for Boston or more eager to begin the journey. Joan was especially excited about the crowd that she knew would greet her at the midway point. Thirteen years earlier, she had graduated from Wellesley College, the women-only university that sits beside the Boston course. Yet, even then, she had been blissfully unaware that the students cheered for the runners every April or that it was one of the marathon's cherished traditions. "I suppose a few of the girls watched the marathon back then, but only the very, very athletic ones," she recalls. "I wasn't in that crowd. I never heard anything about the marathon."

Running past Wellesley in the 1974 Boston Marathon, Joan allowed herself to appreciate the familiar locale and the boisterous support. "The crowd at the campus was incredible, and the noise they made was just about deafening," she says. "There were only a couple dozen women or so in the marathon that year, so the girls at Wellesley could spot each of us in the distance. When we got closer, they went crazy for every one of us."

Seven miles past Wellesley, Joan began the climb up Heartbreak Hill. The storied slope had deflated many a first-time Boston runner, but Joan had no problems. She knew how to pace herself, and her coach, a veteran Boston runner named Ron Daws, had insisted that she include lots of hill running—both uphill and downhill—in her training. He said it was the best way to prepare the leg muscles for the treacherous course. Joan sailed up and over Heartbreak and continued running strongly on the slightly downhill final miles. She finished in 3:17:10, good for 13th place among women runners. "The crowds were tremendous all the way, and it was great fun to run on territory I knew so well," she says. "Boston quickly became my favorite marathon. I ran it 12 times, including the 100th anniversary race in 1996." But how did she come so far in those five short years after 1969?

Joan was born on July 1, 1940, in Chicago, Illinois. Her father, an army pilot, was killed in a plane crash when she was just two years old, so Joan was raised in an all-female family—her mother, grandmother, and sister. She likes to joke that even the family pets, a cat and dog, were female. But an all-female household can have its tentative side. Her mother proved initially overprotective of her daughter's activities. Eventually, with a bit of Joan's persuasion, she would think better of it, and then loosen the reins. "I'm not so sure about it, but that sounds like a wonderful idea, and your father would want you to do it," Joan's mother might begin. "In fact, I'm wishing I were young enough to do it with you myself."

At home, sports didn't exist, not even after the family moved to outdoorsy Pasadena, California, when Joan was nine. Neither her mother nor her grandmother did anything athletic, and Joan simply had no role models from the sports world. She enjoyed school, reading, and other indoor activities. But she also thought it fun to race around the neighborhood with her pals, playing a variety of tag- and hide-and-seek-like games. "I was good at all the running stuff, and I could outwrestle every boy on the block," she told magazine writer Molly Tyson.

The good times ended when Joan and friends became teens. At that point, peer pressure ruled their every move. It was not right for girls to play serious sports. Perish the possibility that you might start sweating! "My friends all started to wear heels, slips, stockings, and lipstick," Joan says.

They had grown into a life stage where looking good was all-important and physical activity was frowned upon. Joan fell in with the crowd. But she possessed a feisty intelligence that made her a classroom star. She attended a girls-only private school in Pasadena—the Westridge School—where the prevailing attitude battled the cultural norm that women were second-class citizens. Instead, the girls were taught to aim high and follow their ambitions. "I had terrific teachers at Westridge, and they probably had more effect on my life than anyone else," Joan recalls. "They taught us that we could do and become whatever we wanted, and the all-girl environment meant that we learned lots of leadership skills. When others said, 'Women can't do such and such,' our attitude was, 'Well, screw that.'"

After Westridge, Joan attended Wellesley, a women's college just west of Boston. She focused on her academic life, particularly her love for languages and government. Following graduation, she passed an entrance exam for the U.S. Foreign Service, and then sat down for her interview. "Do you understand that women in the Foreign Service can't get married?" she was asked.

"What? What about men in the Foreign Service?" she replied.

"Oh, they have to get married. They need their wives to support them in their work."

"Screw that," Joan thought. Besides, she had recently developed a new academic interest: health and physiology. Although she had taken few science and biology courses at Wellesley, she now set her sights on becoming a doctor. She spent the next year meeting her premed requirements at Columbia University and Barnard College in New York, then over the summer at Harvard. The next spring, she was admitted to Harvard Medical School. She graduated in 1966.

———

In mid-1969, Joan moved to San Francisco when her husband accepted a new job. People in Northern California seemed very outdoorsy, and Joan tried to follow their example. She and her husband would take long walks on hilly, wooded trails. But Joan couldn't keep up; she kept falling behind. This troubled the family dog. He'd trot down the hill to Joan and give her a quizzical look, as if to say, "C'mon, why aren't you with us? This is just an easy walk."

Joan had a sedentary job working in a laboratory reviewing pathology slides. Over time she noticed that her body was changing shape—and not in a good way. It wasn't a big shocker to Joan; she was a physician, after all. She knew she shouldn't have been smoking cigarettes, sitting all day, and eating sugary snacks when she grew bored. These weren't healthy activities, but they were habits she had developed over many years, making them that much harder to break. She now calls this time of her life the creampuff stage, an era when she looked and felt like a sweet pastry—too round and too soft in places that should have been firm.

When Joan read Ken Cooper's book *Aerobics* in 1968, she learned that many people had taken up jogging to feel better, to burn extra calories, and to improve their health. She could see that the activity was gaining popularity at the University of California, San Francisco, where she worked. Soon she asked a few colleagues if they wanted to give jogging a try. The memory—the clarity—of her first run stuck with her through the decades.

She and just one friend headed to Golden Gate Park, where they hoped to complete a one-mile loop. In her groundbreaking book, *Women's Running,* Joan writes: "I had never seen a woman run, and felt acutely self-conscious, as did my friend. We had the feeling that everyone passing in a car was staring, pointing, and whispering about us. I tried to look as small and inconspicuous as possible."

But being inconspicuous is difficult when you're 5-foot-9. "I was wearing an old pair of nondescript blue jeans that blended into the dusk and a gray turtleneck that I pulled up over my chin to prevent me from being recognized."

Somehow, the twosome reached their one-mile goal despite the seemingly endless number of steps it required. But afterward, they couldn't contain their excitement about their accomplishment. "I felt like Ferdinand the Bull smelling the flowers," Joan says. "The park was beautiful, and as we ran, we would smell the dirt, the horses, or whatever we passed. I had never thought that a person could get so much enjoyment from a sport. I had thought sports were only about hitting and fighting."

She and her friends became regulars in the park. They increased their distance to three miles at a time and strived (although struggling) each day to beat their previous best time. This proved disastrous. "I got almost every injury in the book," Joan recalls. "It added a lot to my knowledge of anatomy and sports medicine, but kept forcing me to the sidelines."

After repeating the same mistake several times—getting into shape, then rushing to get faster, then succumbing to injury—Joan realized the fault in her training. The truth was, she had more fun and got fitter and healthier when she didn't push so hard. "I was always trying to get into shape too fast," she says. "I didn't have enough patience. I didn't realize that I was meant to go long and slow rather than short and fast. As a result, I kept getting hurt one place or another."

Once she realized that slow, steady, consistent training produced better results, Joan stuck with the formula. Over the next 25-plus years, ending with the Centennial Boston Marathon in 1996, she produced many spectacular results, including 80 marathon finishes. Never a skinny, lightweight speed-demon like the track racers or marathon champs, she nevertheless ran dozens of marathons under or right around the three-hour mark. And she continued improving for many years, recording her personal best (2:47:39) 15 years after her first attempt at a marathon.

———

Joan ran her first marathon in 1973. She approached it with her natural self-confidence that was supported with a base of solid long runs of up to 20 miles. She decided that she was built for distance. "If you can't go fast, go far," she figured. She started the marathon at an 8:00-minute pace and finished at about a 7:30 pace for an overall time of 3:17:10. "It was a five-lap course, and I'll admit the last lap got tough," she says. "But it felt easy up to the 20-mile mark, and then I just had to gut it out to the finish line from there."

By the following summer, Joan had cruised through three more marathons, including her first Boston, and lowered her personal record to 3:08:40.

In September 1974, she experienced an epic, life-changing event. A German doctor and promoter of women's marathoning, Dr. Ernst van Aaken, was organizing the first international women's marathon in his hometown of Waldniel, West Germany. It included entrants from around the globe. Joan wasn't fast enough to make the U.S. team, but the team needed an interpreter, and since she spoke fluent German, she was able to join as the official translator.

Dr. van Aaken proved to be a marvel. A former distance runner himself, he had lost both legs when a car struck him during a training run. But the loss didn't diminish his energy or vision. More than anyone else in the sports world, he believed in women's endurance capacities. Better still, with his medical background and his fondness for the press, he garnered considerable attention. Newspaper reporters listened to him, whereas they outright scorned just about anyone else who preached the gospel of women's distance running.

Joan was a doctor herself. She was smart, assertive, and learning fast about women's fitness and athletic potential. In Dr. van Aaken, she found a kindred spirit and the perfect mentor. Thanks to her German language skills, the two had no trouble conversing at length. "He was such an amazing man, so funny and so athletic even without his legs," she recalls. "He was always the life of every party. He'd swing over to the piano and start playing and singing until he had us all involved. He got all these reporters to come to Waldniel, and he played them with his knowledge and enthusiasm."

Joan was entertained, enthralled, educated, and inspired by Dr. van Aaken. She later described him as an "eternal rebel," a spirit close to her own. In her 1980 book, *Running Free,* Joan paid tribute to Dr. van Aaken with the following passage: "I, and many other sports physicians, have learned much from the van Aaken Method. He was the first to insist, forcefully and in the face of conventional therapy, that our bodies are constructed for movement and use, and that inactivity is the cause of most illnesses."

Apparently, Dr. van Aaken proved a great coach as well. In the weekend's marathon, Joan reduced her personal record to 2:58:10, a significant 10-minute improvement on her previous best. And this was only 15 months after her first marathon.

More important, Dr. van Aaken encouraged Joan to take a leadership role not just in women's marathon racing but also in explaining the whys and wherefores behind the growing women's running movement. The more women clawed their way out of the kitchen and began to participate in running and racing, the more they would face potshots from various critics. Someone had to put these naysayers in their place. Joan was perfect for the job. With her medical knowledge and her transformative personal experience, she could debunk old beliefs about women and sports.

Some physicians claimed running long distances would harm a woman's reproductive organs, prevent pregnancy, and cause missed periods, anemia, and varicose veins. Many also implied women who did sports, like men, would develop more masculine features. But, there was no science to support any of these theories. Joan became the authoritative medical voice to refute all the alleged ills.

Her bestselling book, *Women's Running,* was published in 1976. Point by point, and chapter by chapter, she explained how and why each "threat" was actually baseless. "These guys writing the articles at that time simply didn't know what they were talking about," she notes. "So what if someone misses a few periods? Who wants them? We all had plenty of women running friends who had babies, even the fastest and tiniest like Miki Gorman. When it came to a woman's breasts, a bra was good for comfort, but that's all we needed. Sagging breasts? That's just not the way breast tissue works. And if sagging breasts is such a problem, why wasn't anyone writing about sagging testicles? They hang a lot looser than breasts.

"I regarded all these people as propagandists. They had other reasons for not wanting women to run. That's why Ernst van Aaken was so important. He looked at women runners and saw all the positive health outcomes that came with their running."

Joan's book struck a chord among women runners of her time. Previously, they had almost no credible reference for the health aspects of their running and their well-being. "The purpose of the book was to tell women what they could do in running, not what they couldn't do," Joan says. "I wasn't campaigning for the Olympics. I was more interested in telling average women, 'Yes, you can run.' You're not so different from men, and you might even have some advantages at longer distances."

The book served as an important reinforcement for many women runners who were inevitably surrounded by family and friends who raised constant questions such as, "What are you doing? How do you know that running is good for you? What if . . . ?" With a copy of *Women's Running* in hand, the early ranks of women runners could provide answers to naysayers at last, and persuade other talented-but-timid women to join them. They could tell everyone, "Joan Ullyot is a Harvard Medical School graduate, and she proves all the hearsay is baloney."

Joan wrote the book that helped tens of thousands of women believe they were right to enjoy running and could gain many physical and mental benefits from the activity. *Women's Running* also provided training advice. Joan didn't want others to get injured as she had, and so she wrote that she and Dr. van Aaken believed in slow, easy-pace running. "All the books and magazines we had at the time were about training like Steve Prefontaine or the guys who went to the Olympics," she notes. "But that wasn't right for most women. We train different. We do better when we train at a modest, steady pace."

She also coined the famous 10 Percent Rule. That is, don't increase your total weekly mileage by more than 10 percent from week to week. This advice also was designed to limit injuries. Joan says she was surprised by her book's impact. She had never known the deep doubts that plagued many other women. But as she traveled, she met thousands of readers who couldn't wait to tell her, "Your book changed my life. It gave me the confidence to keep running."

In 1984, Joan attended the women's Olympic Marathon Trials in Olympia, Washington, to witness Joan Benoit's brave victory. When it came to Benoit's L.A. Olympic win, Joan was watching on TV, like much of the world. "My friends and I cheered enormously for Joan," she recalls. "We were so thrilled and proud. It was amazing how long we had to struggle to get the Olympic Committee to accept women. They were so backward. It took so much hard work."

Even with the Olympic excitement, Joan never lost sight of what she believes is the real wonder of running—the way it helps different people in so many ways. "Running gave me great health," she says. "I feel so much better when I'm running. How could anyone not exercise? It gets me outside every day to appreciate Mother Earth and Father Sky. I had grown up thinking I was terrible at sports, but running taught me that I could be an athlete. I could be successful with my body as well as my mind. And it made me so happy."

Charlotte Lettis wins the 1975 women-only Mini Marathon in Central Park after having finished second in the event's inaugural running three years earlier.

"I found that running gave me a simple way to test who I am. Every time you set foot on a starting line, you make a major date with yourself. You go to the line, then run as fast as you can. Running is hard, and when you push through the pain, you look into the depth of who you are as a person. I found that I was much braver, stronger, more courageous than I had realized."

CHARLOTTE LETTIS

Born: **March 23, 1951**

> **MAJOR ACHIEVEMENTS**

- Ran 3:08:54 marathon in 1974
- Winner, L'eggs Mini-Marathon 10-K, New York City, 1975

CHARLOTTE LETTIS was smoking a cigarette on the porch of her apartment when she saw them—a half-dozen young men running past her. An hour or so later, they ran past again, coming from the opposite direction. She was still sitting lazily on the porch. The University of Massachusetts (UMass) junior had no idea what the guys were doing, where they were going, or that they would soon lead her, literally, toward the rest of her life.

However, she did notice that they were "all cute," and they apparently noticed her as well. After a few days of running past her every afternoon that August of 1971, the young men—all members of the UMass cross-country team—stopped and introduced themselves. They even invited her to join them one day for a run.

Charlotte has no idea what moved her to give it a try. But she said, "Sure," and agreed to run with the team at a later date. On their first workout together, the guys took it easy on Charlotte, who knew nothing about running. They went up the road just a mile, then turned and headed back. As they neared her apartment, the pace picked up. Surprisingly, she hung with them. "Actually, I outkicked most of them at the end," she recalls. Just as unexpected, the two miles didn't feel painful at all. "It felt good," she says. "Anyway, the boys seemed impressed, and I thought it was kind of fun. It seemed like a whole new world, an exciting one. I felt tired afterward, but it wasn't a bad kind of tired."

After the run, she relaxed with her usual cigarette. But her smoking habit didn't last long—not once she began running in the afternoons with the friendly, long-haired members of the team. There was something about the workouts that clicked for Charlotte. She could never have imagined it, and didn't understand it, but running felt like something she was supposed to do. "When I started running, my body just seemed to fall into a relaxed rhythm," she notes. "I seemed to have good natural endurance. When I ran slow, it felt so easy that I slipped into autopilot. It was like being in a trance."

A few weeks later, Charlotte entered a two-mile intramural cross-country race that skirted the UMass athletic fields. With no experience in race pacing or strategy, she started way too fast. After a half-mile, her muscles and lungs burned in pain—she was completely breathless and exhausted. Yet, somehow, she kept going, and she won the race—first female. She was awarded a trophy with an ashtray on the top. Only now she didn't need it—and likely didn't want it. She had stopped smoking to concentrate on her running.

Soon, Charlotte and her best friend among the afternoon runners, Tom Derderian, began planning how she could join the men's UMass cross-country team. At the time, most colleges didn't have women's teams, or any women on the men's teams. Charlotte and Tom carefully followed all the rules and regulations, which included filling out paperwork, getting a physical exam, and paying a $35 student athletic fee. They also took their campaign public, writing letters to the school newspaper and the administration.

Charlotte began to consider her cause almost more important than the sport itself. "It was the year before Title IX, and I was in the first wave of feminists who wanted to change women's role in society," she says. "But I didn't know how. The big issues seemed so much bigger than my small existence. But then running came along, and I saw it as a place where I could make a difference, both as an individual and for other women, too."

As soon as Charlotte was granted permission to join the team, she went to the athletic office to pick up her uniform and towel. "What do I do next?" she asked.

The answer: "Go down to the men's locker room, change into your running clothes, and report to cross-country practice."

Charlotte was shocked but undeterred. After the hard effort she and Tom put into getting her on the team, she wasn't about to back down just because she had to use the men's locker room. Besides, she knew her fellow teammates would be gracious. "They were such gentlemen. They would have cleared out and let me change in peace," she says. "I almost never had any problems with male runners. It was the officials and the institutions that were much more difficult."

As it turned out, she didn't have to use the men's locker room. She quickly discovered a nearby room used by the women's swim team. It served perfectly well. Charlotte raced on the junior varsity cross-country team that fall, finishing last in every race. It wasn't because she was the slowest runner; it was because every time she passed a boy, he would drop out—"injured"—rather than finish behind a girl.

Excited by Charlotte's breakthrough in the college environment, Charlotte and Tom next wanted to see if other women might be interested in running. In 1972, they founded the women-only Sugarloaf Mountain Athletic Club and advertised its first meeting in a local newspaper. They had no idea if anyone would show up, but about a dozen did, ranging in age from high-school girls to one grandmother. Most of them wore tennis shoes and cutoff blue jeans. "We were a completely ragtag group at first, but full of great spirit," Charlotte remembers.

The Sugarloaf Mountain AC eventually became an open club with men and still enjoys an active membership to this day. The running club solidified Charlotte's love of the sport.

"I found that running gave me a simple way to test who I am. Every time you set foot on a starting line, you make a major date with yourself. You go to the line, then run as fast as you can. Running is hard, and when you push through the pain, you look into the depth of who you are as a person. I found that I was much braver, stronger, more courageous than I had realized."

Lettis and her female teammates in the Sugarloaf Mountain Athletic Club organized an indoor mile for women at Amherst College in 1972. Lettis is on the far right.

The Sugarloaf Mountain AC also gave her a sense of belonging for the first time in her life, and a place where she could flourish competitively. That hadn't been the case when she was a kid growing up in upstate New York, where almost everyone skied. "I got good at skiing and felt almost like an athlete, though I never did anything competitive," she says.

Then came an amazing growth spurt in sixth grade. Almost overnight she shot up to nearly 5-foot-10 and towered over her classmates. She lost her skiing coordination, and with it the confidence she had gained from mastering the sport. She even started slouching, trying to make herself appear shorter. "I was teased a lot, and I felt embarrassed about every part of my body," she says. "I fell into a tailspin."

Things changed little in high school. She dressed all in black, smoked cigarettes, and hung out with artistic types who shunned the mainstream. After high-school graduation in 1969, Charlotte left for Europe with $100 in her pocket and spent a year hitchhiking. She reached as far east as Istanbul and then lived for a time on a kibbutz in Israel. After returning home, she felt unbalanced, unhealthy, and disconnected from her large-and-too-lanky self. She was loosely interested in the arts and the hippie lifestyle, but completely unsure what direction her life should take. Her path wouldn't become clear until she discovered running.

Charlotte Lettis and Tom Derderian married in December 1972 and became New England's best-known and most peripatetic running duo. While Tom had his greatest successes in long road races and the marathon—he would eventually write the definitive history of the Boston Marathon—Charlotte was more versatile. She raced the 800 meters and the 1500 meters (or one mile) on the track and also joined Tom for longer runs and races. Like all other distance runners in New England, they focused their year on the mid-April Boston Marathon. Charlotte planned to run Boston in 1972, the first year that women were granted official status of their own.

"In those years Boston was everything," she recalls. "We worshipped it. We considered it the one race you absolutely had to do. I particularly wanted to run in 1972 because it seemed like the last fortress to fall for women runners. I ran a lot of long road races, a lot of 30-Ks."

Unfortunately for Charlotte, the long, hard training led to an injury that kept her out of the historic 1972 Boston Marathon, won by Nina Kuscsik. In February 1974, Charlotte was finally fit and healthy enough to finish her only marathon, a 3:08:54, which was fast enough to qualify her for Boston. But an injury sidelined her once again. "When I look back, I realize that it was crazy for me to force my body toward the marathon," she observes. "I had bad knees, and I tended to break down if I ran more than 60 miles a week."

At more modest road distances, Charlotte continued to improve with training and experience. By mid-1972, she was ready to tackle the first edition of an entirely new event—a women-only 10-K road race in New York City. Sponsored by CrazyLegs, a women's shaving gel, the "Mini-Marathon" was set to take place in Central Park.

Charlotte had mixed feelings about the race. It was great that women runners were getting an event all their own. But her activism was aimed at gaining acceptance for women into the big, traditional races that had long barred

Midway through the 1975 Mini Marathon that she eventually won, Lettis still faced plenty of competition from Doreen Ennis (1) and Jackie Hansen (2).

them. And worse still, the race sponsor hired several Playboy bunnies to participate in an effort to gain more publicity. The bunnies received all the pre-race press and then dropped out immediately after the starting gun was fired.

Charlotte finished second to Jackie Dixon in the first Central Park "Mini." The event was highly successful despite the fact that a random male runner jumped in from the sidelines and ran next to Dixon most of the way. "It was so arrogant of the guy to do that, as if we women needed help to pace ourselves," Charlotte says. "I knew women were strong and strategic and could figure things out on their own. Still, the race was really exciting, and it inspired me to train harder for the next year."

By 1975, the Mini race director Fred Lebow had dropped the bunnies from the roster and instead built up the Mini as an East-West confrontation. He invited the top women from both coasts, including California's Jacqueline Hansen, who had set a marathon world record (2:43:54) six months earlier. On race day, as the women began gathering at the start line, they looked around at each other in rapt amazement. There were 300 of them! No one had ever seen that many women runners together in one place. "It just seemed so enormous back then," Charlotte says. "And I know it sounds corny, but they all felt like my sisters. We hugged each other at the start, even runners we didn't know."

But when the gun sounded, the women changed from comrades to competitors. A tight pack of six battled for the win almost the entire way. "It was amazing for all of us to be racing against each other like that," Charlotte remembers.

In past races, one star generally separated herself early and ran alone to the tape. This time, it was impossible to tell who was going to win. Charlotte used her kick to break the tape first, but she doesn't take much credit for the win: "I just happened to be the lucky one that day."

Her joy and sense of camaraderie was shattered only at the awards ceremony. As she jogged to the stage to accept her trophy, she heard a male voice whisper to a friend: "Thank goodness one of the nice-looking girls won." Charlotte was outraged. "I knew he was totally missing the point," she says. "We were there for a distance race, not a beauty pageant. I always hated it when the sports writers devoted their first paragraph to a description of our physical attributes—tall, thin, willowy, blonde, blue-eyed, good-looking, long-legged, or whatever."

Charlotte ran into trouble from men on several occasions. Once or twice, midway through a New England road race, she found herself being chased by men who randomly emerged from a bar nearby. They would either yell lascivious remarks ("Hey, slow down and give me a kiss!") or attack her femininity. "There must be something wrong with your DNA," she once heard a man yell at her.

But, mostly, it was the entrenched male officials who proved the biggest challenge. This happened when Charlotte entered one six-mile men's cross-country race in Boston as "C. Lettis" and had Tom pick up her number. Things went smoothly until, moments before the starting gun was fired, race officials spotted her on the start line. They charged toward her with the clear intent of yanking her off the course. But Charlotte had friends all around her. The other male runners formed a protective cordon.

Seconds later, the gun sounded and Charlotte took off. She easily outdistanced the officials before anyone could interfere. However, the same officials were ready for Charlotte at the finish. They linked arms and prevented her from crossing the finish line.

The worst scene of all occurred in 1975 in Puerto Rico, where Charlotte had been invited to compete in an international women's road race. It should have been an occasion for celebration. But when the runners checked in, they were asked to remove their clothes from the waist down, and parade in front of a panel of judges. "They were supposed to make sure that none of us was a man," she says. "It was shocking that some people were still stuck in the old way of thinking about women athletes."

Throughout her career, most of Charlotte's competitors would be men. And, as she recalls, they were almost universally supportive, even the ones toward the back of the pack who might have felt the most threatened. They were already running well behind the male leaders, and now a woman or two might finish in front of them, too. "But they understood what it meant to be another runner trying your hardest to improve," Charlotte recalls. "They encouraged me to do my best and treated me with respect."

The mayor of Gardner, Massachusetts, was another such encouraging person. Gardner held one of New England's top-ranked road races. Runners enjoyed the excellent organization and the classic, locally hewn wood rocking chairs that were awarded as prizes. Charlotte ran one year, finished first among women, and was awarded with a miniature doll's chair. "But the mayor realized this wasn't right," she says. "He took me aside and told me that if I came back the next year, I could win a real chair, just like the top men. And I did."

***

After competing in the 1976 Olympic Track Trials, Charlotte earned a job at Nike. She was basically the first shoe company employee whose job description read something like: "Promote women runners and women's running." Since her office was located at a Nike retail store in Wellesley, Massachusetts, near the midway point of the Boston Marathon, she moved there in 1979.

Separated from Derderian, she soon was joined by a handful of other talented young women runners who coalesced in the area. Charlotte, a self-described "mother hen" to them all, suggested they live together. The five women—Ellison Goodall, Liz Berry, Dia Elliman, Charlotte, and Charlotte's sister Paula—moved into a large turreted Gothic house on Walnut Street in Wellesley. They soon became known as the Walnut Street

Gang. They were even featured on the cover of *The Runner* magazine in February 1980.

Five years earlier, post-collegiate women runners were so few and far between that it would've been hard to imagine a group living and running together. The Walnut Street Gang was the first of its kind, where members supported each other as they pursued their individual goals from the mile to the marathon. They believed that, one day, the Olympics might put a women's marathon on the schedule—not to mention the 5000 and 10,000 meters—and they wanted to be ready.

Some outsiders claimed or believed the house on Walnut Street was "a fortress against men." Charlotte demurs, noting that men were often invited for workouts and to house parties. The goal wasn't to keep men out, she explains. The goal was to place women runners in an optimal training environment. "We didn't even do a lot of training together, maybe just long runs, because we were all on different programs for different distances," she notes. "But everyone was very supportive of each other, and we did close the place down most nights. We were five distinct personalities, and we had a lot of things to work out. That was the time when we did our bonding. It was a uniquely wonderful period."

Through much of the 1970s—the golden era of women's running—Charlotte was at the epicenter of the running boom in Boston, New York, and New England. At the time, this was by far the biggest and most vibrant road racing scene in the world. Whether winning races herself or launching women's-only clubs, Charlotte helped build a deep, wide foundation for the women runners who would follow. "Many women runners today would be surprised to learn that, at one time, we weren't able to enter races officially," she observes. "We did our job well. Most of the old restrictions are gone. We fought to get into the races, and now women have the chance to pursue their dreams at whatever distance they choose."

On a hard training run, Jackie Hansen shows the speed and smoothness that carried her to the first-ever sub-2:40 marathon by a woman.

"The key is consistency and hard work. You can't pass the test unless you've done all your homework. Things can go wrong, and things will go wrong. You can't control all the variables in your life. That's why you have to prepare 100 percent. You have to give it your absolute best."

JACQUELINE "JACKIE" HANSEN

Born: November 20, 1948

- Winner, Boston Marathon, 1973
- Two world records in the marathon, and first woman under 2:40 (Nike Oregon Track Club Marathon, 1975)

NEARLY A decade after her most competitive running years, 35-year-old Jacqueline "Jackie" Hansen edged to the start line of the 1984 Boston Marathon feeling more pressure than she had ever known. Two different TV crews would follow her from start to finish. One crew would highlight her role with the International Runners Committee (IRC)—of which she was president—and chronicle its lawsuit against the International Olympic Committee. The IRC wanted the Olympics to include the 5000- and 10,000-meter races for women, in addition to the marathon.

The other TV crew tailed Jackie for a more personal reason—to see if she could qualify as a runner for the 1984 U.S. Olympic Marathon Trials, which would follow Boston in six weeks and precede the Olympic Games by three months. Every talented American marathoner wanted to be present at the first Marathon Trials. All but a half-dozen knew that they had little chance of advancing to the Olympics. Marathoners tend to be realistic about their abilities. But everyone wanted to be able to say that they had participated in the first women's Marathon Trials. They wanted to stand on the starting line with the three superstars who would represent the country in the first Olympic Marathon for women.

Jackie had won Boston back in 1973 and twice set world records in the marathon. But that was then, this was now, and her chances to qualify in 1984 didn't look good. She had leg surgery in 1983 and had to fight hard to get back in shape. What's more, she had already tried two other marathons in early 1984 and, both times, had fallen short of the 2:51:16 needed to qualify for the Olympic Trials. Boston would be her third marathon in four months, which was not an optimal approach. And it was the last day on which a runner could qualify for the Trials.

To make matters worse, the Boston conditions—cold and rainy—were abysmal for a Southern California runner like Jackie. She hadn't even packed the right gear for this kind of weather. Fortunately, other Trials hopefuls had come better prepared, and they willingly loaned each other hats, gloves, tights, and more. "One for all, and all for one," that seemed to be their attitude. Jackie put together a mishmash of clothing for marathon day.

For 25 miles, everything went better than she could possibly have expected. She ran smoothly, felt strong, and calculated that she might finish in about 2:44—beyond her wildest dreams and fast enough to get her into the Trials. Then she noticed a little numbness in her arms. Next her legs grew weak, and she began to feel that she was wobbling down the road. Boston turns especially chilling in the last miles, as runners encounter an east wind off the harbor. Jackie started trembling with cold. Next . . . darkness. "I became totally hypothermic and blacked out," she recalls. "When I came around, I was on a cot in the medical tent at the finish, wrapped in blankets, teeth chattering, and an IV in my arm."

Her condition and location didn't bother her. They seemed unimportant. Jackie had just two questions for a nearby doc: "Did I finish?" and "What was my time?" He couldn't help chuckling. What weird questions for a runner who had collapsed and been hauled into the medical tent. She must be quite a competitor, this lady. The doctor sent an assistant to seek answers.

These took a few minutes to ascertain, as Jackie remained huddled under several wool blankets. The assistant returned. Yes, Jackie had crossed the finish under her own power. She had an officially recorded time of 2:47:48. That did it! She was headed for the Olympic Trials. She had achieved her last big goal in running. "I don't know what happened to the four minutes I lost in the last mile, but I got there somehow," Jackie recalls. "I was determined to make it to the Trials, come hell or high water."

Jackie was born in upstate New York but moved to Southern California when she was eight. A child of divorced parents, she never had a father figure in her life and believes this might have contributed to her independent spirit. She had to figure out most things on her own. Eventually, her older sister and brother-in-law adopted her. "They had their own children later, but I felt like an only child growing up," she says. "I loved everything that happened outdoors, especially hiking and backpacking in the hills."

In high school, she developed a program to take kids from children's hospitals out on hiking trips. She also became a voracious reader, drawn in particular to biographies of famous women. She read about Florence Nightingale, Marie Curie, Eleanor Roosevelt, Amelia Earhart, and many others. Struck by the way they established "firsts" among women, she thought: "Someday, I'd like to be the first woman to do something special."

Jackie was certain that she wouldn't achieve any firsts in the sporting world. She hated physical education classes and was the last girl picked when teams were selected. She couldn't catch, couldn't throw, couldn't hit, and was too short for basketball. "I was always the benchwarmer," she remembers. The annual fitness test wasn't much better. The push-ups and pull-ups required more strength than Jackie had in her skinny arms and shoulders. The running requirements were the only saving grace. "I actually liked the running," she says. "I seemed to be pretty good at it."

During her final year in high school, Jackie joined the first girls track and field team at Granada Hills High School in Los Angeles. For some reason, she chose to run the hurdles, and specialized in spectacular falls that left her with arm and elbow scars that she would carry for the rest of her life. On weekends, she invented her own private kind of running game. It was totally different from the sprints and hurdles. She called it "How many laps can you run?" In her memoir, *A Long Time Coming,* Jackie writes: "My highest total was 17 laps. I did this before my graduation picture was taken. I'm the one with the red face and the track shoes beneath the gown."

After high school, while studying at San Fernando Valley State College in the late sixties, Jackie fell in with several campus runners who told her about a nearby track club. They said the club had an unusual coach—a fantastic one. He would even coach women runners, which no one else wanted to do. Jackie soon attended her first practice and met Hungarian coach Lazlo Tabori—the third man to break four minutes in the mile, after Roger Bannister and John Landy. The practice began with a dozen 150-meter strides, interspersed by light jogging. After this, Jackie followed the other runners back to their bags. She thought the workout was over, so she pulled on her sweatpants. "No, we're not leaving," someone said. "That was just the warm-up. Now we're changing into our spikes to begin the real training."

Such was Jackie's introduction to the famous Hungarian system of long, varied interval workouts. She found Tabori strict, charismatic, and utterly devoted to his athletes. His own strong will added to her determination. He became her lifetime running coach. She never felt a need for any other. "Lazlo had a presence and discipline that inspired me," she says. "He always knew what I needed to improve and could sometimes sense more about how I was feeling and performing than I realized myself."

Under Tabori, Jackie's training and fitness increased dramatically. She also began entering more cross-country and track races in Southern California. In late 1971, she heard that her friend Cheryl Bridges was running the nearby Western Hemisphere Marathon. Jackie knew nothing about the marathon but figured she should turn out and cheer for any woman runner who dared to attempt the 26.2-mile distance. Cheryl set a world record that day, running 2:49:40, and made a big impression on Jackie. "She was so graceful, she made it look easy," Jackie recalls. "I started thinking back to those high-school days when I ran as many laps as possible. It rekindled my interest in running longer distances."

Besides, her occasional weekend long runs with friends were proving to be a revelation. They were fun—social, full of rambling conversation—and often ended at the beach with a beer and more talk. The miles passed in what seemed like minutes. Ten miles? No problem. The next fall, 1972, Jackie asked Tabori if she could try the Western Hemisphere Marathon after completing her cross-country season. "You always asked Lazlo if you could do something," she says. "You never told him. I expected him to yell at me, but he turned philosophical. He said, 'You have to find out these things for yourself. You are the most stubborn runner I have ever coached. I believe you will go far.'"

He was right. Jackie won the marathon in 3:15:53, much slower than Bridges had run the previous year, but still a victory. She was accustomed to finishing in the middle of the pack in track and cross-country races, so the first-place finish represented an emotional high. Nonetheless, the last 6 miles were horrendous. "I had some friends riding alongside me on their bicycles," she recalls. "But the last six, they had to get off and walk. They couldn't go slow enough on their bikes and still keep their balance."

Yes, Jackie hit "The Wall." But she also experienced the thrill of a success such as she had never known before. This marathon distance was different. It beckoned. It teased her with the notion that she might explore it deeper and discover new horizons for herself.

After Jackie won the Western Hemisphere Marathon, her friends started pestering her. "You should run the Boston Marathon," they told her. And she couldn't resist the adventure. Her biggest problem would be training in the wintertime darkness. With college classes and a part-time job, Jackie was forced to train early in the morning and late at night. "The buildup was so tough," she remembers. "I was running 13 workouts a week, and 11 of them were in the dark. Lazlo gave me more and longer intervals than anyone else, so I was always the last to leave the track at night."

She had no idea how to dress for the random New England weather of mid-April. She heard that Boston celebrated Patriots' Day, and decided that she wanted to honor the occasion. To attire herself appropriately, she packed red, white, and blue colors, her shorts constructed from terry cloth. This might have worked well enough on a cool day, but Jackie ran smack into that unpredictable Boston weather on her first Boston Marathon attempt.

The day turned hot and steamy, and the trees had not yet leafed out enough to provide roadside shade. A full sun seared the black asphalt roads and the thousands of runners making their way from Hopkinton to Boston. Luckily, Boston's veteran spectators understood what they were supposed

The Boston Marathon media interview Hansen, looking remarkably fresh and relaxed, after her 1973 Boston Marathon win.

to do on days like this. They brought water and hoses to the course and sprayed the passing runners.

That was fine. Up to a point. After a few hose sprayings, Jackie began to notice that her water-soaked terry-cloth shorts were sliding southward. She had to grab them every few strides to tug them up over her hips. It didn't help that she was wearing heavy training shoes that grew waterlogged from all the excess spray. Slosh, slosh, hitch up the shorts. Slosh, slosh, hitch. That was the sound of Jackie running the 1973 Boston Marathon. Still, she won, and set a new Boston course record, 3:05:59. "I had such an extreme focus that I was able to block out everything else like the shoe and clothing problems," she recalls. "That was one of my best running traits—the way I could eliminate everything else but the effort I needed."

Winning Boston changed everything. "I knew I was a marathoner now," she notes. "People recognized the Boston Marathon and runners who won it. I got invitations to run other races, which had never happened before. Success breeds success."

A year later, in September 1974, Jackie ran another strong race at the International Women's Marathon in Waldniel, West Germany. She placed fifth overall, and first among American women in a personal-best time of 2:56:25. She hadn't planned on going—too expensive—but friend, film star, and fellow marathoner Bruce Dern paid for her travel at the last moment. "Waldniel amplified what I had learned at Boston," Jackie says. "Plus, it showed me that I could run with the best in the world."

After Waldniel, Jackie raced a 15-K in Italy, winning the women's division and beating all but seven men. She laughed at her funny prize: a heavy steam iron—not exactly what a backpacking runner needed while hiking around Europe. But she has always remembered a comment she received from one of the Italian runners she had beaten. "This Italian guy sought me out very specifically," she remembers. "He said, 'I always told my wife that the day a woman beat me was the day I would quit running. But today, you showed me that is the wrong attitude. You beat me because you are very good, so I will keep running.'"

On her return to Southern California, Jackie decided to run the Western Hemisphere Marathon again, two years after her first appearance there. This time, she put everything into it. "I had gotten very good at setting goals, and working back from them," she says. "I knew I had to do long runs for the marathon but also maintain my speed with intervals on the track. I knew how to build the two up gradually, like climbing stairs one step at a time. I had gained confidence in my preparations."

She tried to keep it quiet, but everyone knew she planned to attack the existing world record, 2:46:24. The more she heard people talking about her and her not-so-secret goal, the more anxious she became. She knew she had to run relaxed to run fast, but that was looking like a difficult assignment. Before the marathon, she was helped by a conversational warm-up with her friend Dern. "He said he was so happy he had given me the backing to go to Waldniel," she recalls. "He said I had proved myself there by running like a true champion. That calmed me down. It made me believe I could run strong again."

The result? A new personal record—her fourth in succession—and, a new world record as well. Jackie crossed the Western Hemisphere finish line in 2:43:54. "I did everything a little better than before," she says. "I trained more efficiently, reducing my mileage from more than 100 miles a week to more like 85. That turned out to be my sweet spot. I was stronger and more energetic at that level of training. I knew the pace I wanted in the marathon, and I stuck to it."

The women's marathon movement mushroomed in the mid-1970s, with more and better runners joining the cause. As a result, performances got faster and faster. By summer 1975, the marathon world record had dropped to 2:40:15, almost 4 minutes faster than Jackie's time at the Western Hemisphere Marathon. But she wasn't done yet. She wanted another crack at the record and chose the first Nike Oregon Track Club Marathon in Eugene, Oregon, in September.

Jackie arrived a week early, which gave her time for a few training runs with locals—all fast male marathoners. They passed the miles yakking about their hoped-for times on race day. Jackie joined the banter. "I blurted out that I wanted to hold a 6-minute pace the whole way," she says. "Suddenly everyone got very quiet."

The runners in the pack surrounding her knew what *6-minute pace* meant. They knew it equated to a 2:37 marathon—nearly unimaginable. Marathoners of that era never boasted about their training or fitness. In fact, they undersold themselves. It was considered smart to stay quiet. Otherwise, you might jinx yourself. The marathon could humble you, big time.

Besides, you didn't want your competition to know how fit you were. Jackie followed a different approach. She wasn't bragging. She simply wanted to use her own words and thoughts to bolster her determination. "I had been studying sports psychology, and I learned that it could be helpful to make your goals public," she says. "That made them real, and that meant you were going to truly go for it."

In Eugene, Jackie had her one "peak performance marathon race." Usually, a marathon seemed to last forever. This one passed quickly and

Hansen is still running strong near the end of her world record 2:38:19 at the 1975 Nike Oregon Track Club Marathon.

effortlessly. "I didn't struggle at any point," she remembers. "I was in this state of perfect flow. I could even do math—my split times—in my head, which never happened in any other marathon. For the first 21 miles, I ran every mile between 6:02 and 6:10, then I sped up to 5:55s for the last 5. When I hit the finish, I felt I could have run the full distance again at the same pace."

In her fifth marathon, Jackie had established her fifth personal best and her second world record. She ran 2:38:19, becoming the first woman to break the 2:40 barrier. "I knew my record would be erased soon enough [it lasted 18 months]," she says. "But it was still a thrill to crack 2:40. And I didn't scrape under 2:40 either. I really landed it. I had finally achieved my childhood dream of being the first woman to achieve some significant goal."

The Nike marathon had taken place in September 1975—just a year before the 1976 Olympic Games in Montreal. Without question, Jackie was one of the top women marathoners in the world. With her new record, she could even call herself the best. Period. In a different era, with more opportunities for women marathoners, she would have spent the next year of her life in a dedicated quest for an Olympic gold medal.

But she couldn't. There was no such outlet for women—no Olympic Marathon for them. Most of the great women runners who preceded Jackie never even pondered their loss. A decade earlier, it was almost impossible to even think about a women's Olympic Marathon. But the times had changed more rapidly than anyone could have imagined, and Jackie realized the injustice.

She knew the Olympics were a one-of-a-kind event that helped many athletes soar to their greatest performances. Yet the door remained locked and barred for women marathoners. It practically had a sign hanging on the outside: "Ladies, Do Not Enter." Jackie felt completely stymied, with nowhere to turn. "Here I was, the world record holder, and I had no place to take my dreams," she recalls. "I didn't necessarily think that I would win the Olympics, but I thought all the women runners like me deserved the right to try."

———

After her second marathon world record, Jackie continued training hard and racing marathons, but could never improve on her 2:38. She won major marathons in Honolulu and Cleveland, and three times nabbed first in the gorgeous but super-hilly Catalina Island Marathon.

During the late 1970s and early 1980s, Jackie poured time and energy into the International Runners Committee (IRC) and its efforts to gain Olympic equality for women runners. On the day of the 1984 Boston Marathon—the day when she blacked out but still qualified for the Marathon Trials—she learned the IRC had lost its battle to include the women's 5000 and 10,000 in the Olympics. "We were too little, too late for that year," she laments.

However, change did come. The 10,000 was added in 1988, the 5000 in 1996, and the 3000-meter steeplechase in 2008. Women now have full parity with men in Olympic distance events. The work that Jackie and others began in the 1970s bore fruit decades later.

When the first women's Olympic Marathon Trials were held in May 1984, Jackie was on the start line. She realized that she was burned out from the IRC work and her three previous marathons earlier in the year. But that didn't matter. She simply wanted to participate and celebrate with her sister runners. She finished in 3:00:28, slowing in the second half. "It seemed that every woman who passed me had a kind word," she remembers. "The camaraderie was wonderful. We were all bonded together in this historic event."

At the 1984 Los Angeles Olympics, Jackie helped Joan Benoit secure a clean-air, oceanside apartment in Santa Monica. On the long-awaited marathon day, she volunteered to organize and transport the women's equipment from the Santa Monica start to the finish in the Los Angeles Coliseum. Between start and finish, she picked up her four-year-old son, Michael, to share the momentous occasion with him. He wasn't very appreciative. When Joan entered the Coliseum all alone, Michael was terrified by the tumultuous cheering. He also noticed the tears in his mother's eyes and naturally concluded that something bad must be happening. He began wailing uncontrollably.

"That's our friend Joan, and she's winning the Olympics," Jackie explained. "Everyone's cheering for her because they are so happy." Michael was too young to understand.

Jackie couldn't help reflecting on the potential impact of this first Olympic Marathon for women. "It occurred to me that women all over the world were watching Joan Benoit on their TVs," she recalls. "Some of them must have been thinking that they could one day grow up to be an Olympic Marathon champion."

Jackie had been to the mountaintop in her own racing career and had also labored long and hard to give other women more opportunities than she enjoyed. She says she learned the same thing from both pursuits. "The key is consistency and hard work. You can't pass the test unless you've done all your homework. Things can go wrong, and things will go wrong. You can't control all the variables in your life. That's why you have to prepare 100 percent. You've got to give it your absolute best."

Forty-two-year-old Miki Gorman en route to victory in the 1977 New York City Marathon. She had also won the previous year.

"Running gave me so much more self-confidence that my daily life became totally different. I wasn't timid anymore. I said what I believed in and what I wanted. I was still shy perhaps. That is my nature. But I didn't have fears any longer that kept me from speaking up for myself."

MICHIKO "MIKI" GORMAN

Born: August 9, 1935
Died: September 19, 2015

MAJOR ACHIEVEMENTS

- Marathon world record, 2:46:37, Western Hemisphere Marathon, 1973
- Winner, both Boston and New York City Marathons, 1977
- First over-40 marathon champion

SHE STOOD only five feet tall. She weighed all of 88 pounds. And she didn't start running until she was 33. But Michiko "Miki" Gorman made huge strides in the world of running.

As a child growing up in Japan, Miki was embarrassed about being short and thin. She wanted to look like the dancers she read about in magazines. They were tall, willowy, and graceful—everything she was not. That was the kind of body Miki idealized and wanted. Instead, she often felt that she disappeared in elevators and public places where people talked to each other over the top of her head. It was like she was invisible to the world above her. But all of that changed after she moved to the United States.

In 1969, she signed up for a strength-training class at the Los Angeles

Athletic Club (LAAC), hoping to add a few pounds of muscle. The instructor told everyone to warm up with a mile on the indoor track. The track measured 160 yards per lap. To complete her mile, Miki had to struggle through 11 laps before launching into the strength-training regimen. After a few weeks, however, something changed. She began to like the lap running better than the weight lifting. She stopped going to her class and spent the extra time running more laps.

One day, she came across an announcement. The LAAC would be holding an annual contest to see who could run the most miles in the month of October, and also who could cover the most miles on the last day of the month. Miki decided to give it a try. She began pushing much harder and farther in her lap running, and she enjoyed watching her name climb ever higher on the leader board, which was updated daily. "My feet were getting more swollen, and I endured a lot of pain," she remembers. "But I kept running like crazy because I wanted to win a trophy."

To succeed, she needed a seemingly impossible performance in the last 24 hours, but she persevered, and nailed it. Miki tallied 86 miles on the small indoor track during the last day of October. While disappointed not to hit three digits—she had hoped for 100 miles—Miki was thrilled by the huge first-woman trophy the club presented to her. She even dressed up in a kimono for the awards ceremony to honor her Japanese heritage.

The next four years, Miki won the same annual contest, running as many as 911 miles in a month, all on the LAAC's indoor track. She got faster, too. On the last day of October in 1972, she reached the 100-mile mark in 21 hours and 4 minutes. "I don't know where my competitiveness comes from," she says, "but I am very stubborn and a very hard worker. Unless I was sick with a fever or had a broken leg, I wouldn't let anything stop me. Once I decide to do something, I give it my absolute best, no matter what it is."

These were prodigious endurance performances that Miki racked up. And still she had not run anywhere but on the LAAC's tiny indoor track. She had no notion about the road races she could enter. In fact, she didn't know that road races existed. She certainly didn't realize that she possessed the talent and dedication to run with the best long-distance women in the world.

Miki was born Michiko Suwa in China, but to Japanese parents. After World War II wound down, her parents moved the family back to Japan, where they settled in a remote and impoverished area. "We had nothing, and there was nothing there," Miki recalls. "No TV, no trains, no buses. Occasionally, we would see a plane fly overhead."

There were only two businesses in town, a bicycle repair shop and a barber. The nearest school was three miles away. Miki had to walk there, and back, every day. Food was always scarce. The family had little except for small bowls of rice and soybeans. It was not uncommon to eat them in their hard, uncooked state. "We were always hungry," Miki says, "and always very thin."

When the Olympics rolled around every four years, her father would get excited and attempt to listen to Japanese coverage on a shortwave radio. Reception was poor, and trying to follow the events often proved frustrating. Still, the Olympics were an enthralling, worldwide event that brought a buzz to the impoverished household. They made the outside world seem just a little bit closer. "We were always hitting the back of the shortwave, trying to make it work better so we could hear more," Miki recalls of the 1948 London Olympics. Anything to relieve the grim tedium of everyday life.

Miki's father died a few years later, and the family's meager fortunes sank still lower. Several local boys seemed to be attracted to her, and she could imagine a marriage that might bring a happier future. But this kind of arrangement, in Japanese culture, demanded a payment from the wife's family to the new husband. As soon as the boys realized that Miki's family had no money to contribute, they lost all interest in her. "I hated my life in Japan," Miki says. "There were no opportunities at all. I worked three jobs, as a secretary, a store announcer, and a coffee shop DJ. And I still had no hope of improving my life."

Her dismal prospects changed when an American army colonel offered her a babysitting job. The work paid little, but provided a chance to learn some English. She hoped to move to the United States when the colonel returned home. In the United States, she thought, who knew what might be possible? Miki's sponsor was transferred to the Army War College in

Carlisle, Pennsylvania, and his family invited her to go with them. Miki's own family disapproved, but she was determined. She had her sights set on pursuing her future in America.

As it turned out, her life in Carlisle was tough. She worked seven days a week from sunrise to 10:00 p.m. taking care of the house and the children. She had no extra time to attend English classes, her greatest hope. Therefore, she mastered only a handful of English words—her name and address—and was perpetually confused by American culture and habits.

When asked if she was hungry and wanted food, Miki would always answer no. That was the way all well-mannered Japanese answered the question, even if they were, in fact, ravenous. As a result, despite living in the land of plenty, she was often as hungry as she had been in Japan. She yearned to see bigger, more-exciting American cities—gleaming, glamorous places like those pictured in the magazines she flipped through. So when another military family asked if she would like to move to Los Angeles with them, she readily signed on.

Miki soon found a private job with a Japanese import company. It paid $300 a month, while her room and board at the Salvation Army cost just $80 a month. She felt like she was living in luxury. She saved enough every month to send money home to her mother.

In Los Angeles, Miki also met and married Mike Gorman, an athletic businessman who helped her transition to American culture. She couldn't have been happier. Driving on the L.A. freeways with Mike, Miki would raise her arms upward and sing out, "I love living in America. I love living in America."

Mike encouraged her to join the Los Angeles Athletic Club, where she gravitated to the annual endurance running contests and racked up impressive victories. Eventually an LAAC coach asked Miki if she had ever considered entering an actual running race. No, she hadn't. But if someone would explain the procedures involved, she might give it a try.

Before long, Miki signed up for a local cross-country race. While warming up for the event, she spotted a tall, athletic-looking woman, and decided to run with her. "No, that's not a good idea," a friend said. "You won't be able to stick with her."

"Yes, I can," Miki insisted. But her friend was right. Shortly after the start, the tall woman disappeared out of view. Miki was alone with the wind in her hair, the sun on her face, and the challenge of battling up and down hills. It was freeing, and so different from the thousands of laps she ran on the indoor track.

Miki fell in love with the change. "It was so nice to be out there in the open air," she recalls. Near the end of the race, she caught up with and passed the tall woman, who had slowed down while Miki managed to hold her pace. This would soon prove to be her signature strength as a runner. You could rush away from her at the start, you could build a lead in the middle, but it was very difficult to get to the finish line ahead of Miki. She ran steady throughout her races—not faster at one point, not slower near the end—falling naturally into the even-pace approach that distance-running experts have expounded for 40 years.

The cross-country race also erased some of her body-image problems. "I learned that the looks and size of one's body are not important, and that anyone can be competitive," she says. "I gained so much confidence from my running. I finally realized that being small didn't have to hold me back."

———

Encouraged by her first cross-country race, Miki decided to attempt a marathon in December 1973: the famous Western Hemisphere Marathon, also known as the Culver City Marathon. The race had been held since 1948. Four-time Boston Marathon champion Gerard Coté of Canada won it that first year. What's more, a number of pioneer women runners had recorded important marathon performances at Culver City: Merry Lepper, Cheryl Bridges, and Jackie Hansen.

On December 2, 1973, Miki added her name to the list. She trailed several other women for 20 miles, but then finished with her trademark strength to win in 2:46:37. Unbelievably, it was a new world record. She wasn't just the fastest ever to hold the record but also the oldest (38) and the smallest. Not that it came easily. "The last six miles, I was so tired I was worried I was going to fall down," she recalls. "I just wanted to stop and sit down."

Though previously unknown, Miki was now an international marathon sensation. This required that she venture more often into the racing world and test herself at major events. She set her sights on the 1974 Boston Marathon, doing much of her training with two male buddies, Myron Shapiro and Luan Dosti. They were experienced runners who shared their wisdom with her. Sometimes, they'd argue about the best sports drinks, sometimes about racing strategies. But they were always there, even when fierce storms forced the threesome to seek shelter. "It was such a delight to have company," Miki remembers. "They would run one on each side of me, and I felt almost that they were lifting me off the ground with their presence. But the bad-weather days were so difficult. We had to huddle in the bathrooms at gas stations, and our shoes and cotton sweat suits got very heavy in the rain."

Whenever she had to train alone, without her pals, Miki felt more isolated. People stared and yelled, and cars honked. She was so tiny, so Asian-looking, and such a rarity—a woman running alone on the streets of Los Angeles. "I got such strange looks when I was out training," she says. "No one at that time understood anything about women running. It was the same at races. You'd see all these big trophies for the men, but nothing for the women."

Several times a week, Miki also did track workouts under her coach, Lazlo Tabori, the famed Hungarian speed-work master in the Los Angeles area. With his heavy Hungarian accent, and her soft Japanese lilt, they often didn't understand each other. But Miki followed every instruction that came through. "I was always trying to improve my speed," she says. "I had lots of endurance, but I hoped the Tabori workouts would give me more speed like the other girls."

From the start at Boston in 1974, Miki ran with a rare confidence. It was built on her Western Hemisphere Marathon success, the Tabori speed work, and the legend of Japan's Keizo Yamada, who had won Boston in 1953. "In Japan, probably 90 percent of the people knew Mr. Yamada," she says.

The cheering Wellesley women raised her spirits even higher, but Heartbreak Hill soon brought them down. "I tried to save myself for Heartbreak Hill," she says. "But when a hill like that comes at 20 miles, it is just so hard. I could not look ahead. I could only look down at the road."

Miki might have slowed on Heartbreak Hill, but you couldn't tell it from the results. She set a new Boston course record, 2:47:12, and won by almost six minutes. Ten months later, in January 1975, Miki gave birth to her daughter, Danielle. She and Mike had been trying to have a child for some time, but it apparently took a Boston Marathon win to move things along. "Physically and mentally, I was just very relaxed then," she says. Once again, the silly old medical myths concerning women runners and childbearing were proven wrong.

During her pregnancy, Miki continued running until the last several weeks before delivery. "I just felt that I needed to stay active," she says. "Without it, I wasn't my usual self. I felt like I was a water pipe clogged with sewage." Danielle was born completely healthy, and eventually became the professional dancer Miki had once imagined for herself.

———

Miki did her best running after Danielle's birth, even though she was closing in on and then crossing over the 40-year mark. She attributes her lasting endurance, in part, to the joy she felt having the complete family life she always dreamed of—a supportive husband, a daughter, and the chance to continue pursuing her running talent. She had a small-but-dedicated team to support her. And her husband, Mike, was at the helm. "He was like the engine to my car," she explains. "He'd pull me out of bed to train, but when I was exhausted after a marathon, he took care of everything. I didn't even have to move. Without him, I could never have done everything I did in running."

In the fall of 1975, eight months after Danielle's birth, Miki finished second in the New York City Marathon—the last to be held in the confines of Central Park. The next year, she was invited to the first New York City Marathon to weave through all five of the Big Apple's boroughs. The excitement over this new urban marathon concept far exceeded anything that had come before. TV stations followed the action, their helicopters buzzing overhead like mosquitoes, zigzagging back and forth to gain the best vantage points.

Miki marveled at the huge Verrazano-Narrows Bridge, where the marathon began, and the thick and varied spectator crowds. Each borough presented its distinctive ethnic heritage, from orthodox Jews to Latin immigrants to African-Americans to the wealthier folk who lived near Fifth Avenue in Manhattan. At points, her feet hurt desperately because her thin-soled racing shoes didn't offer enough protection from the potholes and rough patches of New York's city streets. "There was no carpeting on the bridge grates that year, so my toes felt like they were on fire," she recalls. Other times, she had to laugh, especially when the course made a 180-degree turn on itself, or when a gigantic St. Bernard dog came bounding up to her. "The dog didn't actually bother me, but it was funny because he was almost as tall as I was."

Miki had raced enough by now to know her best tactic. It was one of the major lessons of her career. "I went into a sort of meditative state," she says. "I'm sure there were many other things to see on the streets of New York, but I was concentrating so hard, I didn't notice a lot. In all of my best races, I have few memories of the course or the sights. That's because I was focusing so hard on every mile of the race."

Less than a half-hour after Bill Rodgers broke the finish-line tape in Central Park (2:10:10), Miki became the first women's champion of the five-borough marathon when she crossed the same line (2:39:11). She was 41 years old—a "masters" runner—and her time was the second fastest ever run by a woman marathoner. The world record had been set the previous year by a 26-year-old Jacqueline Hansen; Miki was 15 years older than that.

In 1977, Miki won both Boston and New York. It was an epic year. She was the queen of marathoning; not as celebrated as Rodgers, perhaps, but nonetheless the woman to beat in any competitive race. Remarkably, she was more than 10 years older than Rodgers and many of the top women runners she competed against.

She set a standard for women runners over 40 that paved the way for many to follow in the coming decades. Miki considers her 1977 New York City win one of her proudest moments. That day, she beat Kim Merritt, who she considered a "blonde goddess." On a sunny, breezy day, when runners faced headwinds much of the distance, Miki lost sight of Kim shortly after the start and never expected to see her again. Kim was almost 20 years younger and had beaten her in the 1975 marathon in Central Park. As usual, Miki just plugged along at the best pace she could maintain, adopting a smart strategy for the day. "It was so windy, I tucked behind the bigger runners whenever I could," she remembers.

Only in the last miles, as the runners entered hilly Central Park after their long winding route through the five boroughs, did Miki finally catch sight of Kim. Miki was gaining and decided she needed a strategy to pass Kim. "I still had somewhat of a complex about the runners who looked so much different from me," she admits. "The ones who were taller, had longer legs, even bigger breasts."

As she edged up on Kim, Miki figured she had to run stronger than she felt and looked. She wanted to portray a runner in complete control, even at the end of a long, windy, hilly marathon. She decided not to pause at Kim's shoulder. Not to say hello. Not to slow down and enjoy a brief respite. Instead, she steamrolled past, untouchable.

The tactic worked. Kim let her pass without a struggle. While Miki's time was slower than the previous year, everyone agreed that the day's weather conditions made the race far more difficult than in 1976. Rodgers also won again that day, as he had six months earlier in Boston. Both he and Miki helped launched the era of mega-marathons. Their victories and their stories played a big role in catapulting the urban marathon to international renown.

After her brilliant Boston-New York double of 1977, Miki won no more major marathons. She began to have intermittent injury problems, which she says did not result from running but from some dance classes she took. "I had a few little running injuries when I was training hard, like everyone, but nothing serious," she says. "I was proud of my strong bones. They were hardened by all the hills and mileage I did. I never had serious problems until I took tap-dancing lessons after my second New York City win."

In 1978, Miki strung together several months of consistent training in preparation for that December's Honolulu Marathon. A month before Honolulu, she broke the half-marathon world record by more than two minutes, lowering the mark to 1:15:58 (at age 43). She didn't recover well, however, and opted not to compete at Honolulu. While her racing speed inevitably declined, Miki held on to the lessons she had learned through her years of strong performances. "Running gave me so much more self-confidence that my daily life became totally different," she says. "I wasn't timid anymore. I said what I believed in and what I wanted. I was still shy perhaps. That is my nature. But I didn't have fears any longer that kept me from speaking up for myself.

"People have told me I should be proud of my times, and my victories, but I don't feel exactly that way. I was always very humble. If I am proud of anything, it is simply that I worked very hard for what I achieved."

Gayle Barron wins the 1978 Bonne Bell 10-K race in Toronto.

"It made me mad when people criticized me for my look. What right did they have? Besides, my race times were the important thing. Later, I heard from many women, particularly in the South, who said that my example encouraged them to begin running. They considered me a role model because I started from nothing and showed that a woman runner could be athletic and feminine."

GAYLE BARRON

Born: April 6, 1945

MAJOR ACHIEVEMENTS

- First winner Peachtree Road Race 10-K, Atlanta, 1970; four more Peachtree wins
- Winner, Boston Marathon, 1978

GAYLE BARRON always looked forward to Sunday mornings. She could sleep a little later, read the newspaper, and enjoy a leisurely breakfast with her husband, Ben. The other days of the week were busy, but Sunday was hers—a day to relax and unwind. However, in December 1972, one of her quiet Sunday mornings switched gears fast. One minute, she was poaching eggs at the stove. The next minute, Ben looked up from the newspaper and announced: "They're having a marathon at Westminster School today. I think I'll run it."

It didn't take Gayle long to respond. "Ben, that's crazy," she said. They had been married for three years, and running together for five, but rarely tackled more than five miles at a time. Besides, they always ran on a track—not on Atlanta's infamously hilly roads. But Ben persisted. He was the athletic one, the dreamer. Gayle simply enjoyed tagging along. "I'll start with you," she said. "But there's no way I can go the whole distance."

When they reached the start, Ben and Gayle realized that they were the least experienced of all the gathered road racers. They didn't even understand why the other entrants in the Peach Bowl Marathon kept swigging a yellowish liquid from plastic bottles. The brew looked disgusting. Wouldn't it just give everyone stomach cramps? They certainly weren't going to try any.

The Peach Bowl course was a two-looper. Ben set a slow pace the first half, as he and Gayle ran side by side. He figured that an easy jog would help the two of them continue as long as possible. At the end of the lap, he asked her: "How are you feeling? We can stop now if you want to."

Gayle gave an unexpected response: "No, I feel pretty good. Let's keep going."

She continued feeling strong for another seven miles. Then things changed quickly—so fast she couldn't believe it. "I felt miserable," she remembers. "I had pains everywhere—in my legs, my lungs, my arms."

Eventually, they had to walk a few times. That didn't help much. It just meant that they would be out on the course longer. Gayle thought about stopping. All the other runners were far ahead of them now. To continue didn't make sense. Then she had a revelation, which she wrote about later in her book *The Beauty of Running*. "I thought, *Why quit now?* Six more miles weren't going to kill me. And if I make it, I'll be the first woman in the state of Georgia, and possibly the entire South, to complete a marathon."

She pictured a big celebration to denote her historic achievement. It didn't happen that way. By the time she and Ben reached the finish in 4:15:25, they were met by only one person, the timer, who was eager to pack up and leave. Gayle hobbled to the gymnasium, where the awards ceremony was almost completed.

There, she discovered that officials had saved a first-woman award for her, and she got a big round of applause from her fellow runners. The thrill didn't last long. The next morning, she couldn't walk. "I had to go to the bathroom," she recalls. "But I couldn't move from bed. I couldn't even sit up. I had to roll out of bed and crawl to the bathroom."

A local newspaper report didn't make her feel any better. It said that she carried a stick when running to ward off any men who might notice her—a too-typical Southern stereotype. "It was true about the stick," Gayle says. "But I carried it as protection from dogs."

Gayle was born and raised in Atlanta. Her father worked first for Westinghouse and later in a family furniture business. He developed multiple sclerosis when Gayle was young, and his physical abilities gradually deteriorated over 25 years, forcing him from a cane to crutches to a wheelchair, as his condition worsened. An athlete in his youth, he could no longer play sports with Gayle and her younger brother. Instead, the family enjoyed board games and card games. Fierce ones. "I think I got my competitiveness from my dad," Gayle says. "He always tried to do his best at whatever he could do. He told me that if I did the same, I'd get good results."

But Gayle loved playing outdoors and wasn't afraid to challenge the neighborhood boys to races from one street corner to the next. Once, on a zoo visit, she tried to race a cheetah along the length of its wire fence. She lost this race, but still impressed everyone who saw her at full speed.

Gayle also enjoyed exploring the local glens and streams, becoming very fond of snakes and lizards. In fact, she raised small snake families in shoeboxes in her bedroom. No one thought too much about this until the evening she let several snakes loose while her mother was entertaining friends at the card table. "There were ladies running all around the house," Gayle reported. "I thought it was pretty funny. My mother didn't."

Druid Hills High School didn't offer any sports opportunities for girls, but that didn't bother Gayle. Like other Southern girls, she enjoyed dressing up, and "loved, loved, loved" cheerleading and drill team. The members got to wear cute, color-coordinated outfits. This seemed to offer the best of both worlds: bright costumes and finely honed athletic movements.

She craved attention and got it. "I was always one of those people who just wanted to please everyone," she says. "A girl couldn't get recognized for being successful in sports back then. You had to turn to dancing or cheerleading. I did those kinds of things, and got compliments, and it meant a lot."

Gayle took shorthand and typing classes, hoping to become proficient enough to land a secretarial job someday. That was what women did when they grew up, according to the Southern culture that enveloped Gayle.

Besides, office work had another big benefit: It was a great place to meet potential future husbands.

The University of Georgia didn't offer any sports for girls either, so Gayle stayed active on the university's cheerleading team. Her senior year, she noticed a strange sight in the football stadium. A blond-haired guy was running steps, up and down, up and down. Gayle decided she could use more exercise herself. She asked the stadium runner if she could join him, and he said, "Sure." Soon she, too, was going up and down, up and down—and trying not to notice the many strange looks being cast her way. "People thought we were crazy," she recalls. "It was unusual enough to run stadium steps then, but when a girl did it, that really stood out."

Some days, Gayle stayed down on the flat track and tried to run a mile. She couldn't make the four laps around the track—not for a long time. But she stuck with it, just as her father had advised, and she eventually completed a mile without stopping. Then she raised her goal to three miles and reached that one as well. "I also started eating better and losing weight," she says. "I found myself craving healthy foods, not junky foods."

After getting married, Gayle and Ben Barron, the blond-haired man she had joined for the stadium-steps routine, continued their habit of running together several times a week. They always ran on a track, which they considered the only appropriate place for running in shorts and thin jerseys. "It was five or six years before we ran outside the track," Gayle recalls. "It never occurred to us at first. We didn't want to be seen. It would have been too embarrassing."

Gayle never considered running alone. She ran with Ben. Period. "I would have felt like an idiot to go out running by myself," she remembers. "It wasn't something a single girl would do."

In 1970, Atlanta held its first big road race—the Peachtree Road Race 10-K on July 4. Ben told Gayle that he was going to enter. She laughed. "I thought it was the stupidest thing I had ever heard of," she remembers. "But if Ben was going to run it, so was I."

They finished together in 49:13, about 17 minutes behind winner Jeff Galloway. The performance earned Ben no particular fame, but it made Gayle the first woman winner at Peachtree, which later developed into one of the nation's biggest and most successful road races. "They gave me a trophy with a male figure on top," she says. "It's one of the few trophies that

I've kept." Gayle also won four of the next five Peachtree 10-K races, improving her best time to 38:04 in 1975. But a year after her Peach Bowl Marathon victory in 1972, she didn't even make an appearance at the 1973 race. She had decided she wanted nothing more of the 26.2-mile distance.

———

Gayle began to change her mind in 1974, after her Peachtree 10-K time dipped into the high 38:00s. A training partner, Tim Singleton, kept telling her that she could run a good marathon if she would only log more mileage in training. Gayle decided to test the waters by joining Singleton and six of his male buddies on their weekend long runs.

And she made a surprising discovery: While the guys covered longer distances than she was accustomed to, they did so at a pace that felt comfortable enough. She only had to tag along beside them and stop for the occasional, reenergizing Coca-Cola breaks. (Coke was Singleton's preferred running drink.) "I learned that if I persevered and stuck with it, I got stronger and stronger," Gayle says. "It was my father's message, proven through long-distance running. I got up to 40 or 50 miles a week, and all of them were up and down the Atlanta hills. That really built my strength. I owed a lot to the seven or eight guys in our training group. Without them, I would never have progressed as far as I did."

To join Singleton and her other Atlanta friends on the Boston Marathon start line, Gayle first had to run a Boston qualifying time (then set at 3:30 for women) in a prior marathon. That took her back to the Peach Bowl Marathon start line again in 1974. Gayle superseded her target time by a ridiculous margin. Hoping for a 3:30 in only her second marathon, she crossed the finish line in 3:06:40, winning her second Peach Bowl. Her time represented a huge and unexpected breakthrough. "I was totally shocked to run that time," she admits. "I never expected anything like it. My time gave me a new confidence. I began to understand that I could run well at distances when I had prepared myself sufficiently for them."

Next Singleton added interval workouts to his group's training. One day, Gayle completed 20 repeats of 400 meters in 90 seconds each. She wasn't sure how intervals would make her a better runner, but Singleton insisted they would build strength and speed. And, good Southern girl to her core, Gayle always did as instructed. The plan worked.

At Boston, Gayle once again improved her personal best by a big margin. This time, she chopped off 12 minutes, crossing the fabled Boston finish line in 2:54:11. That earned the unknown runner from the South third place in the world's most-competitive marathon. Best of all, it felt easy. "Boston was a piece of cake compared to running in Atlanta," Gayle says. "I particularly enjoyed running fast down hills, and I passed a lot of runners going down the Boston hills at about 21 miles. It was such a wonderful race for me. I didn't know who was ahead, and I didn't care. The encouragement of the crowd was an entirely new thing—I had never experienced crowd support like that before. And the girls in Wellesley! They went absolutely bonkers. I couldn't believe it."

There was only one sour note. After the marathon, she kept hearing stories about her good looks and the ribbon she always wore in her hair. The implication? That she wasn't a "serious" runner. The comments stung her. Gayle wasn't trying to impress anyone, or to strut her attractiveness.

"My mother taught me to always dress well," she says. "I enjoyed having a color-coordinated look. It made me mad when people criticized me for my look. What right did they have? Besides, my race times were the important thing. Later, I heard from many women, particularly in the South, who said that my example encouraged them to begin running. They considered me a role model because I started from nothing and showed that a woman runner could be athletic and feminine."

After Boston, Gayle became a regular on the major-marathon circuit. She finished third in the 1975 New York City Marathon and won Peach Bowl for a third time that December. The next year, she placed fourth at Boston and prepared for the 1976 International Women's Marathon in Waldniel, West Germany.

Running for the first time in a USA singlet, Gayle felt nervous to be among such a glittering group of fast women runners from around the world. Many of them could speak some English, but they couldn't understand her Southern drawl. She was also one of the few top runners with no previous experience competing in track races. For a variety of similar reasons, she was "a nervous wreck" before the marathon. "I was intimidated," she admits.

Her fears melted away after the start, however. Following her usual strategy of beginning slow and finishing strong, Gayle gradually moved through the pack of 50-plus runners in Waldniel. She enjoyed the colorful, winding course in the countryside, except when overpowering cow-dung odors forced her to the far side of the road. Eventually, she surged into third place with a new personal-best time, 2:47:44. In less than four years, dating back to her first Peach Bowl Marathon in 1972, she had cut nearly 90 minutes from her marathon time. "I was stunned to finish third in Waldniel," she says. "I didn't expect it because I knew many of the other runners were very fast. Also, this was probably the most significant and competitive women's marathon until the first women's Olympic Marathon in 1984."

In the fall of 1977, Gayle ran three marathons in three months—the Nike Oregon Track Club Marathon in Eugene, Oregon; the New York City Marathon; and the Honolulu Marathon. She finished second, third, and second. Not bad. But it was beginning to gnaw at her that she could never win any of the big-time marathons—only Atlanta's own Peach Bowl Marathon, practically in her backyard. She wanted to do better, so she set her sights on the 1978 Boston Marathon.

Several unexpected circumstances interfered with her plan. First, she caught the flu and missed a full month of training in February. Then, friends and newspapers began saying that she should run the Avon International Women's Marathon being held in Atlanta in mid-March 1978. She hadn't previously planned to enter this event, feeling she needed time to recover from her fall marathons. Her springtime goal was always to peak for Boston. You couldn't do that by running a hard marathon in March.

The pressure got to Gayle. She ran the Avon Atlanta marathon on a hot day and finished fifth behind two Americans and two Europeans. With Boston just a month away, she figured she had no time to recover and run strongly. Worse, she suffered a calf strain after the Avon race, and as a result, lost more training time.

Still, her husband, Ben, and her other training buddies were headed to Boston, per their custom, and she didn't want to miss the fun weekend. Gayle and her mother joined them for the travel escapade. Her father was failing badly at this point, too weak to accompany the crew. But before Gayle left Atlanta, he told her: "I'm very proud of your marathon successes. I know you haven't won a big marathon yet, but you're a tough cookie. Why don't you go for it at Boston?"

Not a chance, Gayle thought. She expected to cover the now-familiar Boston course purely as an easy long run. She knew she wasn't ready for a top-notch performance. She didn't even register until the last moment, when she was given number 229.

Surging away from the start in Hopkinton, Gayle started faster than she had planned, but only to avoid being steamrolled by the hard-charging men all around her. Soon, she settled into a comfortable rhythm. Gayle never worried about her early split times. She waited until she passed five miles. That was the point where she could tell if she was having a good day or not. When Gayle didn't see a clock at 5 miles, she asked one of the nearby men about their time. "We're on about 2:38 pace," he responded. Uh-oh, way too fast. She was shocked. It didn't feel like she was running that fast, not at all. Gayle hadn't even brought her lightweight racing shoes to Boston. She was wearing heavier, more-cushioned training shoes.

With just 229 women runners among more than 4,400 men, Gayle didn't see any other women in the early miles and couldn't tell what place she was in. Third? Fifth? Tenth? At 10 miles, she spotted the swishing blonde pony-tail of Kim Merritt—a 2:37 marathoner. Oh, my. Gayle held her pace and caught Kim in another mile. Kim's husband was surprised to see Gayle. "Do you have any idea how fast you're going?" he asked her. It was a warning: Be careful, you better slow down. But Gayle had never felt so smooth and effortless in a marathon. "Yes, I know it's fast," she replied to Keith Merritt. "But I feel really good."

Gayle and Kim ran the next 10 miles together, occasionally giving each other pep talks, but mainly concentrating on the inner struggle. They thought they were leading the women's division. They didn't know that for certain, however, and wondered what it meant when spectators told them they were battling for second place.

In the middle of Boston's famous Newton hills—a torturous four-mile stretch culminating with Heartbreak Hill—they spotted Gayle Olinek up ahead. She was fading badly after a too-aggressive start, and they quickly swept past her. Gayle and Kim led the women's field to the top of Heartbreak Hill.

Going down Heartbreak into Boston proper, Gayle cut loose. "I flew down the hills," she remembers. "It was hard on the quads, but I trained for it. The crowds were so thick, we were running single file. It was hard to pass anyone. I'd storm up behind these guys, and have to say, 'Excuse me, but I'd like to get by.'"

No one was more
surprised by her
1978 Boston Marathon
victory than Gayle
Barron. Or more
reluctant to get down
from the victory stand.

The last four miles, Gayle had to shimmy around other runners and squirm her way through spectators who had crowded into the streets. She couldn't believe she was ahead. She thought of her father back home in Atlanta, and how, even through his failing health, he had encouraged her to be strong and become a winner. (He passed away several weeks after her Boston race.)

Gayle ran the last mile in a physical and psychological haze, panicked by the thought that there might still be another woman ahead of her, or that someone would catch her from behind. No one did; she crossed the finish line in 2:44:52. Two policemen grabbed her and led her away, like an escort service. What did that mean? "Did I win?" she kept asking them. "Did I win?"

She didn't know for sure until she was eased up onto a victory podium and introduced to the mayor of Boston. He placed a medal around Gayle's neck and a laurel wreath on her head. When she looked out from the podium, Gayle was amazed to behold a crowd of cheering spectators. They had to raise their eyes upward to see the newest Boston Marathon champion.

"That was like my Olympic Marathon—the race we never had back then," she recalls. "If there had been an Olympic Marathon for women, I would have trained so hard to make it. I wanted to stay up on that Boston podium forever. I never expected to win Boston, certainly not that year. I just wanted to be the best I could be. I hope I'll also be remembered as one of the pioneers, particularly in the South, where sports and running weren't considered feminine back then."

Marilyn Bevans, the first African-American woman to run a marathon, holds the silver cup she received for winning the 1979 Maryland Marathon.

"Running gave me a sense of pride and self-esteem. Sometimes, people wouldn't believe what I had done because no other black women were running. I would even hear whispers, like, 'She must be lying.' But I knew what I had achieved."

MARILYN BEVANS

Born: October 4, 1949

> MAJOR ACHIEVEMENTS

- First African-American woman marathoner, with a personal best of 2:49:56
- Top finisher in several Boston Marathons, including second, 1977
- Winner, two Baltimore Marathons

TWELVE-YEAR-OLD MARILYN Bevans had never participated in a track meet, but she took the starting line with a confident feeling in her first race. In fact, she figured she would win this first race. It was a 100-yard dash at a meet in her hometown of Baltimore, Maryland.

Her family included a number of track fans, and she had watched her share of meets on TV with them, especially with her uncle, who often attended the famous Penn Relays in Philadelphia. From watching these meets, Marilyn knew what happened in sprint races: Black women dominated every sprint she had seen, particularly at the 1960 Rome Olympics, where Wilma Rudolph won three gold medals. Now, as Marilyn stood on her own starting line, she surveyed her competition. This looked like her lucky day. She was the only black girl in the race.

But, appearances can be deceiving, as Marilyn soon learned. "The starter fired his gun, and all I saw the rest of the race was everyone's backside," she recalls with a chuckle. "It was evident right away to me that I wasn't cut out to be a sprinter."

The alternative didn't hold much promise either. Few women ran long distances, and none of them were African-American. Fortunately, Marilyn's neighborhood environment offered many outdoor opportunities. Near the family's row house, she saw and bumped into friendly people everywhere—on the stoops, in the streets, in the parks. There was no shortage of trees and greenery, nor opportunities to frolic in the fresh air.

During the summers, her horizons expanded even farther when she attended a camp in the country. At camp, her days were filled with activity—picking berries from thorny bushes, chasing butterflies across large meadows, or pushing, pushing, pushing against a heavy merry-go-round and jumping onboard to spin wildly. She was always on the go, always running from one place to another.

Back home in Baltimore, Marilyn kept moving at high speed. However, her junior high school and high school had no track team for girls, so she could only watch from a distance, looking on wistfully as the boys trained for their events. On her own, she began to explore other outlets. Wearing long pants on even the hottest, most humid days, she took walks to a reservoir a mile from her home. Once there, she would strip down to shorts and jog several laps around the reservoir. Then she'd slip back into her long pants for the walk home. She didn't want anyone to see her in her shorts.

"That would have been very embarrassing to me," she says. "At the reservoir, I never saw anyone else, so I felt okay running in my shorts there. But not when I got back out on the streets and near my neighborhood. Then, I wanted to cover up my legs again." It was what proper young Baltimore ladies did.

During her teen years, Marilyn realized that she was a girl who wanted to run but had yet to prove herself in the only available events—sprints. She sensed that she might be good at longer distances, but there were no distance events for women. This unwritten rule applied especially to black women. No black women, absolutely none, participated in long-distance running events. Someone had to be the breakthrough pioneer. That someone would be Marilyn.

After graduating from high school in 1967, Marilyn attended Morgan State University in Baltimore, which, likewise, offered no distance running for women. Next, she attended Springfield College in Springfield, Massachusetts, to pursue a master's degree in physical education. Again, no track or running teams for women. Unlike Baltimore, however, Springfield was a hub for talented male distance runners.

What's more, the men's coach, Vern Cox, was the warm and encouraging type. When he noted Marilyn running solo laps at the track, he couldn't just ignore her. He walked over to strike up a conversation and even issued an invitation. "Would you like to train with our teams?" Cox asked.

Marilyn didn't have to think twice. She said yes almost immediately. It was the first time someone had welcomed her to a distance-running group. She had been happy enough running by herself—she enjoyed it, in fact. But there is a lot to be said for having company on a long run, especially if you want to learn about the sport, challenge yourself to run farther, and improve your pace. She wanted all these things, and she knew she needed role models.

Improvement didn't come fast or easily. There was no way she could match paces with Springfield's varsity runners. She couldn't even keep up with the second- and third-string distance runners. But in the back of the pack, she found some friends. They belonged to the group that had embarrassed her in that first 100-yard dash—the sprinters.

"The only guys I could stick with were the short-distance runners," she recalls. "They couldn't go very far, and they couldn't keep up with the faster distance guys. They ran along behind everyone else, and I just fell in with them. It was nice to have someone to run with. They could have told me, 'Get lost,' but they didn't. They let me join their workouts." The pack also offered protection from snarling dogs, one of her great fears.

Some of the better runners seemed strangely larger-than-life to Marilyn. In those days, she was shy and quiet, by her own admission. Several of the runners had big personalities. They could be loud, and they didn't mind calling attention to themselves. One of the best actually ran with a bell attached to his waist. It rang incessantly as he ran. While the ringing drove other teammates crazy, it didn't bother Marilyn. "For me, it just made me smile," Marilyn remembers. "I thought it was funny. Besides, I appreciated anything that put attention on someone else, not me."

Soon she could run four miles at a time, and then six. She never caught the runners up front, but she could see and feel herself growing stronger. That was her only goal. She didn't dream of winning major races. She didn't even think about entering them, since she had never heard of women running road races. She was just curious to see if she could apply her personal determination to improve her endurance. "All my life, I believed if you trained hard, you could get better," she says. "You might never be the best, but at least, you would be learning. At Springfield, we trained hard, and I picked up lots of new training methods. When you have a solid work and learning ethic, it always pays off one way or another."

Eventually, Marilyn started to learn about local races in western Massachusetts. Eastern Massachusetts, with its annual Boston Marathon, was situated 90 miles east of Springfield. The races in western Massachusetts bore no resemblance to the famous marathon. These races often covered odd distances like 4.3 miles or 5.8 miles. They tended to make a small loop around a modest town, and then return to the American Legion home where they had begun. They cost 50 cents to enter. What did she have to lose?

When Marilyn arrived at these races, she always found herself the only black woman. And, often, she was also the only black runner, period. No matter. She got used to it, never caring to make a statement or create a scene. She just wanted to run, and pursue her personal goals.

The races had long tables full of trophies and prizes for the top male finishers. On occasion, they had one prize—just one—for the first female finisher. Sometimes, Marilyn would take home that singular prize, but even when she didn't, she considered herself victorious. "There weren't many women at the races, maybe one or two, and I was the only black female," she recalls. "You had to be fast to get a prize, because they only had one prize for women. But even when I didn't win, at least I got a chance to enter races. That was the important thing."

Still, she never lost sight of the reason she was attending graduate school: to continue her education. One fall, Coach Cox invited her to join the team on its travels to a Van Cortlandt Park cross-country race in New York. Van Cortlandt boasted one of the most historic and famous courses in the United States. The invitation was tantalizing, but Marilyn turned it down. Her family had taught her to put her studies and grades before all else. "I had a big paper coming due, and I wanted to be sure to give it my best attention," she says. "I worked hard as a student and always put my classroom work and other assignments ahead of my running."

During summers and academic breaks from Springfield, Marilyn began to meet some of the early road runners back home in Baltimore. They were all men, of course, but they welcomed her to their training runs. Several times a year, they would increase their weekly mileage as they prepared to enter marathons in Boston or New York. "I fell in with some guys who had more experience than me and just tagged along with them on Saturday mornings," Marilyn remembers. "The runs got longer and longer, and they would talk about running-related stuff as we were training. I was a good listener. I soaked up a lot from them. They said you could run farther if you made sure you didn't go too hard on the runs, so that's what I did."

Several of the training group, members of a small club called the Baltimore Road Runners Club, decided to organize a local marathon. They called it the Maryland Marathon, and the first one took place in November 1973. Kathrine Switzer, already famous for her runs in Boston and New York, won the first female title. Marilyn entered and finished second, clocking a 3:31:45. It wasn't fast enough to make the newspaper headlines, but it was more than enough to make her feel proud of what she had accomplished. "It was a positive experience," she recalls. "I had put in the miles, and I paced myself well. I found out that the marathon distance wouldn't kill me. In fact, the marathon encouraged me. I was happy and proud to finish second. It motivated me to train more to see if I could improve myself."

Marilyn began looking for more marathons. Three months after her debut in the Maryland Marathon, she ran the Beltsville Marathon, improving her time by five minutes. Two months later, she made her first trip to Hopkinton, Massachusetts, the starting point of the Boston Marathon. She knew she had reached the big time now, and she was scared. In particular, she worried about Boston's torturous Heartbreak Hill. Everyone talked about Heartbreak Hill, almost to the point where it sounded insurmountable.

Concerned that she would run out of steam before reaching Heartbreak Hill at the 21-mile mark, Marilyn decided to double down on her usual strategy: Start slow, and pace herself as intelligently as possible. She felt strong running through the Newton hills that preceded Heartbreak, passing dozens of fading runners. Still, she held back, worried about the mountain ahead. When it didn't materialize, she asked another runner where it was.

"Oh, we already went over the top of Heartbreak Hill," he informed her. At that point, Marilyn realized for certain that she had a particular talent for strong marathon running. She didn't seem to "hit The Wall" in marathons, as so many others did. "I thought to myself, *Oh, I can start running faster now,*" she remembers. "I had been saving myself for so long that I had quite a bit left."

She finished in 3:17:42, another personal best.

As she increased her weekly training mileage, Marilyn became even stronger and faster. More distance, more distance—that's what seemed to work for her. She wanted to see if she could run even faster marathons, so she began training twice a day, put in longer runs, and ran more total mileage. Over the next several years, she logged 80 to 100 miles a week. For a while, her tougher regimen worked. In the 1975 Boston Marathon, she finished fourth among women, and lowered her personal record to 2:55:52. The following year, in extreme heat, she faded back to sixth among Boston's women. That's when, always a student of the sport, she realized she had been driving herself too hard. To improve further, she would paradoxically have to train easier.

"Eventually, I realized that I was doing too much, especially when I was running twice a day, day after day," she says. "I wasn't giving myself enough rest between workouts and between hard days. As soon as I switched to more of a hard-day/easy-day pattern, my times got better. Once I figured this out, I stuck to the program because it worked so well."

Running in the annual Boston Marathon every April was how runners measured themselves against each other. The country's top marathoners always put Boston on their schedule, and where you finished at Boston was more or less who you were in the U.S. marathon world. Boston defined runners. It put them in a pecking order. Marilyn wanted to move up the ladder, so she focused on running her best at Boston. She hit her highest rung in the 1977 Boston, placing second to Miki Gorman, and she lowered her time to 2:51:12.

"I knew I was ready to run strong that day, though I didn't consider myself a competitor to Miki," she remembers. "I had my splits written down on my wrist, and I ran hard to hit those times. I was aiming for 6:30 per mile, and I had an almost perfect day. I couldn't have been more pleased. I was still the only black woman at Boston, and I ran entirely on my own."

At some other races during this era, the top women were paced by friends or even their husbands. This rankled Marilyn. She was an independent soul and believed women's running should teach, among other things, that women could race on their own. They didn't need men at their sides; they were strong enough to go it alone. She rarely expressed her opinion aloud, but this issue compelled her to speak her mind. "I thought it was pathetic when men paced women," she says. "It was pathetic that the men needed this kind of attention, and pathetic that the women runners would tolerate them."

Later in 1977, Marilyn finished second in the Chicago Marathon and won the Baltimore Marathon, now renamed for its host city. On both occasions, she broke 2:55. There could be no question about her consistent, high-ranking marathon racing abilities. While she didn't come from one of the great distance-running centers—like Boston, New York, or California—and couldn't model herself on other successful black women marathoners, Marilyn was racing with the best.

She didn't hesitate to go it alone, and she wouldn't settle for mediocrity. She wanted to explore her own boundaries and see how far she could go. Yes, there were obstacles. Marilyn doesn't speak about racism in running with any rancor or bitterness. She simply wonders why certain things turned out as they did. "Some of the other women seemed to ignore me, though Miki Gorman and Kathrine Switzer were always very warm and friendly," she notes. "And I wondered why no one ever stepped forward to coach me the way they coached other women.

"Sure, I was independent, but a coach probably would have helped me develop into a better athlete. It just never happened. I think that might have been a subtle form of racism. It's also why I'll remain a coach all my life. I want to be there if someone needs me." By then, she had started a teaching and coaching career in Baltimore that would span four decades.

Marilyn hadn't yet tapped her full running potential, so she remained intent on improving her marathon best. In the 1979 Boston Marathon, she reached a big goal: She broke the 2:50 barrier, hitting the finish in 2:49:56. The following December, she won the Baltimore Marathon for the second time, with a 2:54:35.

Bevans runs alone, but strongly, en route to her victory in the 1979 Maryland Marathon.

"I had learned what I needed to know by reading and listening to others," she says. "Running gave me a sense of pride and self-esteem. Sometimes, people wouldn't believe what I had done because no other black women were running. I would even hear whispers, like, 'She must be lying.' But I knew what I had achieved, and I could produce the proof anytime I wanted to."

In September 1979, Marilyn entered one of the most infamous road races ever held in the United States—the Catoctin 10-K. Catoctin remains the only American race entered by a sitting president—President Jimmy Carter. Carter had taken up running for personal fitness and decided that he wanted to run the Catoctin 10-K. It was located near Camp David, Maryland, the presidential retreat about 60 miles outside Washington, D.C., and 10 miles farther from Baltimore.

The race proved too much for Carter. Undone by the humidity and hills, he collapsed midway through the course, his demise caught in a dramatic series of photos. Marilyn had no such problems, winning the women's division, though she remembers how difficult the race was. At the post-race awards ceremony, a revived Carter put in an appearance, handing Marilyn her prize. She was impressed with the blue running shoes that bore his name and by the braveness of his effort. "I give him a lot of credit," she says. "It was a no-joke course, practically all up and down. He was one of the first presidents to believe in physical fitness and to support it."

With the beginning of a new decade, the 1980s, Marilyn set her sights on the same target that motivated so many women runners of the era: She wanted to qualify for the first U.S. Olympic Marathon Trials of 1984. She had no thought that she could finish in the top three to make the Olympics, but that wasn't important. She simply wanted to be part of the pageantry, competition, and celebration.

However, a case of adult-onset exercise asthma caused her to fall short. Her asthma proved particularly troublesome because it took a long time to get a proper diagnosis. Even though Marilyn stopped racing marathons at a high level, she continued running and entering races for the next 30 years, and counting. Eventually, she saw a trickle of other black women join her, though African-Americans remained vastly underrepresented at road races. The tide has turned somewhat in recent years, thanks to groups like the National Black Marathoners Association and Black Girls Run!, both of which have honored Marilyn's pioneering role.

At any rate, Marilyn never let her relative isolation in the sport detract from her enthusiasm for running. "Running is such a healthy, positive activity," she says. "Maybe it can't always prevent cancer and other serious stuff, but it prolongs life and makes you feel better every day. It gives you strength and a can-do attitude.

"In my life, it also gave me peace, quiet, and thinking time. When there was a lot going on, it got me out into nature and away from the chaos. It makes you tough, too, from battling with the cold, the wind, the rain, the blizzards, the hills, the heat, and all. You learn that you can get through stuff. It helps you see what else you can achieve in your life."

Patti Catalano can't believe her eyes—can't even open them, in fact—as she becomes the first American woman to break 2:30 in the marathon, New York City, 1980.

"I basically ran myself blind the last six minutes. I sprinted out of my mind. I gave it absolutely everything I had, and when I hit the finish line, I couldn't even see the clock overhead. My face was a mess of sweat, salt, and tears. Finally, someone told me my time, 2:29, and it felt so great to know I had done it."

PATTI CATALANO

Born: April 6, 1953

MAJOR ACHIEVEMENTS

- Three straight second-place finishes in the Boston Marathon, 1979 through 1981
- Four straight wins, Honolulu Marathon, 1978 through 1981
- Five wins, Ocean State Marathon in Rhode Island
- First American woman to break 2:30 in the marathon, New York, 1980

IN 1976, at just 23, Patti Lyons thought her life was over. She had a lousy job at a nursing home in Quincy, Massachusetts, and couldn't see a way up and out. She was stuck—stuck with 154 pounds on her modest 5-foot-4 frame, and stuck with no apparent future. The weight was easy to understand, given her diet of doughnuts for breakfast, nachos and Pepsi for lunch, more chips and more Pepsi for dinner, and late nights in a local bar.

Exercise? No way. Who had time for exercise? One day at work, Patti bumped into an old friend who had found work marketing pharmaceutical products. The friend looked so poised and smart in her business suit. Patti was struck by the stark contrast between the two of them. "I looked at her, and I considered myself, and I realized I didn't know who I was or where I was going in life," Patti recalls. "And it just hit me. It was time to figure out who I was and what I wanted."

She decided to start by losing weight. Walking past a bookstore, she saw Ken Cooper's book, *Aerobics*, in the shop window. She walked in, bought it, and sat down to read a few pages. Right away, she learned for the first time that she could lose a pound of fat by burning off 3,500 calories. This impressed her so much that she strolled to the Baskin-Robbins next door for a cone of her favorite ice cream.

But Patti also resolved to start running to lose her excess fat. Not wanting to attract attention, she headed for a nearby cemetery where no one would see her. The first two miles felt awkward and stupid. In the third mile, she relaxed and noticed the lovely grove of trees around her. Fourth mile, absolute nirvana. "I don't remember anything after the first three miles," Patti recalls. "I was just out there by myself, dependent on no one, running free. It was total bliss."

She completed seven miles—what a high! But she paid the price the following day—she could barely get out of bed. The muscle pains stayed with her a full week. She thought about running again, but there was no way. Still, she held tight to the bliss. "I kept thinking about how good I felt in the cemetery and in the shower," she says. "I wouldn't let it go. I knew I wanted to get back to it."

Soon, she was running each morning from the YMCA. She noticed a group of men—doctors, lawyers, and other professionals—running at about the same time each morning. She let them start ahead of her, and then followed at a respectful distance. At first, they would soon disappear from view. Then one morning, she looked up at the end of her workout and noticed that the guys were just a block ahead of her. They weren't pulling away anymore; she was holding her own against their pace. "I thought to myself, *Okay, that's just what I was hoping*," Patti recalls. "I knew if I kept trying hard, I would get better."

Oh, boy, was she getting better. Less than six months later, Patti ran her first marathon—the Ocean State Marathon in Newport, Rhode Island. She won Ocean State in an impressively fast 2:53:40, despite her complete lack of experience.

"I didn't know what I was doing at all," she says. "I was absolutely terrified, as I truly believed I was going to die of a heart attack during the marathon. Somehow, I got into the zone, and the miles just flew past. When I heard the announcer say I was the winner, I must have jumped 10 feet high."

———————

Patti grew up the first of nine children in Houghs Neck, Massachusetts, on Boston's south side. Her mom had left the Micmac Indian reservation in Nova Scotia when she was 11; her dad never advanced beyond a fourth-grade education. Both worked multiple jobs to support the big family and left many parental duties to their oldest daughter—Patti.

In particular, she had to keep house, prepare meals, and make sure her younger siblings didn't miss school. There was little time for Patti and little support for her interests. She understood only that she was supposed to work hard and never complain. At the same time, she should strive to go harder, farther than others. Her father encouraged her to do ever-longer ocean swims in the nearby waters. "I wasn't just swimming 400 meters or 800 meters," she remembers. "I was out there for two miles, three miles."

She swam for a few years on her school teams, but then let the sport go. She didn't have time. By eighth grade, she was working full-time at a nursing home, punching in at 3:00 p.m. and out at 11:00 p.m. She began those days at 6:00 a.m., getting the younger children out of bed, feeding them breakfast, and shooing them out the door to school. Several summers, she and her father drove north to Maine to work the blueberry and potato fields. Everyone there considered her an outsider—a city slicker who couldn't possibly pull her weight. That soon changed. "After several weeks, they accepted me because I had proved myself, working long days beside them," she says. "It was great. They welcomed me into the group. They respected me for what I had shown them."

Back in Houghs Neck, things deteriorated when her father and mother began fighting, especially nights when her father would stay out drinking with his buddies. Too often, their arguments turned abusive. Patti would cower in another room, listening fearfully. At the slightest break in the commotion, she would rush in and implore her father to back off.

But Patti could prove manipulative as well. One day, she was angry at her mother for giving her puppy to the dog pound, so she called her father for support. He lit into her mother, and Patti stood by quietly. "That was the most devastating night of all," she says, "because I knew I had started the whole thing."

Patti's father died several years later, when she was 17, and her mother soon kicked her out of the house. With no family mooring, not even the eight kids she had raised as her own, Patti fell apart. She worked at the nursing home days and drifted in and out of bars at night. "It was the worst time of my life," she recalls. "I didn't have any direction. I didn't know what I was doing."

***

After winning the 1976 Ocean State Marathon, Patti went back to running at the Quincy YMCA, chasing after the men's training group. Now, however, they knew who she was, so they stopped to give advice. "You're too good for us," they told her. "You could develop into something special. You need to find a good coach." They mentioned a fast marathoner in the area named Joe Catalano.

Patti contacted Joe, but he said he had no interest in coaching her or any other women. Crestfallen, Patti went back to her old running routine. Most days, she simply ran an hour on her own. She didn't have any particular plan. She just traced one or two familiar routes through Quincy. She missed her big goal race, the Boston Marathon in April 1977, due to a leg injury. This was no way to prepare for world-class running, but Patti still felt good about the way her life was changing.

"Looking back, I'm glad that I spent my first 18 months of running basically on my own," she says. "I had to figure out everything by myself—how to improve my diet, what shoes to buy, what races to run, how to get to the races. Running changed my life. It gave me so much more confidence that I started coming out of my shell. I talked to more people and learned how to speak up for myself."

In late 1977, Patti won the Ocean State Marathon again, improving her time to 2:47:20. She decided to recontact Joe Catalano. This time, he said yes to coaching her. (They married several years later, and then divorced in the mid-1980s.)

Joe added many new elements to Patti's training program—speed work on the track, hill repeats, fartlek session—and she kept improving. They focused on the 1978 Boston Marathon, but another injury prevented Patti from running. She had won Ocean State twice, but twice missed the far-more-important Boston Marathon. It was a bit depressing, but Patti refused to get sidetracked. "I always liked the process of picking out a distant goal and going for it," she says. "It's good for the mind. It takes your thoughts away from the immediate stuff, which might not be good, and lets you concentrate on how you're going to get to the next level."

Patti reached that next level in the fall of 1978. In a three-month period, she ran three marathons—the Nike Oregon Track Club Marathon, Ocean State, and Honolulu—finishing second in the first marathon and winning the latter two. In the process, she improved her personal best to 2:41:32 (in Eugene). She was beaten only by Julie Brown, a bronzed California runner considered among the best in the United States at every distance from 800 meters to the marathon. By comparison to Julie, Patti felt small and insignificant.

But she refused to crumble. "All my life, I've believed that hard work trumps talent," she says, "and I was absolutely livid that Julie beat me in Eugene. So I just focused more than ever on my training and on getting better."

In April 1979, Patti finally made it to the Boston Marathon start line, though not in top physical condition. She had an inflamed heel that required a cortisone injection. After missing the two previous years, she felt that she had no choice but to run Boston. "I would have killed myself before missing another Boston Marathon," she admits. "It was like a monster I had to throw off my back."

For 20 miles, she led all women. But then, another first-time Boston runner stormed past her—Joan Benoit. Joan ran strong to the finish, setting a new American record, 2:35:15. Patti placed second in 2:38:22, also under the old Boston course record, and a new personal record by three minutes. She felt she that had given her all on that day. "When Joanie passed, there was nothing I could do to stay with her," Patti says. "My foot hurt so bad, it took all my concentration to keep moving forward."

But at least she finished. Boston acted as a springboard to Patti's first New York City Marathon appearance later in 1979. New York's fame had grown exponentially the previous year when Norway's Grete Waitz ran 2:32:30 in her first attempt at the distance. Grete would be returning in 1979, and Patti wanted to face her. She had lost to Julie Brown and Joan Benoit by now. Why not go up against the best of the best? As a competitor, Patti was fearless.

Grete achieved a major breakthrough at the 1979 New York City Marathon, lowering her own world record to 2:27:33. That made her the first woman to break 2:30 in the marathon. Patti finished fourth, 10 minutes back. But she made note of Grete's barrier-breaking time, and it became her next big goal. She wanted to become the first American woman to run under 2:30 in the marathon. It didn't matter if she won the race or not. She couldn't control what others did—only her own efforts.

So Patti increased her training to a whole new level. She ran 120 miles a week, week in and week out, and occasionally scaled up to 150 miles. At many races, whether 5 miles, 15 kilometers, or any other modest distance, she ran an additional 5 miles before the start, and 5 after. "The extra distance made me tougher mentally," she says. "I proved to myself that I could do things I didn't think I could do."

In April 1980, Patti finished second again in the Boston Marathon. This time, the winner was Canadian Jackie Gareau, though that race will forever be known for Rosie Ruiz's fraudulent appearance. Ruiz was crowned champion for a week before race officials disqualified her for cheating. As it turned out, she only ran the last mile of the course—and possibly even less. Gareau was the rightful champion, and Patti the runner-up. The rest of 1980, Patti was virtually unbeatable. She raced frequently, won just as often, and set many course and American records. Every race, and every mile she covered in training, was dedicated to achieving a sub-2:30 marathon that fall. She picked the Montreal Marathon as her target race.

Patti ran hard from the start, far ahead of any other woman, and well under her planned pace. The spectator crowds roared lustily, which pumped her up. She always responded to loud cheering; the fan support seemed to stoke her own energy supply. Then, just past the 20-mile mark, the Montreal Marathon turned pin-drop quiet. Unbeknownst to Patti, the last 6 miles traced a loop around St. Helen's Island in the Saint Lawrence River. No one lived there, no one cheered there. Patti's spirits sagged just as the marathon reached its most challenging miles. "I was ready to break 2:30 that day, and I was running strong for 20 miles," she remembers. "But then we hit the last 10-K, and I got so lonely, I just fell apart."

She finished in 2:30:57, just a minute off her goal, and four minutes up on Jackie Gareau, who had beaten her at Boston. But the win didn't satisfy Patti. "I was devastated," she remembers. "I was on a mission to break 2:30, and I put everything I had into Montreal. That was supposed to be my day."

What next? Patti couldn't stop thinking about how Grete Waitz had run a 2:27:33 at New York the year before. She knew Grete would be back again for the 1980 New York City Marathon, now barely a month off. "I want to run New York," she told Joe.

"No," he said, "too soon."

Patti didn't listen. She called race director Fred Lebow, who said the marathon had already overspent its budget, but he would arrange a hotel room for Patti and Joe. Faced with her steely determination, Joe had to relent. Patti entered the New York event.

On marathon morning, Patti stuck close to Grete's fast pace for the first 5 miles, and passed the half-marathon just behind her, on a sub-2:26 pace. At 16 miles, she moved up onto Grete's heels again. "I knew I couldn't beat her," Patti says. "I hadn't reached her ability level yet. It was something that I still hoped to attain. But it gave me a boost to run with her for about 30 seconds. Then I refocused on my sub-2:30 goal." Grete would win in yet another world record, 2:25:42.

In the last several miles, Patti hit "The Wall." She could feel her physical reserves ebbing away, and she got cold as her pace slowed. "I was totally depleted," she says. "Just hanging on." She could feel her dream sub-2:30 slipping out of her grasp.

As she turned from Columbus Circle back into Central Park with less than a mile remaining, she heard a familiar voice. It was Coach Bill Squires of the Greater Boston Track Club. "You can still do it," he screamed at Patti. "You just have to run as hard as you can the next six minutes." Patti did exactly that.

"I basically ran myself blind the last six minutes," she recalls. "I sprinted out of my mind. I gave it absolutely everything I had, and when I hit the finish line, I couldn't even see the clock overhead. My face was a mess of sweat, salt, and tears. Finally, someone told me my time, 2:29, and it felt so great to know I had done it."

The bad news: She had finished second again—this time at New York, adding to her two second-place finishes at Boston. Patti was still looking to win one of the major marathons. The good news: Her official clocking, 2:29:34, made her only the second woman ever to break 2:30, and the first American. The Association of Road Race Statisticians lists the 1980 New York City Marathon course, and all prior, as "suspect." In other words, not everyone is convinced that the course was the full 26 miles, 385 yards. Still, most record books credit Grete Waitz for all her fast performances in New York and likewise accept Patti's sub-2:30.

―――――

Now, if only she could win Boston the following April. To prepare, Patti ran more long, hard runs up and over Heartbreak Hill than ever before. Boston is the kind of course that demands a very specific training program. You have to get ready for the endless up and down hills. Patti got ready.

"I thought this was going to be the year for me to win," she says. "Third time's the charm, right? I had prepared so hard for the final stretch run. Joe told me, 'No matter how tired you might be there, you have trained yourself to run through it. You'll go on automatic pilot and keep running strong.'"

This was one Hollywood script that almost came true in real life. Lose once, lose twice, but just redouble your efforts and win it all on your third try. Patti led to the top of Heartbreak Hill at 21 miles, running faster than course-record pace. She continued leading on the down side of Heartbreak Hill that heads into Boston.

Around her, mounted police were struggling to hold back the surging crowds. They were rooting for a hometown win, either from Patti or from Joan Benoit, who was having a rare off day. At one point, the spectator throngs pushed forward so far that Patti literally bounced off the hindquarters of a police horse. She lost her balance and would have fallen hard to the ground except for a nearby runner, Tom Derderian. He caught her, and steadied her.

A decade later, Derderian would write the definitive history of the Boston Marathon. Here's how he described what happened shortly after the horse incident, when New Zealand's Allison Roe came up to Patti's side. "Roe looked like an actress coming on stage to take the leading role. The two could not have looked more different. Blue-black hair versus blonde [Roe], brown eyes versus blue, a dark face with chiseled features versus a pale baby face. As Roe tossed in the gentlest of surges, I looked at Catalano and saw her face frozen like a department-store mannequin. Again, she would be a loser after coming so close so often."

Patti, typically, has a less poetic take. She's more the rough-and-tumble type. "I remember Allison passing me like it was slow motion," she says. "I told myself, *No-o-o-o-o, this can't be happening.* The rest of the way, I chased after her. I was thinking, *Close the gap. Close the gap.* Then, I was in the finish stretch, listening to the announcer say, 'Here she is, your American record holder, Patti Catalano.' The crowd was cheering, but I only remember the silence in my own mind. I swore a little bit under my breath, and thought, *Oh, damn, now I have to wait another year.*"

Patti finished second behind Roe. It was her third straight second at Boston, disappointing despite her new personal best time, 2:27:52. She was just 28 years old and had good reason to believe she would run faster in the future. But she didn't. And she never raced hard again at Boston. That December, after winning the Honolulu Marathon for the fourth straight year, she injured her back in a bodysurfing accident.

In 1984, two-and-a-half years after the surfing accident, Patti mounted a modest comeback. Like so many others, she wanted to run in the first Olympic Marathon Trials that year. But just getting to the Trials required a complete reboot. She had to begin by losing 25 pounds, then she had to pile on the training. She achieved a Trials qualifying time in January, running 2:50:35.

Four months later, in Olympia, Washington, she improved to 2:36:13—good for 16th place in the Trials. "I wanted to be at the first Trials to be part of the celebration with the other girls," she says. "But along the way, I looked at my life and realized I didn't want to do the hard training and racing any longer. It was time for me to move on to the next chapter of my life.

"I'd like to think that I helped lay the bricks for other women to follow and to run on," she says. "I feel like I was a bridge from some of the earlier women to Joan Benoit. The progress we made is so amazing. When I began running, I didn't know anything about women's running. I didn't even know that we weren't supposed to be able to run distances. I just wanted to burn calories and get skinny legs."

Norwegian Grete Waitz won the New York City Marathon nine times. Here, she warms up before the start of the 1983 NYC Marathon (which she won.)

"I just loved being active in sports. Norway provided a good environment, and distance running proved to be my best sport. We ran relay races around the neighborhood, we went cross-country skiing in the winter, and we picked blueberries and raspberries in the summer. I never felt that I trained particularly hard. I just enjoyed being outdoors and running on a consistent basis."

GRETE WAITZ

Born: October 1, 1953
Died: April 19, 2011

> **MAJOR ACHIEVEMENTS**

- Five-time winner, World Cross-Country Championships
- First winner, World Championships marathon for women, 1983
- Silver medal, 1984 Olympic Marathon
- Nine-time winner, New York City Marathon

I FIRST met Grete Waitz in early November 1978—the morning after she won the New York City Marathon in the new world-record time of 2:32:30. She was virtually unknown to me and to most readers of *Runner's World* magazine. Since I was the writer assigned to cover that year's marathon for *Runner's World*, I figured I'd better act fast and get to know her better. So at 7:00 a.m. on that Monday, I called Grete's hotel room from the lobby of the Empire Hotel, where she was staying. A woman picked up the phone. "I work for *Runner's World*," I said. "Could I come up to your room to ask you a few questions?"

I didn't expect a positive response. I figured Grete would brush me off the way most superstars would. Besides, she didn't have a clue who I was,

and I'm not sure she knew much, if anything, about *Runner's World* magazine back in those early days of road running.

"We are a little busy," she told me. "But, sure, you can come up to the room."

Surprised by this unexpected success, I hurried up to her room and
knocked on the door. Grete's husband, Jack, opened it, and welcomed me in.

The room was a total mess, with running shirts, sweat suits, and underwear strewn over every chair, light fixture, and towel bar. In other words, it
looked exactly like every other runner's hotel room I had ever seen. I
thought to myself: *"I guess Norwegian marathon champions aren't much different from the rest of us."* Grete was on the phone again, now speaking Norwegian, apparently to someone back in Oslo. Jack explained that it was the
principal of the school where she taught. The principal had expected her
back in her classroom the next morning, Tuesday. Now she was trying to
explain that the New York City Marathon organizers wanted her to stay in
New York for several days of media appearances.

"Have you ever heard of the *Today* show?" Jack asked me. "Why would
they be interested in Grete or the marathon? And why do we have to get up
at 4:00 a.m. to be on the show?"

Good questions, I thought. They reminded me of my own confusion
about what had happened the previous morning when I snuck into the premarathon breakfast. I headed straight for the table where Germany's
Christa Vahlensieck was enjoying a bowl of hot oatmeal. Christa held the
marathon world record and was a strong favorite to win New York. I pep-
pered Christa with several quick questions. How do you feel? How fast do
you want to run today? Do you think you will have any competition? She
looked at me blankly, then lifted her arm to point across the room to another
table. "If she finishes," Christa said, indicating a slim, blonde woman eating
some toast, "she will win."

What? The world record holder was practically conceding victory to
another runner. One I had never seen before, and who, as far as I could tell, had
never run a marathon before. This struck me as a highly unlikely outcome. But
Christa proved an apt prophet. Grete won, and Christa dropped out.

That's why I found myself having breakfast with Grete in her room the next
morning. We exchanged a few pleasantries, and I began asking questions. She
answered all of them with a short, unvarnished sentence or two. Her English

was good, though clearly not her first language, and she occasionally had to search for the right word. I asked how she felt about her first marathon.

"The last part of the race in Central Park was very difficult," she said. "My legs were cramping, and I wanted to stop. But I didn't know how to get to the finish except by running there, so I just kept going. It was hard, but at least I didn't get lost."

Everything I observed and learned about Grete that morning—her lack of pretension, her warm friendliness, her simple approach to all life and running challenges—remained true throughout the next 30 years. She never changed. She never needed to. She was perfectly happy being the person she was and leading the life she had.

I have never forgotten how she invited me up to her messy hotel room that first morning in 1978. She had nothing to hide, so no reason to fear me or anyone else. She was simply a quiet woman of uncommon determination and courage.

Two years later, I was chasing Grete again. This time we were literally racing each other—in the 1980 New York City Marathon. She started on one side of the Verrazano-Narrows Bridge with the elite women runners. I started on the other side of the bridge with the nonelite masses. My plan couldn't have been more basic.

I told the *Runner's World* editors that this race would provide a rare occasion to watch a world record in the making. In her second NYC Marathon the previous year, Grete had set another record, lowering her time to 2:27:33. There was nothing to stop her from a three-peat. She seemed the closest thing ever to a human marathon machine, and I thought it would make a good story to run next to her and report on whatever happened. While I was confident about Grete's speed and consistency, she was proclaiming no such record-setting ambitions. That wasn't her style. She never talked big; she only ran big.

"I'm running for the win," she said at a prerace press conference. "A record is just a challenge for other runners to break someday. A victory is forever."

Still, I had no doubt that she would run fast. That's why I scooted the first 2.5 miles at 5:30 pace—equivalent to a 2:24 marathon finish. That is, much faster than her previous year's pace. I wanted to make sure I was ahead of her when our paths merged on Fourth Avenue in Brooklyn.

Didn't work. As I approached the merge point, I spotted a number of women runners who I knew would be well behind Grete. She must be up ahead of me! Damn, now I had to run really hard to catch her. I moved strongly through the thousands of runners crowded onto Fourth Avenue. No sign of Grete. I was getting seriously worried. Not to mention seriously tired. Then I spotted the TV motorcycle with Kathrine Switzer in a sidecar, where she was providing race commentary. And I saw a gaggle of male runners, all clustered around . . . guess who?

Finally, I heard resounding crowds in Brooklyn.

"Go Grete," they cried.

"Win it again, Grete."

"We love you Gerta." Close enough.

In the midst of all this, I spotted Grete in a long-sleeved blue jersey, her pony-tailed blonde hair swishing back and forth. She passed five miles in 27:20—sub 2:24 pace. She was running next to a famous 50-year-old Dutchman who had recently finished a marathon in 2:22. Other runners were crowded close around her, as if hoping to soak up some of her magic.

The cheering rained down on her from upstairs apartment windows and nearby stoops, as well as the street side. Grete paid no attention to any of this. She stared straight ahead, running with precision, completely focused on the task at hand—moving down the road, gobbling up the miles, getting ever closer to the finish line. When a portly photographer stumbled toward her to take photos, Grete hopped nimbly around him and held her pace. When she passed Finland's Olympic hero Lasse Viren several miles later, he looked over at her twice. She didn't give him a glance. When Jack emerged from the tumultuous crowd at 16 miles on Manhattan's First Avenue to give Grete a water bottle, she grabbed it and never looked back.

For the first 20 miles, we enjoyed a tailwind. Then we circled Harlem, and turned south toward Central Park, the wind now gusting forcefully into our torsos. It was too much for me; I slowed down. Grete didn't. She seemed impervious to the wind. As she disappeared into the distance, I wondered what her final time would be. Could she hold on against the wind and set another world record as I had predicted?

I found out when I struggled to the finish line almost five minutes behind her. The announcer was screaming as loud as he could that the incredible Grete Waitz had set another world record—her third in a row—in the New York City Marathon. This time she ran 2:25:42.

She was standing next to him, still and quiet. The microphone got passed her way. The contrast in voices couldn't have been more dramatic. Grete spoke barely loud enough to be heard, and with no high-pitched excitement. She wasn't trying to send the crowd into a frenzy. She described her race in a couple of short sentences, as if talking to one or two friends, not to thousands of marathon aficionados.

"I ran faster at the start this year because I was in better shape," she noted. "When I heard my halfway time, I thought I had a good chance at the record."

The next day, I caught up with Grete at the marathon's morning-after press conference. I told her I was impressed by her race-day concentration—the way she managed to block out all distractions and to focus entirely on her running. I added that I hoped I hadn't been a hindrance, the way I stalked her throughout the marathon.

Her eyes widened at my comment and a bemused smile crossed her face.

"I never saw you," she said. "I didn't realize you were running near me."
Of course not. She had more important things to concentrate on.

Grete Andersen was born in Oslo, Norway, on October 1, 1953, the youngest of three children, and the only girl. She probably gained her toughness by chasing after her two brothers, Jan, seven years older, and Arild, two years older. At any rate, she rarely stood still for long.

"We were very active," she told me when I visited her in Oslo in early 1981. "We ran relay races around the neighborhood, we went cross-country skiing in the winter, and we picked blueberries and raspberries in the summer."

Grete's parents weren't athletic in any sense of the word, but they encouraged their children to participate in sports. In his teen years, Jan joined a local track club. Grete naturally followed in his footsteps when she turned 12, noting that she had "grown tired of playing children's games." With a quiet resolve that came to reflect her every action, she simply packed a gear bag, hopped a local bus, and showed up at the club. When she found the coach, she said, "Hello. My name is Grete Andersen, and I'd like to do some running with you."

She started as a sprinter, entranced by the story of Wilma Rudolph, sprint sensation at the 1960 Rome Olympic Games. But Grete didn't have great speed and power. What she had was gritty determination and uncompromising endurance. She didn't quit when she failed at the short distances; she simply tried longer ones.

"We are all alike," Jan told me of himself and his siblings. "We like to press ourselves. We enjoy the fight. And Grete always fought particularly hard because she was trying to match her two older brothers."

Best of all, there was no pressure. No one expected anything. When Grete improved her 1500-meter best to 4:16 in 1972, qualifying for the 1972 Munich Olympic Games, that alone was considered a success. It didn't matter that she failed to make it into the final.

Four years later, at the 1976 Montreal Olympics, her innocent world had changed. By then, she had set a world record for 3000 meters, a product of her own resolve and her afternoon training partners—her brothers. They alternated days at Grete's side—first Jan, then Arild.

"She ran so hard all the time in training," Jan remembers. "Neither of us wanted to run with her every day. But every other day was okay."

At Montreal, all of Norway expected its distance-running star to win a gold medal in the 1500 meters, the longest Olympic distance for women. But the four-lap track event was still too short for Grete, who didn't have the top-end speed to match the muscular Eastern European women. When she got boxed in the semifinal, she failed to advance to the final. She was distraught. Normally stoic, she couldn't hold back the tears. As she left the track, the first Norwegian she encountered was the national TV reporter. He shoved a microphone into her face.

"What happened?" he asked. The cruelest question.

Two years later, in 1978, Grete was similarly beaten at the end of the European Championships races in Prague. She went to dinner with Jack after the last night of competition and said she was ready to retire from her running career. She was a schoolteacher, and she led a hard life: running, teaching, running again, then going to bed early so she could repeat the cycle the next day. Winters in Oslo were especially difficult, with only about eight hours of daylight. That meant she had to run twice a day in total darkness, on ice and snow, in cold howling winds. Jack listened sympathetically, then offered an alternative.

"I think you should enter the New York City Marathon," he said.

"But I haven't done any marathon training," Grete protested.

This was true. She had never run more than 12 miles at one time in her life. She didn't need to run more to compete on the track. She needed to run faster. But that was impossible. Tall and lean, she simply wasn't built for track-racing speed. She didn't run with strong, powerful strides but with a flowing, almost effortless grace.

Jack acknowledged that she hadn't trained for a marathon but pointed out that several former track runners had made successful transitions to the marathon. She might be able to do the same. Besides, the two of them had never been to New York City. It would be nice to have a short vacation there.

Grete decided to call Fred Lebow, the New York City Marathon race director. An assistant answered the phone, didn't recognize her name, and told Grete there were no slots open in the marathon. That might have been the end of things. However, late that evening, Lebow noticed Grete's name among the notes his assistant left on his desk. He *did* recognize her name because she had won the World Cross-Country Championships five times. Based on that, Lebow thought she might make a good rabbit for the serious marathon women in his field.

The next morning, he told his assistant to book a ticket for Grete and Jack. All the low race numbers had already been assigned, so Grete was given F 1173. It seemed an appropriately uneventful number for a runner who would almost surely drop out after 15 to 20 miles.

Grete and Jack had a great time in New York. No pressure. Lebow didn't even see fit to invite them to a press conference. Why present a mere race rabbit to the cynical New York media? That left Grete and Jack free to play tourists in New York and to enjoy the restaurants. The night before her first marathon, Grete dined on steak, wine, and ice cream. Not exactly the dinner of champions.

"Grete never ate pasta," Jack once told me.

Out at the marathon start, no one paid any attention to Grete, who didn't even know where to line up. Luckily, she bumped into another Norwegian runner who pointed her in the right direction. Jack had given her just one piece of advice: "Take it easy at the beginning. Don't go out too fast. Go slow."

Privately, he had his concerns. "Grete has never known how to run slow," he told friends.

Jack could not have known how accurate his words would prove. Grete made history in her first marathon and continued making history for the rest of her marathon days.

After her world record 2:25:42 and third straight NYC Marathon win in 1980, Grete won six more New York City victories—1982, 1983, 1984, 1985, 1986, and 1988—for a total of nine. That's a record that will never be matched. She became the queen of the New York City Marathon, and thousands of fans turned out each year mainly to cheer for her.

Through TV, radio, and print coverage, New Yorkers came to know Grete for her easygoing, no-nonsense ways, and her extreme humility. She was so different from many of their fellow city-dwellers, particularly the big-time sport stars. How could they not love Grete? She never boasted that she would win any given year's race, and she never gloated afterward about the worldwide competition she had bested. She just said before most of her races, "I am in good form, and I hope to run well on Sunday." And after: "I knew I was in good condition, and I felt okay today, so I was able to win."

In 1983, Grete put her name in the record books by winning the women's marathon in the first World Championships of track and field. This international competition in Helsinki, Finland, preceded the first Olympic Marathon for women by a year, and it established Grete as a strong contender for the gold medal in the 1984 Olympics. Once again, her country's expectations grew to a fever pitch as Grete prepared for the Los Angeles Games. Grete and her teammate, Ingrid Kristiansen, were rated highly among a handful of potential marathon winners. Another was American Joan Benoit, although she had barely qualified for the U.S. team after requiring knee surgery several months earlier.

I was fortunate enough to watch the 1984 Women's Olympic Marathon from the best seat in the house: a press-row position high above the finish line. We had TV sets directly in front of us with video of the live, advertisement-free feed. No commercials. When Joan Benoit surged to the front at the 5-K water stop, I thought, *"Oh, no. Dumb move. Grete and Ingrid are going to catch you later."*

Of course, I was dead wrong. Joan ran arguably the most brilliant Olympic Marathon ever that day, building a big margin in midrace and holding on for a comfortable win. She deserved the gold medal. Grete finished second, more than a minute behind Joan, but at least she had an Olympic medal this time. She wasn't going home empty-handed, and she definitely wasn't crying as she left the track.

"I ran the best I could," she said. "I have nothing to complain about. Joanie was just too good for me today."

Grete never mentioned a back injury that had hampered her training before the Olympics and constrained her ability to run aggressively in the race. To do so would be to make excuses, and that just wasn't her style. We learned about the injury much later, and only from Jack, not from Grete.

In 1992, at age 39, Grete ran a NYC Marathon that she termed "more emotional" than any of her nine victories. This time, she ran as a pacer and supporter for Fred Lebow, 62, the marathon's long-standing race director. Lebow had never been able to take part in his own masterwork, because, well, he always had many more important jobs on marathon day. In remission from brain cancer, Lebow decided it was time to run the streets of New York rather than driving them in a police car. After making this decision, he picked up a phone and called Grete to ask her for help.

"Yes, of course," she said. "I will be there. I will be at your side."

With a small contingent of other friends and medical personnel surrounding them, Fred and Grete ran that 1992 NYC Marathon side by side every step of the way. Grete counseled Fred to conserve his energy carefully and to take walking and even sitting breaks (someone supplied a chair in mid-marathon).

"Focus on yourself today," she told him. "Don't worry about anything else. Run comfortably. Rest when you have to. It's okay, I'm with you."

Their shared effort captivated New York's raucous spectators and media throngs. *New York Times* columnist George Vecsey later wrote that Fred and Grete were the "Tracy and Hepburn of New York City sports, he of cragged cussedness, she of willowy strength." Eventually, they reached the finish line, hand in hand, in 5:32:34—about three hours slower than Grete's average marathon time.

"In some ways, it was the hardest marathon I've ever run," Grete said, referring to her extended time on the course and the short, slow stride needed to stay with Lebow. "But it was also the most emotional. The last two miles, Fred and I both had tears in our eyes."

This time, Grete's tears signified a moment of selflessness and mutual achievement. She had helped Lebow achieve his dream. Two years later, he passed away when his brain cancer returned.

In the 1990s and 2000s, I continued to see Grete several times a year, mainly at the Boston Marathon and again at the New York City Marathon. Boston was sponsored by her lifelong shoe sponsor, Adidas, who always brought her to town as a symbol of excellence in both running and character.

Each April in Boston, I would moderate a *Runner's World*–Adidas training clinic that included Grete as the big draw. And she was. Without fail, the room swelled to 500 people eager to see the marathon legend, to hear her words, and to honor her pivotal contributions to women's running. I would usually begin by asking her a few easy questions about her marathon training and her steely race tactics. She answered everything directly, honestly, with no exaggeration or hyperbole, but with plenty of self-deprecation.

"I just loved being active in sports, Norway provided a good environment, and distance running proved to be my best sport," she would say. "I never felt that I trained particularly hard. I just enjoyed being outdoors and running on a consistent basis."

When I sensed that the discussion was getting too serious, I would turn to my trick question: "So, Grete, you won New York City nine times, but you failed in your only attempt to win Boston. What happened?" She loved this question, because it gave her a chance to explain that she could be as mortal as every other runner in the packed auditorium.

In 1982, running in her only Boston Marathon, Grete had started at her usual strong pace. In fact, at 21 miles, she was far ahead of the field and running faster than her world-record pace from the 1980 New York City Marathon. Then, the unthinkable happened: She stopped entirely, and walked off the course.

"There was nothing wrong with me," Grete told the clinic attendees with a sly smile of remembrance on her face. "I wasn't breathing hard or anything. But my legs were completely destroyed by the downhill running. I couldn't move them anymore. There was nothing I could do. I had to drop out."

In 2005, Grete's many fans and friends were shocked to learn that she had cancer. She made the announcement in Norway, but never revealed what form of cancer it was. "That is a private matter," she said. "No one else needs to know." We all nodded in agreement.

Typically, she kept exercising as much as possible through various rounds of treatment. She also formed a Norwegian nonprofit, Aktiv against Cancer, to promote the many ways physical fitness can help individuals with cancer. She continued traveling to the Boston Marathon and New York City Marathon, showcasing the latest wigs she wore to cover her radiation-induced hair loss. No one laughed harder than Grete over the colors and styles she selected.

Grete died at home in Norway on April 19, 2011—the day after the 2011 Boston Marathon. One of her closest U.S. friends, Gloria Averbuch, commented, "I pictured Grete pushing through the Monday race date, because she didn't want to draw attention away from the marathon and its winners."

Her great rival and even better friend Joan Benoit Samuelson said, "To me, Grete always stood for goodness, greatness, graciousness, and generosity. She exuded all those qualities."

I spent that morning of April 19 at the Bill Rodgers Running Center in downtown Boston. At noon, Bill's brother Charlie invited a few of us back to his office, where he kept a bottle of his finest Scotch. Charlie picked a thick tome of Robert Burns poetry off his dusty desk and shuffled through it to find the page he was looking for. Then he began reading:

> *Few hearts like hers, with virtue warm'd,*
> *Few heads with knowledge so inform'd,*
> *If there's another world, she lives in bliss;*
> *If there is none, she made the best of this.*

With that, Charlie poured us a round of Scotch. Bill Rodgers was first to raise his glass. "To Grete, absolutely one of a kind," he said. "We were privileged to know you."

Joan Benoit hits the finish line in the historic first women's Olympic Marathon in Los Angeles, 1984.

*"I consider myself part of the next generation.
I'm not in the same league as the pioneer women
runners who came before me. They were part of the
process of history changing. They brought progress
to the sport. They are in a league of their own.
They had guts, they had talent, and, most of all, they
had the passion to pursue the sport they loved."*

JOAN BENOIT

Born: **May 16, 1957**

MAJOR ACHIEVEMENTS

- Winner, 1979 and 1983 Boston Marathons (world record, 2:22:43, 1983)
- Winner, first Olympic Marathon for women, Los Angeles, 1984

IN THE early months of 1984, 26-year-old Joan Benoit prepared herself for the most important day of her life—the first U.S. Olympic Marathon Trials for women on May 12th of that year. One moment, she was in the best of shape. The next moment, she was in the worst. Joan hadn't expected a smooth path to the Olympics, but this was ridiculous.

Through the dark, cold winter months, she had hunkered down in her newly bought, half-falling-down home in Freeport, Maine. There she knocked out week after week of incredible training runs. Nothing deterred her from her two-a-day workouts, many of which were longer and more grueling than she had ever run before.

Joan knew she was in fantastic shape. The year before, she had raced to a world record 2:22:43 at the Boston Marathon. And now, she could feel herself growing even stronger, even faster. She thought she was riding the perfect wave toward the Olympics. But nothing is guaranteed in running.

One day, you're the best; the next day, you're seeking emergency medical treatment.

On March 17, 1984, less than two months before the Marathon Trials, Joan set out on yet another hard 20-miler near her childhood home in Cape Elizabeth, Maine. For 17 miles, she ran smooth, almost effortless. Then, suddenly, she felt something come unhinged in her right knee. She hobbled another 2 miles before she had to stop and walk. Joan never walked. This was trouble. Her knee felt "alarmingly, paralyzingly different" from any previous running injury.

"I remember the fear vividly," she wrote in her autobiography *Running Tide*. "I felt like an artist who crafts a masterpiece over 10 years, and then sees it consumed in a sudden fire. She wonders what the ashes will reveal and is afraid she won't be able to replace the work of art."

Joan had two months to deal with her knee injury. It didn't go well. She rested for a week, received a cortisone shot, and had a few good training days. She felt a bit relieved. Then came a major setback. On her next workout, the knee totally locked up. There was no way she could run. She was reduced to a halting walk.

In mid-April, now just four weeks before the Trials, she flew to Oregon for a consultation with a renowned orthopedist. The doctor and Joan agreed that surgery was too risky. It seemed much smarter to give the knee more time off and hope for the best. Joan rested, and took heavy-duty anti-inflammatories to curb the pain. No luck. Her knee refused to heal.

So, on April 25, Joan went into the hospital for arthroscopic surgery to release a tight plica band in her knee. Her coach, Bob Sevene, attended the surgery and said the plica "twanged like a bowstring" when it was released. The next day, Joan began rehab. Famed exercise physiologist Jack Daniels suspended an inverted bicycle from the ceiling of his Nike lab. When Joan lay on her back under the bike, she could "pedal" it with her arms. This workout didn't strengthen her legs at all, but at least made her feel that she was doing something to stay in shape for the fast-approaching Trials.

The last two weeks before the Trials were like an out-of-control roller-coaster ride. Joan had good days and bad. On May 3rd, she managed a solid 17-miler with no knee pain. But the workout caused a compensation injury to her left hamstring. Again, she couldn't run for several days. A week before the Trials, she couldn't even climb the stands at Eugene's Hayward Field to watch a track meet.

The day before the Marathon Trials, she attended a press conference in Olympia, Washington, the site of the race. She looked wan and weary. "This has been a very emotional period for me," she said, stating the then obvious. "I just about packed my bags and went home to Maine three times.

"But I'm not thinking about my knee and my hamstring today," she continued in typically resolute Joan fashion. "I'm trying to divorce my mind from them so I can concentrate on what I have to do."

Joan was born in Cape Elizabeth, Maine, the third child (and only daughter) of Nancy and Andre Benoit. She spent a lifetime chasing after her older, stronger brothers, and she grew dedicated to the proposition that there's no place like home. She developed an abiding love for everything connected to Maine, from the simple, hard-working people to the craggy-but-beautiful environment.

Joan's father was a former member of the U.S. Army's 10th Mountain Division, trained to perform in cold, mountainous regions. He was also a stylish dresser. After leaving the army, he owned and operated a men's clothing store in Portland, Maine. Her mother enjoyed the arts and culture. The Benoit parents practiced an egalitarian attitude toward the children and everyone else. "No one had any special privileges," Joan recalls. "We all had to be at dinner at the same time every night. The values of our house were fairness, accountability, and support for each other."

With her father leading the way, the family took every occasion to go skiing during Maine's long winters. On the slopes, Joan tried to keep up with her older brothers. That was impossible, but she never considered backing down.

The T-bar lift proved a special obstacle. Everyone was expected to ride it with a partner. So tiny little Joanie, half the height of grown skiers, had to stand at the bottom, and work up the courage to ask others to ride with her. It took a while, but she didn't quit until she had mastered the art and practice of using it.

"I didn't want to look ridiculous, I didn't want people to laugh at me, and I didn't want to talk to strangers," she says. "But I knew if I was going to ski, I would have to master the T-bar. I didn't realize I was learning lessons. Later, I found that if I wanted to run a faster marathon, I'd have to cope with the occasional discomfort of long-distance running. By then, I knew the end result would be worth the effort."

In fourth grade, Joan's report card showed nothing but Cs for her efforts in physical education. Her teacher noted that she failed to impress in team sports. On Field Day, at the end of the year, Joan did better, winning several individual races and receiving a certificate with four blue stars. "I stuck it in my scrapbook," she remembers. "But I wanted to be the best in everything. The idea that I could have done better obsessed me."

Downhill skiing continued to be her favorite sport, and she had high-level aspirations. "I can't say I had a lot of heroes or role models at the time, because there weren't many women in sports," she says, "but I followed some of the women tennis stars and the women skiers who went to the Olympics. That became my goal. I wanted to go to the Olympics in skiing."

When she was 14, however, Joan had a skiing accident and broke her leg. She would recover and continue skiing, but never again with the reckless abandon of the great downhillers. She needed another outlet to which to direct her energy, and running more than fit the bill. Although her high school didn't have a cross-country or track team for girls, she could compete as an individual. By her senior year, even though field hockey had become her latest passion, she improved her mile time to 5:15. Her successes on the track began to attract local attention. A newspaper reporter came to interview her. When his story was published, it quoted Joan as saying: "I have to run every day. If I don't, I feel guilty."

Joan has spent a lifetime talking about the importance of balance in life—school, family, parenthood, community—but there is no doubt about her ability to laser focus on athletic goals. "My body may fail me, but my head never has," she wrote in *Running Tide*. "There's a switch I can throw that puts me into high concentration, so I don't feel pain. I can focus 100 percent on the immediate goal."

This doesn't mean that she craves attention. That has never been the case for Joan. She runs to her own drummer, following her own instincts. Back in those early high-school days, she actually tried to hide the fact that she was training. "I didn't feel comfortable being seen on the roads around Cape Elizabeth," she says. "Running wasn't something normal girls did back then. When I spotted a car coming along, I would often pretend that I was collecting bottles or admiring the roadside flowers."

During college at Bowdoin College in Brunswick, Maine, and at North Carolina State, Joan enjoyed periods of strong running, and not so strong, perhaps because she was still trying to do everything she enjoyed all at once. She was slow to give up field hockey, determined to convince her coaches that she deserved a spot on the first team. Later, injuries interfered with her running progress. During the summer of 1976, she tried a couple of road races. She finished fourth in the L'eggs Mini-Marathon in Central Park and first in the inaugural running of the Falmouth Road Race on Cape Cod. The roads beckoned.

In January 1979, Joan ran and won the Bermuda 10-K. The next day, a friend suggested that they should run the marathon together as a long workout. Sloshing through a cool rain, her friend noted, "Joan never got tired." She finished second overall in 2:50:54, good enough to qualify for that spring's Boston Marathon.

Joan not only entered Boston, but, at age 22, she won the 1979 Boston in 2:35:15, a course and American record. At the marathon's 23-mile mark, a college friend emerged from the spectator crowd and held out two items for her. One was a beer, the other a Boston Red Sox cap. "Take one or the other," the friend said. Joan selected the cap and wore it to the finish line. She has been Boston's favorite marathoner ever since.

At the post-race press party, Joan was surrounded by a thick ring of media reporters for the first (but certainly not the last) time in her life. Some snapped photos, some asked questions. "I don't remember saying anything intelligible," she recalls. She didn't have to. Her performance alone was plenty galvanizing. A new marathon star had completed the first chapter of what would become a remarkable history book.

As she stood on the starting line of the 1984 Olympic Marathon Trials, Joan had no idea if her knee would hold up. She might last the whole distance. She might run strong for 15 miles before—twang!—the all-too-familiar knee pain could return with a vengeance. Or, she might have to hobble off the course after just a dozen strides. "The big question," said her coach, Bob Sevene, "is whether or not her wheels fall off between 20 and 26 miles."

What Joan knew for sure was this: If she didn't finish one of the first three in the Marathon Trials, she wasn't going to the Los Angeles Olympics. Many believed this was a harsh and unfair way to pick an Olympic team, especially when there was a special individual like Joan who everyone acknowledged was the best in the United States.

Other countries allowed such athletes a "bye" onto their Olympic teams. But not the U.S. team. You had to finish in the top three in the Olympic Trials. That was the American way. Joan knew that she would have no recourse but to play by the rules. When others argued that she should receive an automatic selection, she disagreed. "Even at my lowest ebb, I knew I should not ask for special treatment," she said. "Other athletes had experienced similar problems in previous years, and the rules should not be changed. The Trials are a tough school, but to choose Olympic teams on the basis of past records is to invite favoritism and politics."

The first two miles of the Trials race passed slowly and without incident, as the runners felt each other out, trying to gauge who was having a good day and who wasn't. The pace was relaxed, 5:45 per mile, or about 2:30 for the full marathon distance. As many as 10 of the women were capable of running faster. Who would make the first big move? Who would be content to follow?

Just past the two-mile point, Joan circled out from the pack and popped to the front. No one expected this, not from a wounded warrior. But then Joan never ran to anyone else's expectations. "I didn't feel comfortable at first," she reported later. "My legs started tightening up. I knew I had to get out there and run my own pace."

Several minutes later, she motored down a steep hill. Then, the moment of terror! Her right foot caught a crack in the road, twisting her leg, knee, and upper body out of alignment. Joan whirled to see what she had struck, her teeth grinding a silent epithet that wasn't learned at her mother's dining room table. She had been running with a look of pale fear, barely controlled. Now, her eyes focused even harder, and her jaw stiffened. Another such slip, and her race would be over.

At 10 miles, collegiate ace Betty Springs surged to the front. Joan hesitated. There was no particular reason to give chase. At the Trials, a third-place finish was as good as first. "I was thinking of letting her go," she says. "But then I realized that if I let Betty go, I might do the same if someone else caught me, so I figured it wasn't a good idea."

Joan moved up to Betty's side. Two miles later, as her foot slapped down on the 12-mile mark, Joan charged to the front. Over the next 8 miles, she gradually extended her lead. "I knew I had to get well in front and hope my momentum would carry me to the finish line," she says. "I could tell my legs wouldn't have anything left for a surge at the end."

That got Joan to 20 miles—the point where her coach had predicted trouble. Twenty miles is the distance that all marathoners fear, because it is at this distance when the leg muscles have depleted all their glycogen—the body's energy source. At the same time, the brain grows feeble as it, too, is denied the fuel it requires. Joan felt the inevitable pain, and dealt with it. "My legs cramped up badly the last six or seven miles," she acknowledges. "I knew I was in big trouble if a pack came up on me, so I focused everything on just maintaining."

No pack appeared. The reason was simple. In Joan's best marathons, she ran the kind of races that left everyone else far in arrears and flagging much worse than she. And at the Trials, against great physical and psychological odds, the pattern held. By the time she reached the finish line in 2:31:04, earning a 37-second win over Julie Brown, Joan's eyes were heavy with tears. She covered her face with both hands and snuggled into the comforting shoulder of her husband-to-be, Scott Samuelson.

"These last two months, I've been up and down, up and down, so many times," she said. "It's been very. . . ." and here she lost words, rare for her, an articulate, straight-talking Downeaster. "I just can't believe I'm going to the Olympics."

Joan had first dreamed of the Olympics as a downhill skiing preteen in Maine. At the time, she didn't know what a marathon was, and that didn't make any difference because there was no Olympic Marathon for women. Now there was, and she would be running in the very first. Years later, she would acknowledge that this Trials marathon, against long odds and the daunting pressure, was her greatest athletic achievement.

"I tell people that the race of my life was the Olympic Trials Marathon in 1984," she says. "It was a pivotal competition, because I had to run well to make it to the Olympics. At the same time, it was really tough because of the knee surgery I had just had."

After the Trials, Joan had three months, until August 5, to get ready for the Olympic Marathon. She returned to Maine to make herself as happy and comfortable as possible. In her favorite environment, she could let the injury pressures drain from her psyche and also begin to rebuild her training.

"I've always gotten the most out of myself when I'm training at home," she says. "I feel more balanced there with my family, friends, and normal activities. I still have plenty of time to train, but I also have other stuff to focus on when I'm not running. I think your training environment is very important to your success, and Maine has always been the best place for me."

The early-summer months proved unusually hot and humid in 1984, and Joan found herself growing lethargic on many runs. Every runner has known this experience—running day after day in the heat tends to depress your spirits, to say nothing of the way it slows your paces. Joan decided that she needed to try a race. So she went to Los Angeles for a 10-K track race. It was organized to support an eventual 10,000 meters for women in the Olympics. And she was able to see the Olympic course.

On June 17, in Los Angeles's warm-but-dry air, she scorched a fast 32:07 on the Olympic track. It was a personal record by more than 20 seconds. She flew back to Maine feeling even happier than usual.

When she returned to Los Angeles on July 23 for the Olympics, Joan was assigned a room in one of the Olympic Villages. However, the Village dorm was big and packed with energetic international athletes. Joan liked the slow life better. She was afraid a 24/7 Olympic environment would push her adrenaline into overdrive long before her August 5th race.

A friend and fellow Boston Marathon champion, Jacqueline Hansen, found her a cottage apartment in Santa Monica, near the Pacific beaches. It was a sweet setup with one distraction: Every time she went out for a run, she was spotted by local runners, who would pick up the pace to pass her. "I felt like Gregory Peck in *The Gunfighter*," she says. "I should have ignored the challenges, but my competitiveness rose to every occasion. Before long, I was tired, and I had to get away."

But she didn't want to miss the spectacular Opening Ceremonies, so she remained in Santa Monica through July 28th. She wanted to march through the Los Angeles Coliseum tunnel with thousands of her fellow athletes from around the globe. It was a long, tedious evening—with more standing and waiting than marching and celebrating—but Joan never regretted it, especially the lighting of the Olympic torch. "To call those minutes electric would be an understatement," she says. "My whole body was tingly with awe and pride."

Moments later, she found herself on the verge of tears as the athletes joined hands and swayed to and fro to the words of the song, "Reach Out and Touch (Somebody's Hand)." The song was written and first performed by Motown star Diana Ross, but L.A. Olympic officials decided to have a local supermarket clerk, Diana McClure, take the stage. It was an inspired decision.

After that emotional high, Joan knew that she needed to escape from Los Angeles during the last week before her marathon. She flew to her adopted second home of Eugene, Oregon, and stayed with friends. Her nervous energy just about drove them crazy. One evening, they tried to slow her down with a calm game of Scrabble, but she jumped up every couple of minutes to complete one chore or another. Another day, she went berry picking for a few hours, then made jam, then went for a run. When her friends saw their kitchen, it looked like it had been struck by a black-berry tornado.

Back in Santa Monica, the day before the Olympic Marathon, Joan couldn't believe how slowly the clock hands moved. Usually, she had too many things to do, and she normally wished that time would slow down. This day, however, was almost torturous. There was nothing to do but wait. She filled the hours with a little reading, a little TV, a little music, and a lot of premarathon hydrating.

That night, she tried to sleep, but to little avail. She had to get up frequently to use the bathroom. When sleep seemed impossible, she listened over and over again to the theme from *Chariots of Fire*. She remembers dropping off to dreamland for just an hour or so, and even that wasn't relaxing. She had a nightmare. She pictured herself trapped in a department store with no escape.

The next morning, Joan paraded single-file with 50 other women to the marathon starting line at the Santa Monica College track. This entrance was conducted by strict Olympic protocols. The runners were organized in alphabetical order by their country's name, with the United States coming last since it was the host nation. Within each country team, the runners were arranged from tallest to shortest. This meant that Joan was last of the 50 runners to march onto the track. Not a good omen, perhaps. But it reminded her of one of her mother's favorite maxims: "So the last shall be first, and the first last: for many be called, but few chosen."

———————

The first three miles of the Olympic Marathon felt awkward and unnatural to Joan. She and the other top women weren't used to racing among women only. They were much more accustomed to running with men in the big mega-marathons around the world. Paradoxically, the small field produced more bumping and jostling. It seemed as if all 50 runners wanted to stick as close as possible to each other. That wasn't Joan's style. "I felt hemmed in with the pack," she recalls. "I couldn't stride properly when I was surrounded by everyone else. The pace was too slow. I wasn't efficient at that pace. I felt it was time to go, even if that made me the pacesetter. Right after I broke free, we reached the first water station, but I was darned if I was going to get in a crowd again just for a drink, so I skipped it."

Much to Joan's surprise, the gaggle of tough, fast women behind her failed to give chase. She feared Grete Waitz, Ingrid Kristiansen, Rosa Mota, and Lorraine Moller, among others. But they chose to stick close together and let Joan gap them. This was a clear calculation that Joan would hit "The Wall" and fade back to them in the late miles.

It never happened. Joan never faltered. She most feared a long stretch of running on the iconic Marina Freeway, but instead it turned out to be a blessing. All alone on the freeway with no traffic or boisterous crowds to break her concentration, Joan actually imagined herself running long and relaxed on a solitary Maine byway. The thick coastal fog began breaking away to admit sunshine, just as it did back in Cape Elizabeth. "It felt like a quiet summer morning run on uncrowded roads back in Maine," she recalls.

Just before reaching the Los Angeles Coliseum, Joan ran past an office building on which Nike had painted a huge promotional mural. It depicted her winning the 1983 Boston Marathon. She had witnessed the mural creation the previous fall and was a little embarrassed by it. But now it pushed her toward the finish line.

Moments later, she veered sharply into the Coliseum's "marathon tunnel" that led directly to the Olympic track. She had passed through this tunnel during the Opening Ceremonies and wondered what it would feel like to be the first runner here on Marathon race day. "I never expected that I would win the gold medal," she says, "but I thought it would be very cool."

Now, her wildest dreams were coming true. She was running through that same tunnel, far ahead of the pack. And she wondered what awaited her at the finish line. She had the clear and not entirely reassuring thought: "When you come out of this tunnel, your life will be changed forever."

She recalled how uncomfortable she had felt in the media's attention after her 1979 Boston Marathon win and wasn't at all sure she wanted to face an even harsher glare. But she kept running—hard and fast and true. She hit the Coliseum track and began circling it. With 200 meters to go, she gave into the roaring crowds, lifted her running cap, and waved to her many admirers. She had so much energy at the tape that she launched into a big bounding leap across the finish line. Later she said, "I was so charged up that I could have run another 26 miles, though maybe not at the same pace."

A Nike employee gave her a huge American flag to carry with her on her victory lap—the first-ever Olympic victory lap for a woman marathoner. At the victory ceremony, she climbed to the awards podium's top level, flanked by Grete Waitz (silver medalist) and Rosa Mota (bronze). With the flag raising and national anthem that followed the presentation of her gold medal, Joan found herself "beyond feeling. I had to take several long breaths to make it through the ceremony."

Later, she was asked how she had survived the tribulations of 1984 to achieve two major victories—at the Trials and at the Olympics. "Faith is the key to everything," she said. "You can never let anyone or anything deter you from your best efforts. There are no shortcuts in life, or in the marathon. The marathon is like a metaphor for life. You have to run your own race at your own pace."

When Joan ran her first Boston Marathon in 1979, she had yet to hear the name Roberta Gibb, or those of the other pioneer women at Boston. However, Joan is a student, a fast learner, and humble to the core. After her Olympic win, she showered praise on those who came before her. "I consider myself part of the next generation," she said. "I'm not in the same league as the pioneer women runners who came before me. They were part of the process of history changing. They brought progress to the sport. They are in a league of their own. They had guts, they had talent, and, most of all, they had the passion to pursue the sport they loved."

After Oprah Winfrey completed the 1994 Marine Corps Marathon, she appeared on the March 1995 *Runner's World* cover. Her marathon success—and the rallying cry, "Oprah Did It, So Can You"—helped launch the women's running boom.

"Life is a lot like a marathon. If you can finish a marathon, you can do anything you want."

OPRAH WINFREY

Born: January 29, 1954

MAJOR ACCOMPLISHMENT

Finishing the 1994 Marine Corps Marathon in 4:29:20

I WISH I had been sitting at my desk the day in April 1995 when Oprah Winfrey called. It would have been great fun to grab the phone and catch up with my marathon partner. Unfortunately, I missed the call. I was out running. That's one of the very few workouts I've ever regretted.

But I do remember the words on my telephone message recorder. And the voice. The voice was unmistakably Oprah's. I knew that voice now. A year earlier, I wouldn't have. But I had started watching her hyper-popular afternoon show with my wife. Oprah and me, we had become friends now. Well, sort of. We had run a marathon together, after all.

Soon after Oprah finished the 1994 Marine Corps Marathon, I began calling her Chicago office. I wanted to know if she would appear on a *Runner's World* magazine cover. This wouldn't take much effort on her part. We only wanted her to pull on her favorite running outfit and jog in front of a camera a few times. That was the easy part. The hard part was getting to yes. Oprah is one of the most sought-after people in the world. Given her diverse involvement in various business and charitable organizations, it was difficult to land Oprah on the cover of *Runner's World*.

Worse still, we had no idea how *Runner's World* readers would react to seeing Oprah on the cover of their favorite running magazine. The readers were far more accustomed to seeing Olympic marathoners and superfit California models. Despite her fame and recognition, Oprah was not an elite athlete and represented a different type of athleticism than was typically depicted on the cover. While *Runner's World* commonly features real life runners on the cover today, this was a novel concept twenty years ago. As such, we were nervous about the reaction of our core readers.

Magazine companies have the normal amount of bean counters, and they were looking over my shoulders. I could sense their presence and feel them second-guessing the Oprah cover. "Amby, are you sure about this?" I decided to plunge ahead anyway. Every once in a while you have to do something bold, right? If you're afraid to fail, you'll never succeed. We've all heard those bromides over and over again. I found that they didn't do much to calm my nerves. Long story short, we landed Oprah as our cover model and feature story. We put a big headline on the cover, "Oprah Did It, So Can You," and hoped for the best.

A few days after the magazine came out, Oprah called my office phone. In the voice message, she said that it was her favorite cover among all the hundreds of magazine covers on which she had appeared. (This was years before she launched her own, self-named magazine.) She said that she was glad she had agreed to participate and thanked me for the opportunity. The message was nice, but I was still holding my breath. In those predigital days, it took months before a magazine received a full tally of its newsstand results. So I had to wait until early summer to find out if readers approved of our new *Runner's World* cover model.

When the results were finally tabulated, someone rushed the spreadsheet to my desk. Oprah was the bestselling cover in the history of *Runner's World* magazine.

I was already in Washington, D.C., for the 1994 Marine Corps Marathon when the news broke. On Friday morning, the *Washington Post* newspaper ran a small story saying that Oprah was expected to run the marathon two days later, that coming Sunday. I was surprised, since we at *Runner's World* had expected her to run the Chicago Marathon a week later.

Winfrey lives and works in Chicago, but pulled a surprise by running the 1994 Marine Corps Marathon in Washington, D.C. Here Stedman Graham and a Marine Corps security corps escort her to the finish line.

But no matter: I happened to be in D.C. to speak at a marathon clinic on Saturday afternoon before the race. I hadn't planned to run the marathon on Sunday, but there was nothing to keep me from pulling on my running gear and wandering down to the Pentagon parking lot to see if Oprah was indeed in the pack.

So *Runner's World* had its bases covered. Not so for the *National Enquirer* tabloid. The *Enquirer,* I learned later, had also expected Oprah to be running the following weekend in Chicago, her home and business center. The *Enquirer* editors had searched its nationwide offices to find a couple of distance-running staffers who could accompany Oprah, on foot, the whole distance. If anything happened, the paper wanted its reporters to be first on the scene. The editors uncovered two experienced runners, one in Southern California and one in Miami. The two were told to set aside the Chicago Marathon weekend to jet to town and run with Oprah. Meanwhile, the *Enquirer*'s photo department also made plans to get a photo team ready in Chicago. This included motorcycle escorts who could weave their bikes through the crowds of runners to get up-close shots of Oprah.

No problem. The *Enquirer* had a big, well-oiled staff, and the plans were soon booked. Then came the surprise announcement that Oprah was fooling all of us by running Marine Corps. This forced the *Enquirer* and its staff to scramble, and they did so impressively. When I first spotted Oprah at the three-mile mark at Marine Corps, she had *National Enquirer* runners on either side of her. The motorcycle photographers joined us a few miles later, when the running crowd got thinner and the roads wider.

The first thing I noticed was that Oprah was not dressed like a typical marathon runner. She wore a gray hooded sweatshirt as protection against a light, cold rain that was falling early in the race. Bundled up in her sweatshirt, she didn't look the least bit happy about the weather and neither were the other runners. Second, I noticed that her trainer, Bob Greene, was following about 10 yards behind her. It seemed a respectful distance, and I mentally applauded him for letting Oprah run by and for herself. I fell in with Greene and introduced myself. He told me that he and Oprah read *Runner's World* cover-to-cover each month, and, just like that, Bob and I became fast friends.

Greene, a 47-year old personal trainer in California, had gotten a call 18 months earlier from Oprah. She wanted him to move to Chicago and become her full-time trainer. He was hesitant at first, unsure how long her resolve would last. But after several meetings, Oprah convinced him that she was serious about using exercise rather than a trendy diet to achieve her goal weight. She wanted to drop 70-plus pounds—from 222 to 150. To get Oprah there, Greene advised a slow-and-steady program that focused on running for fitness and weight loss.

"There were other options, including swimming and cycling," he explained. "But if you want quick weight-loss results, as Oprah did, running is the best."

Not that things moved fast at first. Like most beginners, Oprah started out with a mix of walking and jogging, Oprah could cover only a couple of miles at a time. She averaged 17 minutes per mile. But Oprah was determined. She and Greene stuck with their program nonetheless, even though she had to do most of her workouts at 5:00 a.m. to fit into her long workday. Sometimes, Oprah added an afternoon session, mainly strength training, to boost her metabolism even more. Four months later, Oprah reached the point where she could run five to six miles nonstop at 11 minutes per mile. She had lost about 40 pounds, and the weight kept rolling off. "The body abides by the laws of physics," Greene told her. "The more weight you lose, the faster you can run. And the faster you run, the more weight you lose."

That August 1993, Greene entered Oprah in the America's Finest City Half-Marathon in San Diego. She finished the 13.1-mile distance handily, clocking a 2:16. Flush with her success, an excited Oprah told Greene that she wanted a new challenge—a bigger one. In fact, she wanted to tackle the full marathon distance. She had watched the Chicago Marathon several times in her home city, cheering enthusiastically for the mass of runners who streamed in front of her.

Oprah found herself particularly drawn to the diverse field of marathoners, as there are distance runners of all sizes, shapes, and ethnicities. Some were fast and looked like the Olympians she had often seen on TV. Most didn't, however. They seemed to represent a true cross-section of humanity—a melting pot. From her position on the sidewalk, Oprah watched them churn past, and she realized for the first time that the marathon was a true Everyman and Everywoman event. That held great appeal for her. She began to think that perhaps she, too, could complete a marathon if she trained sufficiently.

Greene may have been a Hollywood celebrity trainer, but when it came to the marathon, he insisted on a serious, long-range plan. He told Oprah: "Fine, I'll get you in shape to run a marathon, but you need another year before you are ready."

No problem. Oprah had a head of steam now, and she was ready to agree with Greene's assessment. She just kept chugging along. By November 1993, Oprah reached her goal weight of 150 pounds, and she ran a five-mile workout at an 8:00-minute pace. "I was so proud of her," Greene says. "Some people think Oprah's got it easy, with her personal chef and personal trainer. But that's baloney. She worked herself as hard as any athlete I've ever seen, and she deserved the results she achieved."

———

Now, nearly a year later, Oprah was headed toward the 3-mile mark of the 1994 Marine Corps Marathon. She wore race number 40, in honor of the

40th birthday she had celebrated 10 months earlier, and a black baseball cap with a red bill. While nearly everyone else in the marathon wore shorts, Oprah wore long gray sweatpants down to mid-calf and a hooded sweatshirt. Her outfit was reminiscent of a neighborhood jogger running to the end of the street and back. I hate to admit it, but I wouldn't have bet on her chances of going the full 26.2 miles. Still, I trotted onto the road a few yards behind her and settled in for the long haul. Whatever happened, I would be there along with the *National Enquirer* twosome to follow the outcome.

From this close-up position immediately behind Oprah, I decided to check out her stride. That's the first thing I analyze when evaluating another runner. Right away, I saw that Oprah had a solid, determined stride, obviously earned on many long training runs. She moved in a strong and somewhat automatic manner, pumping her arms with particular vigor. Her form displayed her level of determination and commitment. Even though she did not move as fast or as gracefully as the elites, I was impressed. Nothing was going to stop her from reaching her goal. She kept her head down for the most part, or looked directly ahead, trying to ignore all the distractions around her.

Oprah had locked herself in the zone. She clearly felt that there was no other way to get through the intimidating marathon distance. The marathon had a long, glorious history, from Pheidippides to Frank Shorter and Joan Benoit Samuelson, to the great Kenyan and Ethiopian runners of the modern era. Oprah was on a mission to rewrite that history and make a mark for everyday runners no matter their size, gender, or race. There was only one way she could succeed: by completing the marathon and leading by example.

In addition to some of the obstacles I've just mentioned, Oprah also faced an issue the likes of which I had never seen in a marathon before, and haven't witnessed since: her fame. While she wanted to focus on her quiet, solitary journey, every runner who passed her wanted to blurt out a loud "Hello."

"Hi, Oprah, I watch your show every day."

"Hi, Oprah, I lost 110 pounds after I started running. Stick with it."

"Hi, Oprah, you're looking good at the 45-minute mark." Oprah had a funny response to this last comment: "Honey, I'm always looking good at 45 minutes. It's three hours from now that has me worried."

Early in the marathon, Oprah tried to acknowledge all the attention—the constant stream of comments—much as any friendly runner might do. She lifted her gaze, turned her head to make eye contact, and gave a cheery wave with her hand. After a dozen or so miles, however, the fatigue settled more heavily on her.

She was getting greeted by hundreds, if not thousands, of runners. It seemed that all of them had read the *Washington Post* article on Friday, and they were running every step of the marathon with both eyes peeled for Oprah. When they spotted her, they weren't about to pass without some kind of acknowledgement. After all, this was the sort of running experience none of their training partners back home had ever had—"I ran with Oprah!"

But Oprah could no longer respond to all the cheers and the claps on her back. She had no superfluous energy for social engagement. Moving ever forward, holding pace, required 100 percent of her effort. Oprah plodded past the half-marathon mark at Capitol Hill in 2:04. It was way too fast. She would likely pay a price later. Her suffering would increase as her miles grew ever slower.

And then things got worse. As she began the parts of the Marine Corps course that were jam-packed with spectators—the areas adjacent to the National Mall and all its historic landmarks—word traveled up the road that Oprah was coming. This set off a near riot among onlookers who edged forward into the road despite the best efforts of Marine security guards to hold them back. When they actually spotted Oprah, they couldn't withhold their excitement. The tumult from the sidelines was far greater than that within the race. I had never seen anything like this, even for the most famous elite runners in the world.

"Oprah, I loved you in *The Color Purple*."

"Oprah, you're an inspiration."

"Oprah, my daughter beat cancer, and you can beat the marathon."

A guy darted in front of her—a tactic intended to make sure she would see the words on the back of his running shirt. The words said: "I only want to beat Oprah." That evoked a reaction from her. She couldn't hold back: "And I only want to beat at least one other runner in this race."

There was no way Oprah could respond to the constant acknowledgment. She was in the marathon's middle miles, and it was time to begin digging deep. It didn't matter that she wasn't trying for a Boston Marathon qualifying time or to make it to the Olympics. She was simply hoping to finish. And that would require her complete attention. Every step. And every mile.

Just when I thought Oprah was lost in her focused thoughts, one of the *National Enquirer* reporters sidled up to her side and said something. He seemed to be pointing back at me, a few yards behind them. "I told her there was a *Runner's World* editor and Boston Marathon champion right behind her," the reporter explained to me minutes later.

Oprah slowed briefly, turned sideways, and held out her right hand in my direction. I reached forward to shake her hand. The *Enquirer* later sent me a copy of the handshake photo snapped by one of their photographers. It has been hanging proudly in my office ever since.

Near the 15-mile mark, Oprah slowed to get a drink. All around her, other runners did the same. They walked and drank rather than spilling water all over. But Oprah refused to walk. She seemed worried that if she walked just a step or two, she might never begin running again. She kept running, sipping a little water, and spilling some. But always running forward.

Five miles later, I noticed Oprah behaving a little strangely. We passed the 20-mile mark, still moving along steadily, when I saw her staring at a row of portable toilets set back slightly from the road. She looked like she wanted to use one, and probably needed to, as she had been drinking regularly.

But another thought deterred her. If she headed into one of these toilet units, the *National Enquirer* photographers would jump off their nearby motorcycles and race after her. They'd snap a hundred photos as she lurched into any available portable potty, and more as she emerged.

Not the kind of media coverage she wanted. So she forced herself past the toilets. She trotted ahead, ever onward. No potty break.

Her pace kept slowing. At 23 miles, we were barely moving. I wondered if Oprah would be forced to walk since this often happens to first-time marathoners do. They run as far as they can—beyond the edges of their training—and then walk the last 3 miles, or 6, or sometimes 10. This has happened to many of my first-time marathoner friends.

By this point, I was rooting hard for Oprah, but I was also a little concerned. If she could finish the marathon, she would become an outstanding role model for all runners—principally women, but also men—who may have never believed themselves capable of such an endurance achievement. If she didn't finish, she might instead become an embarrassment or a symbol of those who fall short when they reach outside their comfort zone.

Oprah had only 3 miles to go. But those are by far the toughest miles of a marathon—much harder than the previous 23—and nothing is guaranteed until you cross the finish line. She resisted the urge to walk. She faltered but didn't give in. Her stride was now slow and exhaustive but she trudged onward, her head never lifting to look ahead. She looked straight down at her shoes perhaps encouraging her feet to shuffle onward.

Once or twice, Oprah forced her forearm in front of her eyes to look at her watch. Clearly, she was hoping to see that a few more, seemingly endless minutes had passed. Every marathoner has had this experience. In the last miles, time seems to stand painfully still.

The 25th mile was the worst. It seemed to go on forever. When we finally reached the small roadside mile marker with a "25" on it, Oprah looked at her watch, and groaned. "There goes my hopes for a sub-4:30," she muttered. I checked my watch, too, saw that 16 minutes had passed since the last mile-marker, and immediately realized that the 25-mile marker was way off its correct location. For all their military efficiency, the Marine Corps Marathon organizers had badly misplaced this marker. I sped up a little to reach Oprah's side, and told her: "Don't worry. That mile marker was wrong. Stay relaxed. Keep running. You're doing great."

I don't think she heard me. How could she? The other runners around us were all babbling in her general direction.

"Oprah, you're the only TV star who could run a marathon."

"Oprah, you've come so far, and now you're almost there."

"Oprah, I'm right behind you. I'm going to finish this marathon for my mom, and you're going to finish it, too."

We turned up the steep finishing hill toward the Iwo Jima Memorial in Arlington National Cemetery, and Oprah impressively picked up the pace. She began to run faster than at any previous point in the race. When she saw the finish line banner, she accelerated again. Then—bam!—it was done. Oprah crossed the line in 4:29:20, beating her goal by more than 30 seconds.

I have been lucky enough to run with many Olympians, Boston Marathon champions, and other world-class marathoners. All had far more speed and athletic talent than Oprah. But I've never seen any of them run a race more courageous and impressive than Oprah's 1994 Marine Corps Marathon. She didn't share their abilities and she faced significant obstacles of her own but her drive and willpower were on par with any professional athlete.

She also realized that if she committed herself to the starting line, the eyes of the world and particularly the *National Enquirer* would be on her. A failed marathon effort would attract massive public humiliation. Yet she went to the start and ultimately proved triumphant in her quest—as she had done in life and show business—because she possessed the most important runner qualities of all: vision and determination.

As it turned out, Oprah's marathon finish had a galvanizing effect on millions of women runners around the world. Joan Benoit had won the Olympic Marathon a decade earlier, but her great victory produced few new women runners. Most women realized, no doubt, that they had little in common with an Olympian. Quite simply, it was much easier to relate to an Oprah than to an Olympic gold medalist. "If Oprah did it, so can I," these women assured themselves. That was the rallying cry that launched the huge boom in women's running that began immediately after Oprah's marathon finish.

Twenty years later, women made up more than 50 percent of the total running population, and as much as 40 percent of marathon runners. Many weren't fast, but they were smart, determined, and goal-oriented. Just like Oprah. In addition to her personal transformation, Oprah provided words of inspiration. Running a marathon can serve as a metaphor for much more, she explained. "Life is a lot like a marathon," she said. "If you can finish a marathon, you can do anything you want."

AFTERWORD: WHERE ARE THEY NOW?

HERE ARE BRIEF UPDATES on the women featured in *First Ladies of Running* and their lives after the prime years of their racing careers. In alphabetical order:

Gayle Barron continues to live and run in the greater Atlanta community. In the 1970s and 1980s, she worked in TV and radio and, since then, has coached various charitable running groups. She was inducted into the Georgia Sports Hall of Fame in 2003. Gayle currently serves as a corporate fitness consultant.

Sara Mae Berman and her husband, Larry, have been married more than 60 years and continue to live in Cambridge, Massachusetts. They have made many key contributions to the local and national fitness communities. They founded the Cambridge Sports Union athletic club in 1962 and also published *Orienteering North America* magazine for many years. Both remain active in Nordic skiing. They have three children and six grandchildren.

Marilyn Bevans still lives in Baltimore, where she coaches track and cross-country and serves her Catholic church community. She runs and strength trains, and enjoys entering the occasional short road race. In 2013, she was inducted into the National Black Marathoners Association Hall of Fame.

Julia Chase Brand lives in New London, Connecticut, and has begun writing articles about her early days in women's track and field. In midlife, she changed career paths from zoology to psychiatry, receiving her MD from the Albert Einstein College of Medicine. She continued running through 2011, when she ran the Manchester Road Race on the 50th anniversary of her historic race in 1961.

Grace Butcher taught English at Kent State University until her retirement in 1993. She competed in masters track championships through 2003 and has written six books of poetry and one collection of motorcycle riding columns. She lives on the family farm in Chardon, Ohio, where she acts in community theatre and tends to Spencer, her quarter horse gelding.

Patti Catalano Dillon became a stay-at-home mother of two in Connecticut. She and her husband, former elite runner Dan Dillon, also directed a Home School Harriers running club for six years. Patti won her first national championship medal—third place in her age group in snowshoe-ing in 2014—and continues running more days of the week than not.

Bobbi Gibb is an attorney and sculptor who splits her time between the coasts, always living near the ocean. She has continued running all her life, mostly alone. In 1996, at the 100th anniversary of the Boston Marathon, marathon officials finally awarded her a medal for her three wins from 1966 to 1968. Bobbi completed that year's centennial race in 6:02:09.

Miki Gorman lived her later years mostly in the Pacific Northwest—Vancouver, British Columbia, and Bellingham, Washington—to be near her daughter Danielle, who became the dancer-actress Miki wanted to be as a child. Miki was elected to the National Distance Hall of Fame and the New York Road Runners Hall of Fame. In 1981, the movie *My Champion* was made about her life. Miki died in Washington State on September 19, 2015.

Jackie Hansen won the World Masters Track and Field Championships titles at 1500 meters and 5000 meters in 1987. She no longer runs, due to severe arthritis, but tries to exercise up to an hour a day by walking and using an ElliptiGo. She lives in Los Angeles, has written a memoir called *A Long Time Coming*, teaches health education, and coaches high-school runners and marathoners of all levels.

Doris Brown Heritage served as women's distance coach for the U.S. teams at the 1984 Olympics and 1987 World Championships. She continued running at Seattle Pacific University through 2014. Since then, her running has been diminished by knee-replacement surgery. She lives on Whidbey Island, about 30 miles north of Seattle, Washington—a place that she describes as "Heaven on Earth."

Judy Ikenberry ran to stay in shape until about 1995 and then switched to bicycling. With her husband, Dennis, she formed Race Central, a pioneer-ing race-registration and race-timing business that she has controlled since Dennis's death in 2012. She lives in Crestline, California.

Nina Kuscsik, after her competitive racing career, served until 1985 as chair of USATF's Women's Long-Distance Running Committee. She worked as a patient representative at Mount Sinai Hospital and raised a daughter and two sons. She continued entering recreational road races until she had a knee replacement in 2009. She still walks, gardens, and rides her bicycle.

Francie Larrieu earned a master's degree in sports management from the University of Texas and has been the head men's and women's cross-country and track coach at Southwestern University since 1999. She lives in Georgetown, Texas.

Merry Lepper, after her breakthrough marathon of December 1963, turned her attention to academic challenges. She received advanced degrees in zoology, plant ecology, veterinary medicine, and epidemiology. In 2012, she moved to New Mexico (on the Arizona border), where she is building a house, living on solar power, and taking care of three horses, two burros, two cats, and one dog. For exercise, she rides an indoor bike (there are no roads near her home), hikes in the mountains, rides her horses, and does a lot of barn work.

Charlotte Lettis Richardson continues to run, bike, and recreate with her husband and sons all over the Pacific Northwest and beyond. Coaching is now her passion, and 2015 marked her 43rd season of coaching at Lincoln High School in Portland, Oregon, where she lives. She produced and directed a short film, *Run Like a Girl*, about the early days of women's running.

Joan Benoit Samuelson promotes sustainable living projects in Maine and still lives in the coastal Maine house that she bought in the early 1980s. In 1998, she founded the internationally famous Beach to Beacon 10-K in Cape Elizabeth, Maine. Joan has continued running sub-three-hour marathons into her late fifties. She's also a worldwide women's running ambassador for Nike.

Mary Decker Slaney retired from competitive track and road racing in the late 1990s, beset by continued injuries. She lives in Eugene, Oregon, where she has found a new athletic life on the ElliptiGo, completing charity rides as long as 525 miles (San Francisco to Los Angeles). She has also begun entering a few recreational road races up to the half-marathon distance.

Kathrine Switzer, after helping to create the Women's Olympic Marathon in 1984, wrote three books and worked on several Emmy-award-winning TV broadcasts. She has recently launched 261 Fearless, a global movement that uses her famous 1967 Boston Marathon bib number to empower women through running. "Running always changes women's lives," she says. "We're using the fearless to help the fearful." She lives with her husband, runner-writer Roger Robinson, in New Zealand and New Paltz, New York.

Cheryl Bridges Treworgy lives in North Carolina. She's a professional photographer of track meets and road races. Her daughter, Shalane Flanagan, won a bronze medal in the 2008 Beijing Olympic 10,000 meters and ranks as one of America's top marathoners.

Joan Ullyot, the women's running doctor, ran her last marathon in 1996 at the 100th anniversary of the Boston Marathon. She retired from her Jungian analytical practice in 2005 and spends much of the year in Scottsdale, Arizona. She still runs most days, aiming for three to five miles. "It stimulates my heart, legs, and mind," she says, "and reminds me that the world is still beautiful. I particularly enjoy the smells, and listening to the birdsongs and the breezes."

Grete Waitz died at home in Oslo, Norway, on April 19, 2011. She is survived by her husband, Jack, and her two brothers. Her record of nine New York City Marathon wins will never be equaled. Beyond her unmatched running accomplishments, her name lives on through a number of fitness events and organizations, particularly Aktiv against Cancer.

Oprah Winfrey once commented that she might attempt another marathon at age 60 to bookend her Marine Corps Marathon race at 40. Might. Although no longer hosting *The Oprah Winfrey Show* on national TV, she has remained a powerful force by way of the cable TV channel Oxygen, filmmaking, and promoting women's projects worldwide, including a school in South Africa. A number of international magazines have termed her "the world's most powerful woman."

MORE FIRST LADIES

THE WOMEN CHRONICLED WITH full chapters in this book were by no means the only pioneer runners. Many others made important contributions. They include the following women, who ran and advanced the cause during the 1960s, 1970s, and 1980s.

Ruth Anderson was one of the first and most prolific over-40 women runners. She ran her first marathon at age 44 in 1973, finishing in 3:52:36. Two months later, she would win the Fiesta Bowl Marathon in 3:26:07. By 1978, at age 48, she had improved to 3:04:19. The San Francisco–area resident then moved up to ultramarathon distances and enjoyed even more success. The annual USATF woman ultrarunner award is named after her.

At age 17, New Zealand's **Anne Audain** finished ninth in the 1973 World Cross-Country Championships. In the 1976 Olympics, she ran both the 800 and 1500 for New Zealand, setting a new national record in the 1500. Audain ran her first 5000 meters in 1982, setting a new world record of 15:13.22. Later, she turned to the roads, achieving a marathon best of 2:31:41 in 1990.

Laurie Binder was a frequent winner of women's road races in the late 1970s and early 1980s and a winner of masters division titles a decade later. She won the Bay to Breakers 12-K in San Francisco four times and set an American record for the marathon, 2:35:08, in 1982. She ran her personal best, 2:33:36, in early 1983.

In 1968, at age 5, **Mary Etta Boitano** was the first female finisher in the famous Dipsea Race, a trail race, in Mill Valley, California. Five years later, she won the (handicap start) race outright. She ran a 3:46 marathon at age 8 and a 3:01:15 at age 10. Now Mary Blanchard, she is still running strong in San Francisco area races.

In 1971, 18-year-old **Beth Bonner** set a marathon world record, 3:01:41, at the Eastern Regional AAU Marathon Championships in Philadelphia, Pennsylvania. Later that year, the West Virginia–born runner won the New York City Marathon in Central Park, running 2:55:22—the first sub-three-hour marathon by a woman. She died in 1998 when hit by a truck while bicycling.

Wisconsin's **Cindy Bremser** was a top cross-country and track runner in the late 1970s and early 1980s. She won a silver medal in the 1983 Pan American Games 1500 and finished fourth in the 1984 Olympic 3000-meter race in Los Angeles (the Zola Budd–Mary Decker collision race). In 1986, Bremser clocked a fast 15:11.78 for 5000 meters.

Julie Brown was one of America's top track, cross-country, and marathon runners from the mid-1970s through the mid-1980s. Montana-born, but mostly living in the Los Angeles area, she won the World Cross-Country Championships in 1975. Brown won three silver medals in the 1979 Pan American Games, and qualified for the 1980 Olympics in both the 800 meters and 1500 meters (but did not compete due to the U.S. boycott of the Moscow Games). In 1984, she placed second in the U.S. Olympic Marathon Trials and 36th in the Olympic Marathon.

Lyn Carman became the third American woman runner to complete a marathon (after Merry Lepper, 1963; and Roberta Gibb, April, 1966) when she ran the Santa Barbara Marathon in 3:57:51 in October 1966. She also won the Santa Barbara race in 1969 and 1970. Carman and her husband, Bob, a top-ranked marathoner, were a major force in Southern California road running in the 1960s and 1970s. She died in 2014.

While just 16 in 1972, **Eileen Claugus,** a member of the San Jose Cindergals track team, finished second in the World Cross-Country Championships 4-K race. Almost a decade later, she moved up to the marathon, recording several times in the high 2:30s. She placed third, 2:38:49, in the 1983 Boston Marathon.

Western Massachusetts resident **Nancy Conz** won three major marathons: London 1980, Ottawa 1981, and Chicago 1982. She set her personal best, 2:33:24, at Chicago.

Californian **Marty Cooksey** was the surprise winner of the warm 1978 Avon International Marathon in Atlanta, Georgia, where she finished in 2:46:26. Earlier in 1978, she had won the San Diego Marathon in 2:54:06. In November of the same year, she led Grete Waitz for much of the New York City Marathon, running at world-record pace, before she faded to second in 2:41:49. In 1979, she won the London Marathon and, in 1980, improved her personal best to 2:41:01 in the London Marathon (sixth place).

Merry Cushing finished eighth in her first Boston Marathon (3:36:06) in 1973 and improved to 2:56:57 two years later (fifth place). The Western Massachusetts resident won the Framingham Marathon and Holyoke Marathon twice each.

Jacqueline Dixon was just 17 when she won the first Crazylegs Women's 10-K in Central Park in 1972 by a whopping 50 seconds over Charlotte Lettis, who would win three years later. Other pioneer women runners Nina Kuscsik and Kathrine Switzer finished third and sixth in the 1972 race—the first for women only. That same year, Dixon finished second to Cheryl Bridges in the Bay to Breakers mega-race in San Francisco. She trained often with Francie Larrieu of the San Jose Cindergals. In the early 1980s, Dixon ran a 3:12:56 marathon, but then learned she had a cardiomyopathy that forced her to retire from serious running.

Canada's **Jacqueline Gareau** won the 1980 Boston Marathon and finished second in 1982. Her victory in 1980 was clouded by Rosie Ruiz's infamous cheating effort. Ruiz arrived first at the finish line, having run less than a mile, and it took Boston officials more than a week to disqualify her and declare Gareau the rightful champion.

Michigan's **Francie Kraker Goodridge** ran 800 meters for the U.S. Olympic team at Mexico City in 1968 and competed in the first Olympic 1500 in Munich four years later. She had a long and distinguished coaching career at the University of Michigan, Wake Forest University, and the University of Wisconsin.

Californian **Donna Gookin** was a frequent and fast marathon finisher in the 1970s. She won several of the 40 marathons she completed and recorded her personal best, 3:08:26, in placing first in the 1973 Santa Barbara Marathon. She also won her age group in the World Masters Marathon in Toronto, Canada, in 1975, and twice won the Santa Monica 50-mile.

Scotland's **Dale Greig** ran the first sub-3:30 marathon for women in May 1964. Organizers were so concerned about possible medical harm to a woman running such a long distance that they ordered an ambulance to follow her around the Isle of Wight Marathon course, which she completed in 3:27:45. Greig also finished the 55-mile London-to-Brighton race in 1972, seven years before women were officially allowed to enter. In 1974, she won the World Veterans Marathon in Paris.

In 1923, **Frances Hayward** attempted to enter South Africa's famous 56-mile Comrades Marathon. Her entry was refused. She ran anyway, in a green gym tunic, and completed the course in 11 hours, 35 minutes—ahead of two men. Organizers wouldn't give her a medal, but her fellow runners and race spectators pooled funds to buy her a silver tea service. After finishing Comrades, Hayward attended the theater that evening.

In 1967, 11-year-old **Debbie Heald** from Mirada, California, ran the mile in 5:33.9. Five years later, she set a high-school (and world) indoor mile record, 4:38.5. This mark remained on the books for 41 years, until broken by Mary Cain. Injuries and mental illness curtailed Heald's career.

Canada's **Abby Hoffman** participated in four Olympic Games (1964, 1968, 1972, 1976) and four Pan American Games, winning two gold medals in the Pan American Games. She specialized in the 800 meters, with a personal best of 2:00.17. She has held many important positions in Canadian sports and health organizations and serves on the Council of the International Association of Athletics Federations.

South African **Mavis Hutchinson** completed her first standard-length marathon in 3:50 in 1963. Two years later, when she was 40, she finished the 56-mile Comrades Marathon for the first of eight times. In 1971, she set a women's world record for the 100-mile and 24-hour distances. Known in South Africa as the Galloping Granny, in 1978, Hutchinson became the first woman to run across the United States. She covered the 2,871 miles from Los Angeles to New York City in 69 days, 2 hours, and 40 minutes.

Sister Marion Irvine was the oldest qualifier (54) at the first U.S. Olympic Marathon Trials in 1984. Race organizers arranged for her to room with the youngest, 18-year-old Cathy Schiro. A member of the Dominican order, Sister Irvine began jogging in 1978 and two years later, ran 3:01 in the Avenue of the Giants Marathon. In 1983, she improved her marathon time to 2:51:01, a world record for women over 50, and a Trials qualifier.

Helen Klein began running ultramarathons in 1981 at the age of 59. She and her husband, Norm Klein, directed the famous Western States 100-Mile Endurance Run for many years. Klein ran hundreds of marathons and ultramarathons in her sixties, seventies, and eighties. In December 2002, she ran a 4:31:32 marathon to shatter the world record in the women's 80 to 84 age category.

Norway's **Ingrid Kristiansen** won the 1984 Houston and London Marathons, and then finished fourth in the Los Angeles Olympic Marathon that summer. The following year, she set a marathon world record, 2:21:06, in the London Marathon. She was also the first woman to break 15:00 minutes for 5000 meters (1984) and to break 31:00 minutes for 10,000 meters (1985).

France's **Chantal Langlace** twice set world records in the marathon. In 1974, she ran a 2:46:24 in the Neuf-Brisach Marathon in France, and in 1977, she improved to 2:35:16 in the Oiartzun Marathon in Spain.

Diane Leather is the Roger Bannister of women's one-mile running. Just 23 days after Bannister famously broke the four-minute barrier on May 6, 1954, Leather became the first woman to break five minutes for the mile. She ran 4:59.6 in a track meet in Birmingham, England. The next year she lowered her personal best to 4:45. Leather also won silver medals in two European Championship 800-meter races, and twice won the unofficial women's division of the World Cross-Country Championships (1954 and 1955).

Frenchwoman **Marie-Louise Ledru** has been credited by some groups with being the first woman to complete a marathon when she ran a 5:40 in the Tour de Paris Marathon on September 29, 1918. Other groups give first honors to Great Britain's Violet Piercy who may have run a 3:40:22 in England on October 3, 1926. The distances and other details of both runs are sketchy. This book credits Merry Lepper as being the first American woman to finish a marathon, in 1963. She may also have been the first woman worldwide to run a verified marathon.

Chris McKenzie would have been the first finisher (ahead of Julia Chase) in the 1961 Manchester Road Race in Connecticut except that she stepped off the course a block before the finish to avoid possible problems with the Amateur Athletic Union. She feared the group might rule her ineligible for future competitions or take action against her husband, Gordon, a U.S. Olympic runner. Born Christine Slemon, in Great Britain, she was part of a 3 x 800-meter team that set a world record of 6:49 in 1953. She attended one U.S. road race with a T-shirt proclaiming, "If I can carry a baby for nine months, I can run a 10-K."

Brazilian **Eleonora Mendonca** was a key member of the International Runners Committee that lobbied for the 1984 women's Olympic Marathon and other equal opportunities for women runners. She ran in the 1984 Olympic race, finishing 44th in 2:52:19. She achieved her marathon personal record four years earlier at London (2:49:15). She also won the Mount Washington Road Race three times.

At one time or another during the 1970s, Connecticut's **Jan Merrill** held the American record for 1500 meters, 3000 meters, and 5000 meters. She also placed second in the 1981 World Cross-Country Championships.

Wisconsin-based **Kim Merritt** won the 1975 New York City Marathon and the 1976 Boston Marathon. She established an American marathon record with her 2:37:57 in the 1977 Nike Oregon Track Club Marathon.

Kathy Mills won the 1977 Association for Intercollegiate Athletics for Women (AIAW) cross-country title and the AIAW 5000-meter title in 1978. Her 5000-meter time, 15:35.52, was an unofficial world record (official women's records for the distance were not maintained at the time). She also competed in the World Cross-Country Championships in 1977 and 1978. In

1978, she was the women's winner of the first Utica Boilermaker 15-K.

Madeline Manning Mims is the only U.S. athlete to win an Olympic gold medal in the women's 800. The Ohio-born runner did this at the 1968 Mexico City Olympics, setting a new Olympic record, 2:00.9. She also won the Pan American Games 800 in 1967. Over her long career, she qualified for four Olympic teams, won 10 U.S. national track titles, and ran her best time, 1:57.9, in 1976.

New Zealander **Lorraine Moller** began her international track career in 1974, finishing fifth in the Commonwealth Games 800 with a time of 2:03.63. She ran and won her first marathon (Grandma's, Duluth, Minnesota) in 1979 in 2:37:37. She then won her next seven marathons until placing fifth in the first women's Olympic Marathon in 1984. She ran the next three Olympic Marathons, taking the bronze medal in Barcelona in 1992 at age 38.

Portugal's **Rosa Mota** won the first European Marathon Championships for women (1982), finished fourth in the first World Championships Marathon for women (1983), and took the bronze medal in the first Olympic Marathon for women in 1984. She improved to the gold medal in the 1988 Olympic Marathon. She won the Chicago Marathon twice and the Boston Marathon three times.

Fifteen-year-old **Marie Mulder,** from Sacramento, California, burst onto the U.S. track scene in 1965 with double wins (800 meters and 1500 meters) at the National Championships. That summer, she set an American record of 2:07.3 for 800 meters in Kiev, Soviet Union. A *New York Times* newspaper feature story said that she had switched from boys football to track just 18 months earlier and noted, "She would be a hit on the dance floor of the most fashionable discotheques." Mulder finished second to Doris Brown in the 1968 National Indoor Championships for the one-mile distance, but there was no Olympic 1500 at the time, and her career soon ended.

In 1975, Iowa State's **Peg Neppel** won the first Association for Intercollegiate Athletics for Women (AIAW) Cross-Country Championships. The same year, she placed 24th in the World Cross-Country Championships. She was a one-time holder of the world record for 10,000 meters and won the 1977 New York City Mini Marathon.

In September 1967, **Anni Pede-Erdkamp,** a 27-year-old German and mother of two, set a marathon world record of 3:07:27. She was one of the first protégés of the influential German doctor, coach, and race organizer, Ernst van Aaken.

Californian **Sue Petersen** won more than a dozen mostly West Coast marathons during a career that stretched from 1976 to 1987. She achieved her personal best, 2:43:03, in the 1979 Boston Marathon.

Arlene Pieper Stine walked and perhaps jogged the Pikes Peak Marathon in 9:16 in 1959. This makes her, in one sense, the first woman marathon finisher in the United States. She entered Pikes Peak primarily to promote a local gym that she and her husband owned in Colorado Springs, Colorado. This book credits Merry Lepper as the first American woman to run a marathon, as her 3:37:07 finish in the 1963 Western Hemisphere Marathon was clearly a serious running effort.

New Zealander **Allison Roe** won the Boston and New York City marathons in 1981. At Boston, she set a course record by almost eight minutes, running 2:26:46. At New York, she broke Grete Waitz's previous course mark with her 2:25:29. Her New York performance is variously regarded as a world record, though the Association of Road Race Statisticians labels the course as approximately 150 meters short.

In 1981, 80-year-old **Ruth Rothfarb** ran a 2:30 half-marathon. Six months later, she completed her first marathon in 5:28. In 1986, then 84, Rothfarb ran the Boston Marathon in 7:35:31. In 1993, at age 93, Rothfarb completed the Tufts Health Plan 10-K in Boston.

New Zealand's **Mildred "Millie" Sampson** set a marathon world record, 3:19:33, in the 1964 Auckland Marathon. She had been out dancing late the night before, ate no breakfast, and consumed chocolate and ice cream in the marathon's final miles. She also won the New Zealand Cross-Country Championships three times.

Cathy Schiro O'Brien finished ninth (2:34:24) in the U.S. Olympic Marathon Trials of 1984. At the time, she was a high-school student in Dover, New Hampshire. She made the U.S. Olympic Marathon Team in her next two efforts, in 1988 and 1992, finishing as the top American (10th overall) in the 1992 Olympics.

In 1969, **Julie Shea** ran the fastest-ever mile for an American runner under age 10, girl or boy, when she clocked a 5:33.5. She was wearing canvas high-tops. As a high-school senior in 1977, she set a national high-school outdoor record for the mile, 4:43.1. At North Carolina State University, Shea captured eight national titles and, in 1978, finished fourth in the World Cross-Country Championships. She ran 2:30:01 at the 1981 New York City Marathon. Her younger sister, Mary, was also an elite performer.

In 1982 at age 44, Great Britain's **Joyce Smith** won the London Marathon in 2:29:43, a new record for women over 40. She had previously excelled at every distance from 800 meters (in the late 1950s) to 1500 meters (competing in the 1968 Olympic Games) to cross-country, winning the World Cross-Country Championships in 1972. In 1969, she set a world record for 3000 meters.

Germany's **Christa Vahlensieck** won 21 marathons from 1973 to 1989, including five victories in the Kosice Peace Marathon. In 1977, she set a new world record in the Berlin Marathon, 2:34:48.

Oregon's **Caroline Walker** set a marathon world record, 3:02:53, in the 1970 Trail's End Marathon in Seaside, Oregon. She was a 16-year-old junior at Grant High School in Portland, Oregon. While attending the University of Oregon, Walker competed twice in the World Cross-Country Championships. Years later—1984, 1986, and 1987—she won Oregon state titles in the triathlon.

Polish-born **Sylvia Weiner** spent several years in German prison camps during World War II and was with Anne Frank the day the famous Dutch diarist died in the Bergen-Belsen concentration camp. In the early 1970s, living in Montreal, Weiner began running to relieve stress. She won the Boston Marathon's first masters division title for women in 1975, clocking a 3:21:38. Four years later, she improved to 3:15 at the Skylon Marathon in Buffalo, New York. In her mid-eighties she was still running almost every day in either Miami or Montreal.

England's **Priscilla Welch** quit smoking at age 35 in 1980 and entered her first marathon. Four years later, she finished a strong sixth in the 1984 Olympic Marathon despite her age (39) and her previous smoking habit. In 1987, at age 42, she ran 2:26:51 in the London Marathon and won the New York City Marathon.

Canadian **Maureen "Moe" Wilton** had been running for four years but was still just 13 when she set a marathon world record, 3:15:23, in May 1967. Kathrine Switzer finished second to Wilton just 16 days after her historic Boston Marathon debut. Wilton was coached by Sy Mah, who once held the record for the most completed marathons. Wilton stopped running at age 17 in 1971 but returned to the sport in 2009 (in her late fifties), running several half-marathons in the high 1:30s and mid-1:40s. She continues to compete as a top age-group road racer in the Toronto, Canada, area.

TIMELINE OF FEMALE RUNNING HISTORY

Important events in the lives of the
First Ladies of running from 1958 to 1994

1958

FEBRUARY: Grace Butcher wins exhibition 800-meter race at National Indoor Championships.

1959

JUNE: Grace Butcher wins National Championships, 800 meters. Also races 800 in second USA vs. USSR track meet.

1960

FEBRUARY: Grace Butcher wins the National Indoor Championships, 800 meters.

JULY: Doris Severtsen (later Brown) finishes third in the Olympic Track Trials 800. Also competing: Grace Butcher, Julia Chase, Judy Ikenberry.

1961

NOVEMBER: Julia Chase becomes the first woman to finish a road race when she runs the Manchester Road Race 5-miler at 7:10 pace—and ahead of several men.

1963

DECEMBER: Merry Lepper finishes the Western Hemisphere Marathon in 3:37:07, the first American woman to run a marathon.

1966

JANUARY: Doris Brown gets a rare chance to run the mile distance, and she produces a world indoor record, 4:52.

APRIL: Roberta "Bobbi" Gibb finishes the Boston Marathon in 3:21:25, the first of her three consecutive Boston victories.

1967

MARCH: Doris Brown travels to Wales to win the first of five World Cross-Country titles.

APRIL: Kathrine Switzer gets attacked by Jock Semple in the Boston Marathon, producing the most famous photo in the history of women's running. She finishes in 4:20.

DECEMBER: Judy Ikenberry finishes the Las Vegas Marathon in 3:40:51—the first woman.

1968

OCTOBER: Doris Brown finishes fifth in the Mexico City Olympic 800 despite falling to the track en route.

1969

APRIL: Sara Mae Berman wins the first of three straight Boston Marathons. She runs her fastest time, a course record 3:05:07, in 1970.

APRIL: Nina Kuscsik runs her first marathon (Boston) and finishes in 3:46.

1970

JULY: Gayle Barron becomes the first woman to run the Peachtree Road Race 10-K in Atlanta. She clocks a 49:13 to win her first of five Peachtree 10-Ks in the next six years.

SEPTEMBER: Nina Kuscsik is the only woman to start the first New York City Marathon, held in Central Park. She drops out.

1971

MAY: On a lark, 12-year-old Mary Decker runs the Palos Verdes Marathon in 3:09:47.

DECEMBER: Cheryl Bridges becomes the first woman to break 2:50 in the marathon when she runs a world record 2:49:40 at the Western Hemisphere Marathon.

1972

APRIL: In her fourth entry in the Boston Marathon, Nina Kuscsik wins the women's division—the first time women are officially recognized at Boston. Four other women finish.

JUNE: Title IX takes effect.

JULY: Although clearly among the United States' best middle-distance track runners, "Little Mary Decker," 13, is judged too young to compete in the Olympic Track Trials.

JULY: Francie Larrieu (first in Olympic Trials) and Doris Brown (third) qualify for the inaugural Olympic 1500 meters at the 1972 Munich Olympics. Larrieu will qualify for four more Olympic teams.

OCTOBER: Nina Kuscsik wins her first New York City Marathon in 3:08:41 and repeats as the champion the next year with a time of 2:57:07.

1973

APRIL: Jackie Hansen sets a Boston Marathon course record, 3:05:59.

NOVEMBER: Marilyn Bevans becomes the first African American woman to finish a marathon (Baltimore, 3:31:45).

DECEMBER: Miki Gorman sets a women's world record, 2:46:37, at the Western Hemisphere Marathon.

1974

FEBRUARY: Judy Ikenberry wins the first National Marathon Championships for women in San Mateo, California, with a time of 2:55:18. Fourteen years earlier, then 17-year-old Judy Shapiro had run in the 800 meters at the Olympic Track Trials.

APRIL: Miki Gorman wins Boston in first attempt and sets a new course record, 2:47:12.

APRIL: Joan Ullyot completes her first Boston Marathon in 3:17:10.

SEPTEMBER: Seven years after her first Boston Marathon run, Kathrine Switzer wins the New York City Marathon in 3:07:49—more than an hour faster than her 1967 time at Boston.

1975

APRIL: Still improving, Kathrine Switzer finishes second at the Boston Marathon with a personal best time of 2:51:37.

JUNE: Charlotte Lettis wins L'eggs Mini-Marathon 10-K in New York City. She had placed second three years earlier in the first Crazylegs 10-K.

SEPTEMBER: Jackie Hansen runs the Nike Oregon Track Club Marathon in the world record time of 2:38:19. This makes her the first woman to break 2:40.

1976

APRIL/NOVEMBER: Miki Gorman finishes second in the Boston Marathon and first in the New York City Marathon (in the first five-borough marathon). The next year she wins both of these marathons.

MAY: Doris Brown runs her first marathon and wins the Vancouver Marathon race in 2:47:35.

JUNE: Francie Larrieu qualifies for the Olympic team in the 1500 meters.

JUNE: Joan Ullyot's influential book *Women's Running* is published.

NOVEMBER: Doris Brown takes a red-eye flight from Seattle to New York City and, with no sleep, places second to Miki Gorman in the Marathon.

1977

APRIL: Marilyn Bevans finishes second in the Boston Marathon, lowering her personal record to 2:51:12.

DECEMBER: Marilyn Bevans wins the Baltimore Marathon.

1978

APRIL: Gayle Barron wins the Boston Marathon in 2:44:52.

NOVEMBER: Grete Waitz enters and wins her first New York City Marathon, setting a new world record, 2:32:30. She will win eight more times, setting two additional world records.

DECEMBER: Patti Catalano wins the Honolulu Marathon for the first of four straight years.

1979

APRIL: Joan Benoit enters and wins her first Boston Marathon in a course and American record, 2:35:15.

APRIL: Patti Catalano finishes second at Boston, as she also does the next two years.

JULY: Mary Decker wins gold in the 1500 meters at the Pan American Games in Puerto Rico.

NOVEMBER: In the New York City Marathon, Grete Waitz improves her world record to 2:27:33.

1980

JUNE: Mary Decker wins the Olympic Track Trials 1500 by more than 2 seconds, with Francie Larrieu Smith third. But the United States boycotts the Moscow Olympics.

NOVEMBER: Grete Waitz lowers her New York City Marathon time to 2:25:42—another new world record.

NOVEMBER: Patti Catalano finishes second at the New York Marathon, running 2:29:34—the first American under 2:30.

1983

APRIL: Joan Benoit runs 2:22:43 to win Boston, setting a new American and World record.

AUGUST: Mary Decker wins the "Decker Double" (1500 meters and 3000 meters) at the first track World Championships in Helsinki, Finland.

AUGUST: Grete Waitz wins the first World Championships Marathon in 2:28:09.

1984

MAY: Joan Benoit wins the first U.S. Olympic Marathon Trials 17 days after arthroscopic knee surgery.

AUGUST: Mary Decker collides with Zola Budd in the first Olympic 3000 meters for women. Decker falls and is unable to complete the race. Budd fades to seventh.

AUGUST: Joan Benoit wins the first women's Olympic Marathon in Los Angeles with a time of 2:24:52. Grete Waitz finishes second in 2:26:18.

1988

SEPTEMBER: Francie Larrieu finishes fifth in the first-ever Olympic 10,000 meters for women.

1992

AUGUST: After qualifying for her fifth U.S. Olympic team, 39-year-old Francie Larrieu places 12th in the Barcelona Olympic Marathon.

1994

OCTOBER: More than 10 years after Joan Benoit's epic Olympic win, Oprah Winfrey completes the Marine Corps Marathon in 4:29:20. The years following Oprah's successful marathon mark the beginning of the "women's running boom" that has continued to the present.

ACKNOWLEDGMENTS

THIS BOOK WOULD NOT exist but for the twenty-two First Ladies who spent countless in-person, telephone, and email hours responding to my endless questions. I had hoped to visit each personally. This proved impossible, but I did have face-to-face meetings, often at their homes, with Julia Chase, Doris Brown, Merry Lepper, Roberta Gibb, Sara Mae Berman, Judy Ikenberry, Mary Decker, Charlotte Lettis, Jackie Hansen, and Miki Gorman.

I am eternally grateful to all.

In the 1960s and 1970s, I ran many road races where I met and became friendly with most of the First Ladies. This book gave me a chance to get reacquainted with them—a wonderful gift. Grace Butcher is the only one I have never met. I'm eager for the opportunity and hope to make it happen soon.

A number of the First Ladies also have deep file cabinets and memories. They were particularly helpful when I ran into knotty dead ends. Kathrine Switzer is a great source on the history of women's running, as is her husband, the elite marathoner, literature professor, and running writer Roger Robinson.

Nina Kuscsik, Charlotte Lettis, and Jackie Hansen were equally as ready and able to assist. Lettis also made a terrific short film, *Run Like a Girl,* about several of her running heroines.

Since retiring from her psychiatry caseload a few years ago, Julia Chase has conducted new and primary research into the pivotal women's 800 meter race at the 1960 U.S. Olympic Track Trials. She was a participant in that event, along with two other First Ladies (Doris Brown and Judy Ikenberry), and I look forward to reading more from Julia.

Tom Derderian's *The Boston Marathon* book and Peter Gambaccini's *The New York City Marathon* history were never more than inches from my desk. Louise Mead Tricard's two-volume *American Women's Track and Field* is mind-boggling in its length and depth and in the fascinating letters from key women athletes.

Frank Murphy's *The Silence of Great Distance* explores the hopes, successes, and failures of women "running long" in a manner unlike any other book. David Davis single-handedly re-discovered Merry Lepper with his *Marathon Crasher.* Then he told me how I could contact her.

First Ladies of Running was guided from start to finish by my literary agent, Farley Chase, and Rodale book editors Mark Weinstein, Franny Vignola, and Gillian Francella. Project editor Nancy Bailey, a colleague from my own days at Rodale, and designer Carol Angstadt kept the book accurate, consistent, and smooth flowing.

Liz Reap Carlson and I have worked together on many photo projects since the historic 100th running of the Boston Marathon in 1996, and I knew she would be the perfect photo editor for this project. Fortunately, Rodale agreed, and Liz made contributions well beyond simply gathering up old photos.

Of Grete Waitz and Miki Gorman, I can only say: We miss you so much. Your running and your humanity speak for themselves.

As always, I am indebted to John J. and Jacintha Kelley for almost everything, including their early support for women's running. They taught me from my teenage years in the 1960s that there was no reason why women shouldn't join us guys on the start lines. They were right, as they were in so many other arenas.

The First Ladies in my life—my wife, Cristina, daughter, Laura, and daughter-in-law, Kris—cheered me through the years of work on this project. I couldn't have made it to the finish line without them. Best of all, they continue to light up my life on a daily basis.

PHOTO CREDITS

ActionPlus (www.actionplus.co.uk), 99

Associated Press, 196

©Bettmann/CORBIS, 61, 160

Courtesy Larry Berman, 74

Courtesy Marilyn Bevans, 194

Patrick A. Burns/*The New York Times,* 107

Courtesy Grace Butcher, xx

George H. Cook/*Baltimore Sun,* 186

DUOMO/PCN, 120

Bill Eppridge/©Estate of Bill Eppridge, 18, 20

Courtesy Jacqueline Hansen, 132, 163

Courtesy Judy Ikenberry, 76, 82, 84

Walter Iooss Jr./*Sports Illustrated*/Getty Images, 52

Steve Jacobs (www.sjpics.com)/courtesy Freihofer's Run for Women, xii

Jeff Johnson, 22, 54, 66, 93, 129, 134

Fred Kaplan/*Sports Illustrated*/Getty Images, 42, 51

Joe Kennedy/*Los Angeles Times*/Getty Images, xvii

Jerry Kinstler/*NY Daily News* via Getty Images, 144, 150

Chang W. Lee /*The New York Times,* xi

Frank Lennon/*Toronto Star* via Getty Images, 176

Courtesy Merry Lepper, 32

Courtesy Charlotte Lettis, 148

Bill Leung, 154

Rick Levy, 100

David Madison/Getty Images, 218

Courtesy Manchester Road Race, 10

Mitch Mandel, 230

Anthony Neste/*Sports Illustrated*/Getty Images, 206

Courtesy Seattle Pacific University Athletics, 26

Mark Shearman, 88

Paul J. Sutton/DUOMO/PCN, 110, 166

Steven E. Sutton/DUOMO/PCN, 119

Courtesy Cheryl Treworgy, 122

Mark Wilson/AP Photo, 233

INDEX

Boldface page references indicate photographs.